Original Intent and the Constitution

Studies in Social and Political Philosophy

General Editor: James P. Sterba, University of Notre Dame

Social Contract Theories: Political Obligation or Anarchy? (1990)
by Vicente Medina, Seton Hall University

Collective Responsibility: Five Decades of Debate in Theoretical and Applied Ethics (1991)
edited by Larry May, Washington University, and Stacey Hoffman, Purdue University

The Principle of Fairness and Political Obligation (1991)
by George Klosko, University of Virginia

Original Intent and the Constitution: A Philosophical Study (1992)
by Gregory Bassham, King's College

Original Intent and the Constitution

A Philosophical Study

Gregory Bassham

Rowman & Littlefield Publishers, Inc.

ROWMAN & LITTLEFIELD PUBLISHERS, INC.

Published in the United States of America
by Rowman & Littlefield Publishers, Inc.
4720 Boston Way, Lanham, Maryland 20706

British Cataloging in Publication Information Available

Library of Congress Cataloging-in-Publication Data

Bassham, Gregory, 1959–
Original intent and the Constitution: a philosophical study / Gregory Bassham.
p. cm. — (Studies in social & political philosophy)
Includes bibliographical references and index.
1. United States—Constitutional law—Interpretation and construction. 2. United States—Constitutional history. I. Title. II. Series.
KF4550.B285 1992
342.73'029—dc20 91-44467 [347.30229] CIP

ISBN 0-8476-7737-0 (alk. paper)

Printed in the United States of America

The paper used in this publication meets the minimum requirements of American National Standard for Information Sciences—Permanence of Paper for Printed Library Materials, ANSI Z39.48–1984.

For my Parents

Contents

Preface

Over the past twenty years, Americans have witnessed an extensive and spirited debate over the foundations of American constitutional theory. At the heart of this dispute has been a basic disagreement over the nature and source of constitutional meaning. Constitutional "originalists," as they are now generally called, have insisted that constitutional meaning is forever fixed by the original intent of the framers; their "nonoriginalist" opponents have contended that constitutional meaning properly evolves to meet changing circumstances the framers could not have foreseen and perhaps in ways the framers would not have approved. The legal and political stakes at issue in the debate are immense.

In part, these stakes are so high because "virtually all of constitutional doctrine regarding human rights fashioned by the Supreme Court in this century must be adjudged illegitimate"[1] if original intent is the touchstone of proper constitutional interpretation. Over the past three decades decisions by the Supreme Court legalizing abortion,[2] expanding the rights of criminal defendants,[3] barring state support for religion (including prayer in public schools),[4] liberalizing the law on pornography and obscenity,[5] and substantially restricting the circumstances in which states are free to impose the death penalty,[6] have long been prominent targets of criticism by conservatives generally and by originalists in particular.[7] But the stakes in the current debate over original intent are by no means limited to this rather familiar litany of conservative judicial grievances. In the name of original intent, leading conservatives have also criticized landmark Supreme Court decisions in such areas as school desegregation,[8] gender equality,[9] federalism,[10] and the application of the federal Bill of Rights to the states.[11] Some conservatives, more dramatically still, would roll back or eliminate altogether welfare and other transfer payments, progressive taxation, zoning, rent control, workers' compensation laws, minimum-wage and maximum-hour legislation—in short, "many of the heralded reforms and institutions of the twentieth century"[12]—as constitutionally infirm on originalist grounds.[13]

Given the importance of the current debate over original intent, it is surprising that there exists no in-depth examination of the controversy by a professional philosopher.[14] To be sure, some of the key issues in dispute are largely or entirely empirical questions; and philosophers, not surprisingly, have often been reluctant to become embroiled in normative disputes that presuppose specialized empirical knowledge or expertise. Such cross-disciplinary ventures frequently involve both hard work and considerable risks, and the pressures to remain within conventional academic compartmentalizations can be formidable. Increasingly, however, scholars are recognizing that many important fields of inquiry have long been poorly served by excessively specialized approaches and can only be effectively approached through interdisciplinary research and cooperation.[15] The fundamental premise of this book is that constitutional interpretation is one of those fields.

The aim of this book, in brief, is to elucidate and advance the current debate over original intent by bringing to bear on it some of the techniques and conceptual resources of contemporary analytic philosophy. After providing (in Chapter 1) a historical introduction to the current debate, I attempt to sort through (in Chapter 2) the various conflicting ways in which originalism has been characterized in the literature. After clarifying the nature of originalism and presenting a typology of originalist theories, I then seek to determine (in Chapter 3) which of these forms of the theory is most defensible. I argue in Chapter 4 that three standard objections to originalism have little or no force against this most plausible form of the theory. In Chapter 5 I argue that even this most plausible form of the theory is fatally flawed and should be rejected. I conclude (in Chapter 6) by sketching an alternative theory inspired by the broadly pragmatic approach to judicial decision-making set forth in Benjamin Cardozo's 1921 classic, *The Nature of the Judicial Process.*

I owe thanks to far more people than I can possibly name here. But I cannot resist paying tribute to those teachers from whom I have learned most over the years: John Haynes, Joseph Byrnes, Ken Merrill, Ed Sankowski, Stewart Umphrey, Tom Boyd, Chris Swoyer, Steve Wykstra, Paul Brown, Dick Lind, Phil Quinn, Tom Morris, and Alvin Plantinga. Special thanks to Phil Quinn, Neil Delaney, Steve Watson, Sot Barber, and John Attanasio for much-needed encouragement and advice when this book was a mere gleam in its author's eye, and to Jim Sterba, Michael Perry, and Richard Kay for instructive comments on a penultimate draft of the work.

My greatest and most persistent intellectual debt is owed to my dissertation director, John Robinson. John taught me constitutional law and theory from the ground up, and without his patient and expert guidance this book could never have been written.

Finally, to my parents, to whom this work is dedicated, and to my wife, Mia, I can only say, *Cor ad cor loquitur*. My debt to them is greater than I can say.

1

Historical Introduction to the Current Debate

Constitutional scholars are currently deeply divided over both what the U.S. Constitution means and how judges and other political officials should seek to determine what it means. Disagreement over the U.S. Constitution is nothing new to American politics and jurisprudence; from the hotly contested Alien and Sedition Acts in the 1790s, to the monumental constitutional conflicts of the Civil War era, to today's impassioned debates over abortion, flag burning, and prayer in public schools, Americans have regularly disagreed more or less deeply over the meaning of their fundamental charter of government. By contrast, disagreement over the basic principles of constitutional construction is a comparatively recent development in the American constitutional tradition. From the founding era until roughly the New Deal, one model of constitutional interpretation held virtually unchallenged sway in American law. According to one oft-quoted statement of this theory, "[t]he whole aim of construction, as applied to a provision of the Constitution, is to discover the meaning, to ascertain and give effect to the intent, of its framers and the people who adopted it."[1] This traditional theory of interpretation, now generally known to as constitutional "originalism," was largely abandoned by constitutional scholars and by the Supreme Court itself following the triumph of New Deal liberalism on the Court in the late 1930s.[2] However, in recent years, originalist jurisprudence has enjoyed a major resurgence, both in the pages of law reviews and on the Court itself. My aim in this first chapter is to place this resurgence and the controversy it has generated in historical perspective.

FROM ARISTOTLE TO LEGAL REALISM

When American jurists of the founding generation first undertook to interpret their new constitutions, both federal and state, one point on which they readily agreed was that these political compacts should be construed in accordance with traditional canons of legal interpretation. These traditional principles were drawn largely from two sources: common-law authorities on legal interpretation, such as Matthew Bacon, Thomas Rutherforth, and William Blackstone, and Continental authorities on the law of nations and the interpretation of treaties, such as Hugo Grotius, Samuel von Pufendorf, Jean Domat, and Emmerich de Vattel. In both of these interpretive traditions, the cardinal rule was that all legal instruments should be construed in accordance with the intent of their makers.[3]

The remote roots of these two traditions of legal interpretation lie in the Middle Ages, in the systems of "equitable" or "rational" interpretation developed by medieval casuists and jurists. The leading ideas, indeed, go back ultimately to Aristotle, who distinguished "equity" (*epieikeia*) from "legal justice" by noting

> that all law is universal but about some things it is not possible to make a universal statement which shall be correct. In those cases, then, in which it is necessary to speak universally, but not possible to do so correctly, the law takes the usual case, though it is not ignorant of the possibility of error. . . . When the law speaks universally, then, and a case arises on it which is not covered by the universal statement, then it is right, where the legislator fails us and has erred by over-simplicity, to correct the omission—to say what the legislator himself would have said had he been present, and would have put into his law if he had known. . . . And this is the nature of the equitable, a correction of law where it is defective owing to its universality.[4]

Medieval jurists generally followed Aristotle in limiting equitable construction, in the strict sense, to what later came to be known as *restrictive* equitable construction: the "correction" of a law, judged to be deficient by reason of the generality or universality of its expression, on the presumption that the lawmaker did not intend his law to extend to the case at hand.[5] A classic example of such equitable restriction (due ultimately to Plato) is provided by Aquinas:

> [T]he law requires deposits to be restored, because in the majority of cases this is just. Yet it happens sometimes to be injurious—for instance, if a madman were to put his sword in deposit, and demand its delivery while in a state of madness, or if a man were to seek the return of his deposit in order to fight against his country. In these and like cases it is bad to follow

the law, and it is good to set aside the letter of the law and to follow the dictates of justice and the common good.[6]

In the early modern era, this classical and medieval conception of equity as a *correctio legis generaliter latae qua parte deficit* often was broadened to include cases in which a law was judged to be deficient, not because of its universality, but rather because of its excessive particularity.[7] Such cases were thought to call for *extensive* equitable construction: the extension of a legal rule to encompass fact-situations not within the literal words of the rule, but believed to be within the *ratio* or "mischief" that moved the lawmaker to enact it. A famous example from American law occurs in *Baker v. Jacobs*,[8] where the court supported its decision that cigars were "victuals or drink" for purposes of a state statute barring successful litigants from regaling jurors with these amenities by quoting the following passage from an unnamed "old book" (Matthew Bacon's *A New Abridgment of the Law*, 1736):

> In some cases the letter of an act of parliament is restrained by an equitable construction; in others it is enlarged; in others the construction is contrary to the letter. In order to form a right judgement whether a case be within the equity of a statute, it is a good way to suppose the law maker present, and that you have asked him this question: Did you intend to comprehend this case? Then you must give yourself such answer as you imagine he being an upright and reasonable man would have given.[9]

While leading early-modern Continental jurists such as Grotius and Pufendorf discarded or significantly reshaped many features of medieval jurisprudence, they retained the central features of medieval legal hermeneutics, including the basic principle that the lawmaker's actual or presumptive will or intent should prevail over the literal import of his words. These Continental authorities heavily influenced eighteenth-century English common-law discussions of legal interpretation, including those by Bacon, Rutherforth, and Blackstone, the leading authorities on legal construction for American jurists in the founding era and for some decades thereafter.[10] Long before the eighteenth century, however, the basic principles of medieval equity jurisprudence had taken root in the common law through the writings of English jurists such as Christopher St. Germain[11] and Edmund Plowden,[12] who had been much influenced by late medieval Continental jurisprudence.[13]

Thus when Chief Justice John Marshall, writing in defense of his landmark decision in *McCulloch v. Maryland*,[14] remarked that "the great duty of a judge who construes an instrument, is to fit the intention of its maker,"[15] his words reflected an orthodoxy that had prevailed in Western jurisprudence for centuries. This traditional view was widely shared by Marshall's fellow framers and contemporaries. Thus, Alexander Hamilton argued in an important early case[16] that "many things within the letter of a statute are not within its equity and vice-versa"[17] and that "[i]n law as in Religion the letter kills[,] the spirit makes alive."[18] James Wilson taught his law students that "[t]he first and governing maxim in the interpretation of a statute is, to discover the meaning of those, who made it,"[19] and that "[e]quity is synonymous with true and sound construction."[20] Thomas Jefferson urged that "[o]n every question of [constitutional] construction, [we should] carry ourselves back to the time when the constitution was adopted, recollect the spirit manifested in the debates, and instead of trying what meaning may be squeezed out of the text, or invented against it, conform to the probable one in which it was passed."[21] And James Madison held that the "true meaning" of a constitutional provision is that sense in it which was "understood by the nation at the time of its ratification."[22]

Indeed, so axiomatic was the notion that a written constitution, like other legal instruments, should be construed in accordance with the intent of its makers, that it is only in recent decades that one first meets with sustained attempts to elaborate and defend the theory. In part, this may reflect the sheer momentum of a doctrine so long and so firmly embedded in the American constitutional tradition. A deeper explanation, however, would advert to two pictures, one jurisprudential and one semantic, that have long powerfully shaped Western conceptions of law and legal practice, and that continue to exert a strong attraction for many today.

The first picture is that of judges as politically subordinate officials, whose task, as James Wilson said, is "not to make law, but to interpret and apply it."[23] This traditional conception of judges as properly exercising (in Alexander Hamilton's famous phrase) "neither Force nor Will, but merely judgment,"[24] dominated American law for much of our nation's history. Contemporary advocates of "judicial restraint" have made the underlying rationale familiar: since "rule in accord with the consent of a majority of those governed is the core of the American governmental system,"[25] electorally unaccountable judges should limit themselves to ascertaining and applying the policy choices of the elective branches of government, rather than making law or policy themselves. In constitutional law this principle of judicial deference was manifested very early in the form of an adjudicative rule,[26] now widely known as "Thayer's Rule" after the constitutional scholar who argued most influentially for its correctness,[27] that courts should not hold an act of the political branches invalid "unless its violation of the constitution is, in their judgment, clear, complete, and unmistakable."[28] This traditional presumption against unconstitutionality, although widely endorsed by originalists past and present, clearly conflicts with a strict or pure form of originalism, since it requires judges in some cases not to enforce what seems on balance to be the best originalist reading of a particular constitutional provision. Still, many of the same values and concerns that motivate originalism also lie behind Thayer's Rule, and it was only when judges began to develop a more "activist" conception of their political role, beginning roughly around the turn of the century and reaching its peak in the latter years of the Warren Court, that an effective challenge to originalism could be mounted.

In addition to the inertia of precedent and the power of the traditional conception of judicial authority, a semantical theory that for centuries served as the standard account of how words achieve sense and reference may also have contributed to the long dominance of originalism in this country. According to that theory, verbal meaning is, focally, what philosophers of language now call speaker's meaning: "that meaning which the person or persons, who made use of the words, intended to convey to others, whether he used them correctly, skilfully, logically or not."[29] The influence of this traditional picture of linguistic meaning is evident in the ancient theory, apparently accepted by Aristotle[30] and Aquinas,[31] and expounded most influentially in modern times by Locke, that "Words in their primary or immediate Signification, stand for nothing, but the Ideas in the Mind of him that uses them."[32] It is only within the last century or so that scholars working in many different disciplines—literary theory,[33] philosophy,[34] linguistics,[35] as well as law—have begun to develop nonintentionalist interpretive and semantical theories to challenge the traditional speaker-based semantics.

In short, constitutional originalism has long been supported by powerful intellectual currents in political and philosophical theory as well as in law. It should be noted, however, that American judges and commentators have rarely endorsed originalism in a strict or unqualified form. One common qualification of the theory, noted above, is Thayer's Rule. Another is the so-called Plain Meaning Rule, at one time held to be a fundamental canon of constitutional and statutory construction, but now widely rejected.[36] As applied to constitutions, the rule held that

> [w]here the meaning shown on the face of the words is definite and intelligible, the courts are not at liberty to look for another meaning, even though it should seem more probable or natural, but they must assume that the constitution means just what it says. . . . But if the words of the constitution, thus taken, are devoid of meaning, or lead to an absurd conclusion, or are contradictory of the other parts of the constitution, then it cannot be presumed that their prima facie import expresses the real intention. And in that case,

> the courts are to employ the process of construction to arrive at the real intention, by . . . [*inter alia*] studying the facts of contemporary history and the purpose sought to be accomplished, and the benefit to be secured, or the evil to be remedied, by the provision in question.[37]

Finally, most originalist judges and commentators, past and present,[38] would concede that original intent must sometimes give way in the face of long-standing or transformative judicial precedent or practical construction. Indeed, for much of our constitutional history it was generally held that "the principle of *stare decisis* applies with special force to the construction of constitutions, and an interpretation once deliberately put upon the provisions of such an instrument should not be departed from without grave reason."[39]

We saw earlier that the prevailing view during the founding era was that "[t]he real intention [of the lawmaker], when accurately ascertained, will always prevail over the literal sense of the [law's] terms."[40] As the nineteenth century wore on, however, this traditional "intentionalist" approach to legal interpretation came increasingly under fire. Its critics—among them such giants of nineteenth-century American law as Joseph Story[41] and Theodore Sedgwick[42]—charged that the theory was both unworkable and unwise. "How are we to know," for example, Story asked,

> what was thought of particular clauses of the constitution at the time of its adoption? In many cases, no printed debates give any account of any construction; and where any is given, different people held different doctrines. Whose is to prevail? Besides; of all the state conventions, the debates of five only are preserved, and these very imperfectly. . . . How are we to arrive at what is the most probable meaning? Are Mr. Hamilton, and Mr. Madison, and Mr. Jay, the expounders in the Federalist, to be followed? Or are others of a different opinion to guide us? . . . [A]re we to be governed by the opinion of those, who constituted a majority of those, who were called to act on that occasion, either as framers of, or voters upon, the constitution? If by the latter, in what manner can we know those opinions? Are we to be governed by a sense of the majority of a particular state, or of all the United States? If so, how are we to ascertain, what that sense was? Is the sense of the constitution to be ascertained, not by its own text, but by the "*probable meaning*" to be gathered by conjectures from scattered documents, from private papers, from the table-talk of some statesman, or the jealous exaggerations of others? . . . Suppose different persons had different opinions, what is to be done? . . . These, and many questions of the same sort, might be asked. It is obvious, that there can be no security to the people in any constitution of government, if they are not to judge of it by the fair meaning of the words of the text; but the words are to be bent and broken by the "probable meaning" of persons, whom they never

knew, and whose opinions, and means of information, may be no better than their own.[43]

The problems Story draws attention to in this frequently cited footnote—inadequate and often unreliable historical evidence, the difficulty in determining whose intentions should count and how to reconcile or "sum" multiple intentions when they conflict—would later become standard objections to intentionalist interpretive strategies.[44] Story's appeal to the "security" of the people also suggests why a growing number of judges and commentators in his own day were beginning to question the wisdom as well as the practicability of intentionalist approaches to legal interpretation. Both in the United States and in England, rising concern over the wide discretion accorded unelected and life-tenured judges under the traditional theory of equitable interpretation led increasingly to calls for judges to adhere closely to the "plain," "natural," or "popular" import of statutory and other legal language. In England, this trend eventually resulted in the supersession of the ancient "Mischief Rule" of statutory construction by the far more restrictive "Literal" and "Golden" rules.[45] Similar stirrings in American law led to progressively more strongly worded forms of the Plain Meaning Rule,[46] growing distrust of judicial appeals to natural, higher, or unwritten law,[47] increasingly more common disavowals of any judicial power either to extend or to restrict the letter of the law in accordance with its "spirit" or "equity,"[48] as well as to appeals, such as Story's, to prefer the original conventional or popularly understood meanings of legal texts to any private or subjective meanings that may have been intended by their makers. We shall see later that Story's efforts on this score met with only partial success and that the issue of lawmakers' intent versus original public meaning continues to be the focus of lively debate in both statutory and constitutional contexts today.

LEGAL REALISM AND ITS AFTERMATH

> I look forward to a time when the part played by history in the explanation of dogma shall be very small, and instead of ingenious research we shall spend our energy on a study of the ends sought to be attained and the reasons for desiring them.
>
> —Oliver Wendell Holmes, Jr.[49]

The developments noted in the preceding paragraph were all intramural developments within a still thoroughly regnant originalist framework. The revolutionary notion that neither original intent *nor* original textual meaning should be controlling in legal interpretation was first argued with significant effect only in the early decades of the twentieth century. In the forefront of those arguing for this view was a group of reform-minded lawyers and judges known as legal realists.[50] The leading figures in the movement—Oliver Wendell Holmes, Jr., Roscoe Pound, John Chipman Gray, Karl Llewellyn, Felix Cohen, Jerome Frank, and others—scarcely shared a fixed jurisprudential credo. Nevertheless, a number of common themes run through their writings. One of the most important of these was the need to look "realistically" at what judges actually do in resolving legal disputes. In this regard, the realists denied what legal "formalists" were alleged to affirm: that judges seldom make new law, as opposed to merely interpreting existing law; that they routinely "deduce" legal conclusions by more or less mechanically consulting and applying a set of supposedly clear, comprehensive, and consistent legal rules; that they exercise minimal discretion and are rarely influenced by the "felt necessities of the time, the prevalent moral and political theories, intuitions of public policy," or "the prejudices which judges share with other men."[51] Prescriptively, the realists urged judges to acknowledge frankly the extent to which gaps, inconsistencies, and unclarities in the law make hard judicial choices unavoidable; to abandon prevailing laissez-faire models of law and adjudication and conceive of these social instrumentalities pragmatically, as means to socially desired ends; and to exercise unabashedly the discretion they often possess to resolve legal disputes on their merits to achieve just outcomes and advance the common good. An integral part of this ambitious program, not surprisingly, was to undermine the prevailing originalist orthodoxy in both statutory and constitutional hermeneutics.

The main criticisms advanced by the realists against originalist approaches to interpretation have all become familiar gambits in the current debate over original intent. Since these arguments will be examined in detail in subsequent chapters, they can be discussed briefly here.

One common realist argument was to develop and generalize Story's claim that historical evidence of original intent is often unreliable or inconclusive.[52] It was argued by some, for example, that Story's argument is equally valid when the object of historical investigation is not legislative or framers'[53] intent but rather the public meaning or public understanding of statutory or constitutional language.[54] Other critics picked up and elaborated Story's related complaint that originalists have never supplied convincing answers to the questions, "Whose intentions are to be counted?" and "What should be done when the relevant intentions conflict?"[55] Several critics, anticipating later arguments, sought to show that standard intentionalist approaches are actually inconsistent with true fidelity to the Constitution's framers, since the framers' broader, overriding intention was that the document should "be adapted to the various *crises* of human affairs."[56] Others argued on broadly pragmatist grounds that static conceptions of legal meaning are undesirable given the need to keep legal norms flexible and context-sensitive in the face of changing social, economic, and political conditions.[57] Some[58] appear to have endorsed a still stronger argument: that static conceptions of legal meaning are actually incoherent, since, in Bishop Hoadly's famous dictum, "whoever hath an absolute authority to interpret any written or spoken law, it is he who is truly the lawgiver, to all intents and purposes, and not the person who first wrote or spoke them."[59] Thus it was widely argued that the Constitution can "mean one thing at one time and an entirely different thing at another," since "at any given time the Constitution means what the Supreme Court says it means."[60] Other critics, echoing Jefferson's bold declaration that "[t]he earth belongs always to the living generation,"[61] questioned whether it was not anything more than "filio-pietism"[62] to suppose that the intentions of one generation could really bind another.[63] Finally, it was widely urged that the very notion of a collective legislative "intent" or "will" is a particularly barefaced legal fiction.[64] This was thought to be true, generally, for two reasons. First, it was held that talk of intent is reasonably realistic, if at all,[65] only if one is talking about "ideas consciously before the draftsmen, the committee, the legislature: a known evil to be cured, a known goal to be attained, a deliberate choice of one line of approach rather than another."[66] In many cases, however, courts are required to apply statutory or constitutional language to "circumstances utterly uncontemplated at the time of its passage."[67] Second, and more importantly, while talk of a composite legislative intent may be reasonably intelligible in cases in which every member of a lawmaking body has basically the same determinate situations in mind as specific applications of an enacted or proposed law, to attribute any intention whatever to a lawmaking body when it enacts or proposes a law "which some two or three men drafted, which a considerable number rejected, and in regard to which many of the approving majority might have had, and often demonstrably did have, different ideas and beliefs,"[68] is sheer mystification. There is no nonarbitrary and coherent way of combining disparate individual intentions into a composite group intention. And even if such an "intention-voting" schema could be devised, to "fashion monsters and endow them with imagination,"[69] as the orthodox theory of interpretation in effect requires, is hardly a satisfactory way of settling statutory and constitutional issues in a changing world.

Reactions to these far-reaching criticisms were predictably varied. A few, mostly conservatives, but famously including one New Deal liberal, Justice Hugo Black, effectively ignored the realists' arguments. Black, in particular, seemed to believe that a sufficient answer to the realists' corrosive doubts was simply to practice better and more extensive originalist archaeology.[70] Others largely accepted the realists' animadversions against intentionalist approaches, but insisted that these arguments had little force against interpretive strategies that focused, not on any subjective intentions of lawmakers, but on the original conventional meaning or public understanding of the laws they proposed or enacted.[71] Still others suggested that the most serious difficulties raised by the realists could be blunted by adopting what recent commentators have termed an "agency"[72] or "delegation"[73] model of legislative intent.[74] On this model, the collective intention of a lawmaking body (the "principal") is identified with the individual intentions of a small number of legislative "agents"—legal draftsmen, members of legislative committees, bill sponsors, floor leaders, or others—prominently associated with a particular legal measure. The principal advantage of this approach, as its proponents noted, is that there often is reasonably good evidence of the comparatively few "canonical" intentions judges are called upon to ascertain and enforce. This advantage is enhanced when the model is combined, as it sometimes was, with what was perhaps the most common response to the realists' assault on traditional legal hermeneutics.[75] This was to attempt to salvage broader legislative goals from the general ruin of lawmakers' "intent" by distinguishing relatively generalized or abstract legislative intentions (purposes) from other putative entities (legislative "meaning," "will," or "specific intent")[76] that realists had admittedly shown to be suspect or worse. It was suggested that, whatever might be the status of these alternative senses of legislative "intent," general legislative purposes or goals often *are* both widely shared and discoverable, and that these larger purposes or ends, once determined, both can and should play an important role in the interpretation and application of enacted law.

Notwithstanding these various expressions of dissent, the realists' campaign against originalist jurisprudence, particularly in the field of constitutional law, must be accounted a striking success. Remarkably, there was no major counterattack; indeed, not a single sustained defense of the old originalist orthodoxy was written to counter the dozens of attacks on the theory that appeared throughout the 1920s and 1930s. Most of those who responded to the realists sought only to mitigate or qualify the latter's radical conclusions, not to dispute their central thrust. In the law schools, the triumph of the new interpretive approach was swift and pervasive. On the Supreme Court, the triumph was slower and more equivocal but, over time, unmistakable. An early sign of the sea change to come occurred in 1934, when Chief Justice Hughes, speaking for a sharply divided Court, declared:

> It is no answer to say that this public need was not apprehended a century ago, or to insist that what the provision of the Constitution meant to the vision of that day it must mean to the vision of our time. If by the statement that what the Constitution meant at the time of its adoption it means today, it is intended to say that the great clauses of the Constitution must be confined to the interpretation which the framers, with the conditions and outlook of their time, would have placed upon them, the statement carries its own refutation. It was to guard against such a narrow conception that Chief Justice Marshall uttered the memorable warning—"We must never forget that it is a constitution we are expounding . . . [,] a constitution intended to endure for ages to come, and consequently, to be adapted to the various crises of human affairs."[77]

Seven years later, in 1941, Chief Justice Stone expressed clearly the new tone that, by then, had triumphed on the Court:

> [I]n determining whether a provision of the Constitution applies to a new subject matter, it is of little significance that it is one with which the framers were not familiar. For in setting up an enduring framework of government they undertook to carry out for the indefinite future and in all the vicissitudes of the changing affairs of men, those fundamental purposes which the instrument itself discloses. Hence we read its words, not as we read legislative codes which are subject to continuous revision with the changing course of events, but as the revelation of great purposes which were intended to be achieved by the Constitution as a continuing instrument of government.[78]

In the years that followed, while the Court continued to attach considerable importance to historical evidence of the original understanding of constitutional provisions, its attitude toward arguments from history had decisively changed. With increasing frequency, the Justices were inclined to pronounce historical evidence of original intent "inconclusive,"[79] or to hold that fundamental changes in social and political conditions made it impossible to "turn back the clock"[80] to the time when various constitutional provisions were adopted. This was particularly true with respect to the Equal Protection and Due Process Clauses of the Fourteenth Amendment, adopted in 1868. By holding that the constitutional guarantee of equal protection cannot be "shackled to the political theory of a particular era,"[81] the Court was able to brush aside clear evidence that the amendment was not originally understood to prohibit segregated public schools,[82] legislative malapportionment,[83] discriminatory suffrage laws,[84] gender discrimination,[85] or antimiscegenation legislation.[86] Similarly, by adopting the view that "[g]reat concepts like . . . 'due process of law,' 'liberty,' 'property,' were purposely left to gather meaning from experience,"[87] the Court was able to effect a veritable revolution in procedural and substantive due process jurisprudence, without being significantly constrained by historical conceptions of what legal "processes" are "due."[88] Nor were the Equal Protection and Due Process Clauses the only provisions of the Constitution the Court viewed as adaptive or open-ended in this way; the Commerce Clause,[89] the First Amendment guarantees of freedom of speech and press,[90] and the Eighth Amendment prohibition of cruel and unusual punishments,[91] among other provisions, were also viewed as delegations to future interpreters to look beyond the document's intended meaning and scope to contemporary values and circumstances in giving evolving significance to the instrument's "majestic generalities."[92] The "struggle for judicial supremacy"[93] that the legal realists and their Progressivist and New Deal allies had waged had apparently been won.

ORIGINALISM *REDIVIVUS*

There is no remembrance of former things.

—Ecclesiastes[94]

Sen. Ervin: I wish to repeat my question: Is not the role of the Supreme Court simply to ascertain and give effect to the intent of the framers of this Constitution and the people who ratified the Constitution?

Judge [Thurgood] Marshall: Yes, Senator, with the understanding that the Constitution was meant to be a living document.

—Marshall Confirmation Hearings (1967)[95]

Sen. McClellan: Would you be willing, as a judge, . . . to disregard the intent of the framers of the Constitution and change it to achieve a result that you thought might be desirable for society?

Mr. Rehnquist: I do not believe I would, Senator.

—First Rehnquist Confirmation Hearings (1971)[96]

As a presidential candidate in 1968, Richard Nixon promised that if elected he would appoint to the Supreme Court what he termed "strict constructionists": judges "who saw their duty as interpreting law and not making law,"[97] who would "interpret the Constitution strictly and fairly and objectively" and not "twist or bend" its words "in order to perpetuate [their] own personal, political, and social views."[98] In keeping with this judicial philosophy, Nixon later nominated William Rehnquist to the Supreme Court and appointed Robert Bork Solicitor General of the United States. Both would emerge as leading spokesmen for a resurgent jurisprudence of original intent.

It is Bork who has perhaps the best claim to have initiated the current round of controversy over originalist jurisprudence. His 1971 paper, "Neutral Principles and Some First Amendment Problems,"[99] is widely cited as among the earliest and most influential defenses of originalism in the recent literature. The central thesis of that paper—"that no argument that is both coherent and respectable can be made supporting a Supreme Court that 'chooses fundamental values' because a Court that makes rather than implements value claims cannot be squared with the presuppositions of a democratic society"[100]—was hardly new. Nor did the article undertake to refute the standard criticisms of originalism that had been systematically surveyed in the literature for four decades. Its influence lay, rather, in the fact that Bork was believed by many to have expressed forcefully the central, fatal problem that afflicts all nonoriginalist approaches to constitutional adjudication: the subjectivity or undiscoverability of moral truth.[101] In Bork's words:

> Every clash between a minority claiming freedom and a majority claiming power to regulate involves a choice between the gratifications of the two groups. When the Constitution has not spoken, the Court will be able to find no scale, other than its own value preferences, upon which to weigh the respective claims to pleasure. . . . There is no principled way to decide that one man's gratifications are more deserving of respect than another's or that one form of gratification is more worthy than another. . . . There is no way of deciding these matters other than by reference to some system of moral or ethical values that has no objective or intrinsic validity of its own and about which men can and do differ. Where the Constitution does not embody the moral or ethical choice, the judge has no basis other than his own values upon which to set aside the community judgment embodied in the statute. That, by definition, is an inadequate basis for judicial supremacy. . . . The judge must stick close to the text and the history, and their fair implications, and not construct new rights.[102]

This is not to say that, for Bork, matters of political morality are wholly up for grabs; in his view, such judgments properly belong "to the political community,"[103] that is, to the majority, since political truth is precisely "what the majority thinks it is at any given moment."[104] It follows that judicial review of the actions of the elective branches is legitimate only if, as is the case, contemporary majorities consent "to be ruled undemocratically within defined areas by certain enduring principles believed to be stated in, and placed beyond the reach of majorities by, the Constitution."[105] But society cannot be said to have consented to the assumption by the Supreme Court of "an institutionalized role as a perpetrator of limited coups d'état."[106] As Bork notes:

> The Supreme Court regularly insists that its results, and most particularly its controversial results, do not spring from the mere will of the Justices in the majority but are supported, indeed compelled, by a proper understanding of the Constitution of the United States. Value choices are attributed to the Founding Fathers, not to the Court. The way an institution advertises tells you what it thinks its customers demand.[107]

Thus, Bork concludes, "[c]ourts must accept any value choice the legislature makes unless it clearly runs contrary to a choice made in the framing of the Constitution."[108]

In the years following Bork's influential article, originalism gradually began to emerge once again as a major focus of constitutional debate. The resulting controversy, for the most part, was unilluminating, as both sides were generally content to do little more than restate familiar arguments and responses in familiar terms.[109] There were a few outstanding exceptions, however. Ronald Dworkin, for example, in a 1972 critique of Nixonian strict constructionism,[110] brilliantly updated and reinforced the legal realists' argument from the assertedly "open-ended" intent of the Constitution's framers by means of his now widely accepted distinction between abstract "concepts" and concrete "conceptions."[111] And three years later, Stanford law professor Thomas Grey, in an elegant and widely cited article, persuasively argued that an "extraordinarily radical" and politically intolerable "purge" of established constitutional doctrine would be required if judges and other political officials were faithfully to apply a jurisprudence of original intent.[112]

In 1977, with the publication of Harvard historian Raoul Berger's *Government by Judiciary,* originalism moved again to the center of constitutional debate. Berger's positive arguments for originalism can fairly be characterized as pedestrian or simply question begging.[113] What galvanized critics and defenders alike was rather Berger's heavily documented argument that the critical first section of the Fourteenth Amendment[114] was originally intended only to constitutionalize the relatively narrow protections of the 1866 Civil Rights Act, which had guaranteed men of all races equal rights

> to make and enforce contracts, to sue, be parties, give evidence, to inherit, purchase, lease, sell, hold and convey real and personal property, and to

> the full and equal benefit of all laws and proceedings for the security of person and property, [with like punishments for like offenses].[115]

The amendment was not intended to reach beyond these rather limited civil rights, Berger argued. In particular, the amendment was not meant to guarantee equal political rights (the right to vote or hold public office), to incorporate the Federal Bill of Rights, to prohibit state-sponsored segregation, or to guarantee equal rights for women. Thus, the original intentions of those who framed and ratified the amendment were not "vague," "abstract," or "open-ended," as activist judges and commentators often alleged, but rather clear, specific, and relatively narrow. As a result, Berger argued, much of twentieth-century constitutional jurisprudence should be frankly abandoned as the illicit product of a judicial "usurpation" of powers that rightly belong to the citizenry of the several states.

In the years since Berger's book appeared, there has been an extraordinary ourpouring of literature on originalist jurisprudence.[116] Since most of the major arguments advanced by leading critics and defenders during this period will be examined in detail in later chapters, discussion of these developments is best postponed until then. Without question, the high-water mark in terms of both public and scholarly interest in the controversy was reached in the late summer and early fall of 1987, as the United States Senate considered, and ultimately rejected, the nomination of Robert Bork to replace Lewis F. Powell on the Supreme Court.[117] Since that time, however, the controversy over original intent has continued to rage and currently shows few signs of abating.[118] To that controversy we now turn.

2

The Nature and Varieties of Originalism

> [I]t is almost necessary, in all controversies and disputations, to imitate the wisdom of the mathematicians, in setting down in the very beginning the definitions of our words and terms, that others may know how we accept and understand them, and whether they concur with us or no. For it cometh to pass, for want of this, that we are sure to end there where we ought to have begun, which is in questions and differences about words.
>
> —Francis Bacon[1]

This chapter has two connected aims: first, to clarify the nature of constitutional originalism, and second, to distinguish carefully the major contemporary and historical varieties of the theory. Taking such pains at the outset of our investigation is essential, I believe, if we are to avoid a number of common confusions that have contributed to what Ronald Dworkin has fairly characterized as the "lamentable character"[2] of the public debate over original intent.

ON THE GENERAL NATURE OF ORIGINALISM

Following current fashion, I have used the expressions "originalism" and "constitutional originalism" to denote a theory (or family of theories) that has gone by many names in the recent literature, including "interpretivism,"[3] "intentionalism,"[4] "preservatism,"[5] "historicism,"[6] and a host of cognate locutions.[7] Despite the now mountainous literature on the subject, it is no simple matter to state with any precision just what the theory asserts. To get some idea of the difficulties involved, consider the following explications of the theory:

> (1) '[O]riginalist' approaches to statutory interpretation . . . [either ask] how the legislature originally intended the interpretive question to be answered, or would have intended the question to be answered had it thought about the issue when it passed the statute, . . .[or, alternatively, they use] the original purpose of the statute as a surrogate for original intent, especially when the latter is uncertain.[8]

> (2) '[O]riginalists,' or interpretivists, . . . maintain that the provisions of the Constitution mean what the Founders intended them to mean.[9]

> (3) Interpretivist theories of constitutional interpretation assert that a court should declare a challenged state action unconstitutional only on the basis of principles derived from the plain language of the text and/or the intent of those who wrote the words.[10]

> (4) '[I]nterpretivism'. . . [holds] that judges deciding constitutional issues should confine themselves to enforcing norms that are stated or clearly implied in the written Constitution.[11]

> (5) Originalism is the view that constitutional interpreters should be bound by the plain meaning of the text and by the intent of the Framers.[12]

These characterizations clearly reflect distinguishable, and in some cases markedly different, ways of thinking about the nature of originalism. By carefully attending to some of these differences, a clearer picture should emerge of just what I take the theory to assert.

As a start, we should note that while some theorists view originalism exclusively as a theory of *constitutional* interpretation,[13] others[14] characterize it more broadly, in such a way that it makes sense to speak of "originalist" approaches to statutory and perhaps other modes of legal or textual interpretation. In the notes I discuss some issues of analytical detail connected with this terminological difference.[15] Here it will suffice to note that, unless otherwise indicated, I shall use "originalism" to refer exclusively to a theory of how the United States Constitution[16] should be interpreted.

Consider, next, the following additional differences between the foregoing characterizations of originalism: (2) describes originalism as a theory of constitutional *meaning*; (3) represents it as what might be called a theory of *negative judicial review*; (4) treats it as a theory of constitutional *adjudication*; (5) characterizes it as a theory of constitutional *interpretation*. Clearly these are not equivalent. So which of them, if any, represents the best way of understanding originalism?

The problem with treating originalism simply as a theory of constitutional *meaning* is that some originalists clearly hold that it is not so much the original meaning of constitutional language that is now binding as it is the original *intentions* or *understanding* of those who drafted or ratified that language.[17] In order not to disrupt the flow of argument, an extended discussion of these various notions will be postponed until a later subsection of this chapter.[18] Here we can simply note that it is at best misleading to describe something as part of the "meaning" of a text unless there is at least some colorable basis in the text for the expression of that meaning. It may be true, for example, as originalists often claim,[19] that the framers intended judges to exercise no significant policy making role in the nation's political order. But since the text of the Constitution is completely silent on the subject, it seems decidedly strained to describe such allegedly binding but wholly extratextual intentions as somehow part of the Constitution's original "meaning."[20] This strain becomes even more obvious when the "original" "meanings" asserted to be controlling are in fact purely *counterfactual* judgments—most commonly, what the Framers *would have said* if they could somehow have anticipated and answered in their time an interpretive question now at issue in ours.[21] Accordingly, it seems best not to characterize originalism simply as a theory of constitutional meaning.

Similar problems count heavily against characterizing originalism simply as a theory of *negative judicial review*, that is, as a theory of when courts should *strike down* statutes and other political acts as unconstitutional. Certainly all originalists insist that courts not invalidate state actions on the basis of principles neither stated nor fairly implied in the constitutional text or original understanding of those who framed or adopted that text. But virtually all would also insist on something stronger: that courts must ascertain and enforce the original intent of relevant constitutional provisions even when *upholding* challenged governmental actions. Indeed, a fair number of originalists claim something stronger still: that constitutional interpreters *generally*, not simply judges deciding constitutional cases, should understand the Constitution as its makers originally intended.[22] Thus, it seems unduly narrow to characterize originalism simply as a theory of negative judicial review.

A third and more promising possibility is to view originalism as a theory of objectively correct or valid constitutional *interpretation*. On this view, it might be thought that what originalism fundamentally asserts is roughly that

> (P1) For any interpreter *S* and constitutional provision *p*, *S* correctly interprets *p* just in case *S* interprets *p* in accordance with *p*'s original intent.[23]

However, to understand originalism in this way is to misconceive its normative force. Originalists assert not only that originalist constitutional readings are uniquely correct—much as a literary intentionalist might claim that a particular reading of *Hamlet* is uniquely correct[24]—but rather that judges (and perhaps other classes of interpreters) are in some fairly strong sense *bound* to interpret constitutional language in its original sense. This seems to suggest that what originalists really mean to assert is something closer to the following:

> (P1*) For any interpreter *S* and constitutional provision *p*, *S* correctly interprets *p* just in case *S* interprets *p* in accordance with *p*'s original intent; and if *S* is legally subject to constitutional requirements, *S* has *a duty* to interpret *p* in accordance with *p*'s original intent.

On one reading of this principle, it implies that lower courts, public officials, and ordinary citizens have a duty to interpret constitutional provisions as they were originally intended, even when the Supreme Court has decisively adopted a nonoriginalist interpretation of those provisions. Read in this way, (P1*) states what Rawls calls a theory of partial compliance.[25] The theory is intended to apply, that is, even when its own directives are not universally complied with. Understood in this way, however, (P1*) states a principle that few originalists would accept. Most would concede, for example, that whenever the Supreme Court has clearly settled on a rule, lower courts are at least normally bound to apply that rule, even if they correctly believe that the rule is indefensible on originalist grounds.[26] This suggests that (P1*) might better be read as stating a theory of strict compliance.[27] Read in this way, (P1*) simply states an ideal—the ideal, roughly, that courts and others ought to interpret the Constitution in its original sense. Strictly, it says nothing about what interpretive strategies lower courts, nonjudicial public officials, or ordinary citizens should adopt in cases in which politically authoritative interpreters of the Constitution fail to interpret the document as the correct theory requires. Providing answers to questions of this sort is, instead, the task of a large supplemental theory, a theory of what we might call *constitutional pragmatics*. To such a theory falls the difficult task of providing detailed guidance on interpretive responsibilities when problems of partial compliance or other practical problems make it improper or impossible to interpret and apply the Constitution as the theoretical ideal requires.

Perhaps in order to avoid complications of this sort, most recent commentators[28] have preferred to characterize originalism as a theory of constitutional *adjudication*, that is, as a theory of how courts should decide issues of constitutional law. As attempts at definition, such characterizations would clearly be deficient, since at least many originalists have clearly wanted to assert something stronger than simply that judges are bound to adhere to original intent. Because of the many and widely differing varieties of originalist theory, it seems likely that a strict analysis[29] of originalism is impossible—that at most only "family resemblances" exist between the various theories that have been grouped under the label.[30] If this is true, as I suspect, then discussions of originalism are likely to be most illuminating when they focus on particular versions of the theory. Viewed in this way, characterizations of originalism *qua* theory of adjudication have much to commend them. Originalists of all sorts share a core conviction that in deciding constitutional cases the Supreme Court is at least ordinarily bound to adhere to the Constitution's original intent, and that lower courts are likewise so bound (except perhaps when higher courts have clearly settled on a nonoriginalist interpretation). Outside this area of shared conviction, however, there seems to be little agreement among self-professed originalists about what, if anything, the theory requires of nonjudicial constitutional interpreters. Like most recent commentators, therefore, I shall try to avoid needless complexities by discussing originalism only as a theory of how *judges* should decide constitutional cases. In fact, even more narrowly, I shall focus almost entirely on the question of whether the *United States Supreme Court* should accept a jurisprudence of original intent. The claim that it should I take to be the core assertion of originalism, whatever else may be expressly or impliedly asserted by particular versions of the theory.

THE MAIN VARIETIES OF ORIGINALISM

The form of originalism I shall examine, then, directs judges (at least in the absence of strongly compelling arguments from precedent or practical construction)[31] to accord binding authority to the original intent[32] of the United States Constitution. In this section I provide a typology of the principal historical and contemporary varieties of this theory. The importance of carefully distinguishing these various types will become evident in Chapter 3, where we shall see that some forms of the theory are significantly more defensible than others.

Originalism and Thayer's Rule

We may begin by noting one important distinction that has drawn surprisingly little commentary: that between originalist theories that incorporate Thayer's Rule and those that do not.[33] Thayer's Rule, it will be recalled,[34] requires judges to uphold a challenged state action unless that action *clearly* violates a constitutional norm. On this view, it is *not* a court's task in constitutional adjudication "merely and nakedly to ascertain the meaning of the text of the constitution and of the impeached Act of the legislature, and to determine, as an academic question, whether in the court's judgment the two [are] in conflict."[35] Rather, courts are bound to defer to whatever practical construction a legislature adopts unless such an act is clearly *ultra vires*. Since, as we shall see, many of the most heavily litigated constitutional provisions have no clear and determinate original intent, it is of considerable importance whether this requirement of clear mistake is or is not built into an originalist theory.

The Role of Precedent

A second major distinction is between *strong originalists*, who attach little or no weight to prior Court decisions that are inconsistent with original intent, and *weak originalists*, who accord more significant force to such precedents. As a matter of conceptual coherence, of course, no one claiming to be an originalist can uncritically accord binding authority to every nonoriginalist precedent: that would be as senseless as saying that a utilitarian can consistently treat some deontological principle as of coequal weight with the principle of utility itself. Because virtually every extensively litigated constitutional provision is now construed by the court in a manner inconsistent with the provision's original intent,[36] any theorist who accepts all of these interpretations as settled law is by any practical test not an originalist. Simply stated, there would then be too little left to be an originalist about. This said, however, it is certainly true, as Justice Antonin Scalia has recently noted, that "almost every [contemporary] originalist would adulterate it with the doctrine of *stare decisis*."[37] Thus, the important difference is between originalists like Raoul Berger[38] and Richard Epstein,[39] who frankly call for a wholesale repudiation of the present constitutional order, and originalists like Chief Justice William Rehnquist[40] and Robert Bork,[41] whose respect for precedent is considerably greater but still clearly subordinate to their respect for the framers' intent.

Strict and Moderate Originalism

A further important distinction is between what Paul Brest has termed *strict* and *moderate originalism*. The former, according to Brest, either takes the language of the Constitution as the primary or exclusive source of constitutional law and requires interpreters "to construe [its] words and phrases very narrowly and precisely,"[42] or, alternatively, requires interpreters "to determine how the [framers] would have applied a provision to a given situation, and to apply it accordingly."[43] The first variety of strict originalism Brest labels *strict textualism*, the second *strict intentionalism*. Moderate originalism is similarly divisible into textualist and intentionalist varieties. The former requires interpreters to treat the language of the Constitution as the fundamental source of constitutional norms, but unlike strict textualism it recognizes that this language is to be read in its original "social and linguistic contexts" and that much of this language, so read, is "open-textured."[44] The latter asks, not how the framers would have applied a provision, but instead directs interpreters to apply the Constitution's provisions "consistent with the [framers'] intent at a relatively high level of abstraction, consistent with what is sometimes called the 'purpose of the provision.'"[45] Setting aside for a moment the distinction between original textualism and original intentionalism, let us first examine Brest's more general distinction between strict and moderate originalism.

Moderate Originalism and the Role of General Purposes

Here it is important to avoid confusion about what an originalist can and cannot say about "purposes," understood here in Brest's sense as relatively abstract or generalized intentions. No originalist, as such, can assert that judges are free to disregard the clear original intent of constitutional language in favor of some highly generalized purpose the framers may have shared. Because general purposes can be invoked to support almost any position an interpreter chooses to defend, they impose too little constraint, too little that is genuinely *original*, on judges to be regarded by originalists as a surrogate for clear original intent.[46] This has long been recognized to be true of the great general purposes enunciated in the Constitution's Preamble: national unity, justice, liberty, tranquility at home, defense against foreign enemies, and the promotion of the general welfare. Early in this century, the Supreme Court declared that by themselves these broad purposes can afford no basis for a claim either of state power or of private right.[47] For an avowedly originalist Court,[48] there was little choice: to have ruled otherwise would have effectively transformed the Court into a "continuing constitutional convention"[49] and the Constitution itself into a "blank check to posterity."[50] Judicial discretion of such magnitude is clearly at odds with the spirit of originalism.

This is not to say, however, that originalists are bound to renounce all resort to abstract or general purposes. Such purposes can consistently be admitted on at least three levels: first, as an aid to determining the framers' specific original understanding or intent when this is unclear; second, as a way of enforcing the framers' general interpretive intentions; and finally, as an interpretive aid in cases in which it appears that the original understanding was so fractured that no coherent original intent can be recovered. Each of these requires some explanation.

At least since the Middle Ages, it has been recognized that the reason or purpose of the law is not itself the law.[51] Thomas Rutherforth, writing in the middle of the eighteenth century but faithfully reflecting a much older jurisprudence, cautioned his readers "not to confound the meaning of a law with the reason of it."[52] The latter, he explained, "consists in the end which the legislator intended to obtain; or in the effect which he intended to produce by making the law."[53] The former, by contrast, "is the design of the lawmaker in respect of what he commands or forbids."[54] It is this lawmakers' "design," the intended "meaning" or "sense" of a law, which, it was traditionally believed, judges must seek to determine and apply.[55] This should not be taken to mean, however, that inquiries into broad legislative purposes have historically played little role in originalist jurisprudence. On the contrary, as Blackstone noted about the time of the American Revolution, the traditional view was that "the most universal and effectual way of discovering the true meaning of a law, when the words are dubious, is by considering the *reason* or *spirit* of it; or the cause which moved the legislator to enact it."[56] In fact, until relatively recent times, when reasonably reliable and complete legislative histories have at last become available,[57] judges regularly had little else to rely upon in construing obscure laws than known or conjectured general legislative purposes. Certainly in the American constitutional tradition appeals to such purposes have long figured prominently in originalist strategies. Thus we find Joseph Story, for example, in one of his last major Supreme Court opinions, declaring that

> perhaps . . . the safest rule of [constitutional] interpretation after all will be found to be to look to the nature and objects of the particular powers, duties, and rights, with all the lights and aids of contemporary history; and to give to the words of each just such operation and force, consistent with their legitimate meaning, as may fairly secure and attain the ends proposed.[58]

What should be emphasized, however, is that this is consistent with Story's earlier-stated view that "[t]he first and fundamental rule in the interpretation of all instruments is, to construe them according to the sense of the terms, and the intention of the parties."[59] In the great tradition of Blackstone and of classical originalism generally, Story deemed general legislative purposes of importance, not as *substitutes* for the plain "sense of the terms" or the known "intention of the parties," but rather as valuable extrinsic aids in reconstructing the original sense or intention in cases in which these were unclear.

One type of original purpose, the framers' general *interpretive intentions*,[60] may be viewed as especially important by originalists. Generally, such purposes will be distinguishable from the framers' *substantive intentions*,[61] which (roughly speaking) fix the original "meaning" or doctrinal content of particular constitutional provisions. Interpretive intentions, by contrast, are intentions regarding interpretive canons or strategies that judges and perhaps others ought to adopt in construing and applying constitutional rules. Thayer's Rule, for instance, if rightly attributable to the framers, is an example of an original interpretive intention. Similarly, if it could be shown that the Founders intended the elective branches and not courts to be the final arbiter of so-called political questions[62] of constitutional law, this would also be a case of interpretive, rather than substantive, original intent. Finally, some legal historians have argued that particular versions of originalism were themselves originally intended.[63] In some cases, to be sure, the distinction between substantive and interpretive intent may be unclear, or even collapse altogether. But as a general matter originalists are free to distinguish the two kinds of intent and to insist, if they wish, that both be regarded as binding.[64]

Finally, originalists might legitimately appeal to the framers' underlying general purposes in cases in which no single coherent original collective intent is discoverable. In Chapter 4 we shall examine two kinds of cases in which the problem of "summing" disparate intentions is especially acute. The first involves what we might loosely call "paradoxes of voting,"[65] where different majorities of framers "vote" for inconsistent conclusions. The second are cases in which there were a number original readings, none of which commanded a clear majority, and where at least some of these original readings were sufficiently disparate from others that no "core" or "aggregate" meaning is constructible. Later I shall argue that neither of these possibilities may be dismissed out of hand. Here my point is simply that if such cases should be thought to occur, one natural option available to originalists would be to resort to demonstrably widely shared original purposes as standards for deciding which of the rival originalist readings should be enforced as law.

In sum, while originalists can legitimately appeal to the framers' general purposes in a variety of ways and for a variety of ends, it is contrary to both the history and spirit of originalist theory to suppose that they may treat such general purposes as substitutes for the clearly intended meaning of constitutional language. This suggests that Brest's distinction between "strict" and "moderate" varieties of originalism must be either recast or rejected. Shortly, I shall suggest one way in which the distinction might be reformulated. To do this, however, requires that we look more closely at the distinction, noted earlier, between original textualism and original intentionalism.

Original Textualism

Except as straw men, strict textualists seem not to exist.[66] Nevertheless, for heuristic purposes, it is useful to invent them. Their standardly assigned view, roughly stated, is that the meaning of constitutional language is its original "textual" meaning, that meaning it possesses in virtue of the established linguistic conventions at the time the language was adopted.[67] Thus a strict textualist would hold, for example, that where the Constitution mandates that the "trial of all Crimes, except in cases of Impeachment, shall be by jury,"[68] it expressly says (and *means) "all Crimes"*; no amount of extrinsic evidence that the clause was originally understood to exclude petty[69] or juvenile[70] or military crimes,[71] or to permit voluntary waiver of the right to a jury trial,[72] should be permitted to override the clear conventional or textual sense of the words. Similarly, where the Constitution says that "Congress shall have the Power to . . . promote the Progress of Science and useful arts, by securing for limited Times to Authors and Inventors the exclusive Right to their respective Writings and Discoveries,"[73] this protection is expressly extended only to *authors and inventors*; it may not be extended by construction to film makers, artists, photographers, or others not explicitly named.

A moderate textualist, like his stricter cousin, views the clear conventional meaning of constitutional language as fundamental. He differs, however, in permitting *modest* departures from this meaning to avoid inconsistency, obvious absurdity, or to achieve a closer approximation to its apparently intended or generally received meaning.[74] Thus, although the First Amendment clearly states that "Congress shall make *no law* . . . prohibiting the free exercise" of religion, a moderate textualist judge might well uphold laws prohibiting (even religiously based) polygamy[75] or parental denial of urgently needed medical care to their children.[76] However, the powerful gravitational force (so to speak) of the textually absolute "no law" will continually act upon such a judge to ensure that few such implied exceptions are recognized.[77]

Textualism, even in its strict form, should not be confused with what Richard Kay calls a "pure text"[78] approach to constitutional interpretation. On this view, judges are bound to enforce the original *sentence meaning* of constitutional language, that is, that meaning the language originally expressed independently of any particular context or occasion of use.[79]

For reasons familiar to any student of modern philosophical semantics, such an approach is an obvious nonstarter. Few expressions, considered wholly acontextually, express a single determinate meaning. Read abstractly, for example, the sentence-type "No Bill of Attainder or ex post facto Law shall be passed"[80] could just as well express a *prediction* or *exhortation* as it could a mandatory rule of law.[81] Moreover, like almost any document viewed wholly acontextually, the Constitution is replete with ambiguities or indeterminacies of *homonymy* (two or more words having the same pronunciation or spelling),[82] *multivocality* (one word having two or more senses),[83] and *indexicality*[84](one word having an extension that varies from context to context or token to token).[85] Read acontextually, for example, the Article II requirement that the President be a "natural born Citizen" could equally be taken to refer either to his *place of birth* (i.e., the fact that he was not foreign born) or to the *manner of his birth* (the fact that he was not delivered by Caesarian section).[86] This problem of acontextual indeterminacy pervades constitutional language. As a result, sentence meaning provides a hopelessly indeterminate standard for interpreting constitutional language.

More commonly, textualism is said to assert that judges should apply the rules of the Constitution in the sense that a *hypothetical typical reader* of the time would have understood them.[87] Defined in this way, however, textualism becomes, for practical purposes, indistinguishable from a widely held form of intentionalism: namely, that constitutional rules should be applied in the sense in which they were originally intended or understood by the sovereign people, as a whole, who adopted them.[88] In principle, there is nothing distinctively "textualist" about such an approach. Extensive extratextual research would be needed, for example, to determine whether, say, corporations[89] or the unborn[90] are "persons" within the original public understanding of the Equal Protection Clause. More importantly, careful historical investigation would almost certainly produce cases in which the original public understanding of a constitutional provision diverged significantly from the plain textual meaning of its words. The Article III guarantee of trial by jury, mentioned earlier, is a likely example. In cases of this sort, the difference in terms of constitutional theory and practice between a jurisprudence of original textual meaning and a jurisprudence of original public understanding may be substantial. By contrast, there are likely to be few historically confirmable differences between the way the American people as a whole originally understood a constitutional provision and the way the provision's proposers or ratifiers intended it to be understood.[91]

What ultimately distinguishes original textualism from original intentionalism is, rather, this: that textualists stick close to the "letter" of constitutional provisions and eschew more expansive or restrictive interpretations based on the intended meaning, "spirit," or "equity" of those provisions. Textualists are thus what hornbooks used to call "strict constructionists."[92] They believe that constitutional provisions should be read, not so much *narrowly*,[93] as *strictly*, much as an informed literalist would have read them at the time the provisions were proposed and ratified. Intentionalists, on the other hand, tend to be much more hospitable to originalist readings that depart from the letter of constitutional language, so long as these readings conform to the intended sense or spirit of that language.[94]

Original Intentionalism

We turn next to an examination of original intentionalism. In so doing, we enter a minefield of subtle confusions. In many cases these confusions can be traced to overlooked differences in the use of such key notions as "intent," "intention," "meaning," and "understanding." It is therefore important to distinguish carefully these various senses and to make clear how I shall use these and related expressions in the following pages.

As noted earlier,[95] I use "original intent" abstractly, as what Dworkin terms a general "concept" that admits of various competing "conceptions." To illustrate this distinction, consider the notion of social justice. As a general proposition, it would probably be widely agreed that justice consists in giving people their "due," i.e., roughly, what they are entitled to or deserve. There is thus broad agreement on the abstract nature or character of justice, an agreement that serves, as Dworkin notes, as a kind of "plateau on which further thought and argument are built."[96] As one moves away from this plateau of shared abstract agreement, however, toward increasingly more specific theories and opinions about what justice requires, one tends to find less and less common ground among these relatively concrete "conceptions." "Original intent," as I employ the notion, fits this common pattern of abstract agreement and concrete divergence.[97] Originalists, that is to say, agree on some generalized level that the Constitution's original "intent" is binding. They disagree, however, about how best to conceptualize that intent—some emphasizing textual meaning, others intended meaning, still others publicly understood meaning, and so forth. Understanding original intent in this way has the virtue of allowing us to view disputes among originalists as real disputes over a shared interpretive concept, rather than simply semantic disagreements over a word. It also allows us to avoid long disjunctions ("original textual meaning *or* original intended meaning *or* . . .") when speaking about what all or most originalists believe.

We earlier noted that it is important to distinguish the framers' specific intentions from their general underlying goals or purposes.[98] It will be helpful at this juncture if we now distinguish various kinds of relatively specific "intentions" that originalists have often claimed are binding. For our purposes, the most important of these are the framers' original

(a) *scope beliefs*: beliefs[99] about the specific legal *implications or effects* of (correctly interpreted) constitutional provisions (e.g., whether Congress is authorized to incorporate a national bank within the meaning of the Necessary and Proper Clause);[100]

(b) *counterfactual scope beliefs*: beliefs about the specific legal implications or effects of (correctly interpreted) constitutional provisions that the framers would have held if, contrary to fact, they had considered the question at issue (e.g., whether skyjacking is an "infamous" crime within the meaning of the Fifth Amendment Grand Jury Indictment Clause);

(c) *semantic intentions*:[101] intentions regarding the *meaning* of constitutional provisions (e.g., whether an "establishment of religion" means "preferential treatment by the State of some Christian sects over others");[102]

(d) *constitutionalized extratextual intentions*: intentions that have no direct connection with either the meaning or the legal implications of written constitutional provisions but are nonetheless asserted to be binding on judges deciding constitutional questions (e.g., certain interpretive intentions of the sort discussed above).[103]

While other sorts of original "intentions" can no doubt be identified,[104] and may be important in other contexts, these four give us all that we now need to explain the central features of original intentionalism and to distinguish strict from moderate versions of the theory.

We saw earlier that Paul Brest identifies strict intentionalism with the view that judges should "determine how the [framers] would have applied a [constitutional] provision to a given situation, and to apply it accordingly."[105] In terms of my suggested categories, this essentially amounts to the claim that judges should enforce both the framers' scope beliefs and their counterfactual scope beliefs. Understood in this way, Brest's description seems to me to be basically sound, but I would qualify it in two important respects. First, some leading intentionalists[106] are even stricter than Brest's characterization indicates. These theorists accept enforcement of the framers' scope beliefs but deny that judges should attempt to determine or enforce the framers' counterfactual scope beliefs. Second, as we noted earlier,[107] some intentionalists believe that various original extratextual intentions are now binding on judges. To return to an earlier example: imagine that it could be shown that the framers intended only the political branches, and not the Court, to interpret and enforce the constitutional mandate that "[t]he United States shall guarantee to every State in this Union a Republican Form of Government."[108] According to some intentionalists, this interpretive intention would then be binding on contemporary courts. In that case it would be incumbent on judges *not* to attempt to give legal effect to the framers' substantive intentions on the meaning or scope of the clause.

For brevity, we can now introduce the following shorthand. An originalist believes in enforcing the *specific intent* of the framers if he believes that judges deciding constitutional cases should generally seek to ascertain and enforce only the original scope beliefs of the framers.[109] An originalist believes in enforcing the *original understanding* of the framers if he believes that judges should generally seek to ascertain and enforce both the original scope beliefs and the original counterfactual scope beliefs of the framers. An originalist is a *strict intentionalist* if, roughly, he believes in enforcing either the specific intent or the original understanding of the framers. Finally, an originalist is a *moderate intentionalis*t if, roughly, he believes (a) that the framers' semantic intentions (their intended "meanings") sometimes conflict with the framers' specific intent or original understanding, and (b) that judges deciding constitutional cases should generally seek to ascertain and apply the framers' semantic intentions.[110]

The idea that a lawmaker's intended meaning may differ from her specific intent or original understanding is now widely recognized among constitutional theorists. Almost two decades ago, Dworkin made the point clearly in his now-classic attack on Nixonian "strict constructionists." He wrote:

> Suppose I tell my children simply that I expect them not to treat others unfairly. I no doubt have in mind examples of the conduct I mean to discourage, but I would not accept that my "meaning" was limited to these examples, for two reasons. First I would expect my children to apply my instructions to situations I had not and could not have thought about. Second, I stand ready to admit that some particular act I had thought fair when I spoke was in fact unfair, or vice versa, if one of my children is able to convince me of that later; in that case I should want to say that my instructions covered

> the case he cited, not that I had changed my instructions. I might say that I meant the family to be guided by the *concept* of fairness, not by any specific *conception* of fairness I might have had in mind.[111]

In Dworkin's view, the fact that the framers deliberately chose broad, abstract language in formulating various constitutional provisions strongly indicates that they intended such provisions to enact broad concepts, not their own particular conceptions.[112] If this reading of the framers' semantic intentions is correct, then contemporary courts can enforce the original meaning of those provisions only by seeking to determine and apply the best conceptions of those abstract concepts and principles the framers' meant to enact. Inevitably, as Dworkin notes,[113] this will require judges to make controversial judgments of political morality of just the sort that strict originalists condemn.[114]

In fact, even in cases in which the framers did not intend to enact broad "contested" concepts of the sort Dworkin notes, it may be possible to distinguish more or less clearly between the framers' semantic intentions and their specific intent or original understanding. Two possibilities, in particular, should be noted. The first is that the framers may have intended some constitutional expressions to have an *evolving or temporally indexed content*. Thus, the intended meaning of "cruel and unusual punishments" may have been, in effect, "punishments generally considered to be cruel and unusual at the time the interpretive question is asked."[115] If this was in fact how the framers intended the expression to be understood, then enforcing the framers' actual or counterfactual scope beliefs with respect to the clause would violate their semantic intention to give the clause an evolving content. The second possibility, that the framers may have had what Michael Moore terms "spare" semantic intentions, requires more extended discussion.

Speakers have *spare* semantic intentions, in Moore's sense, if their overriding semantic intention is to simply use an expression "in the right way, whatever that turns out to be."[116] Speakers have *rich* semantic intentions, on the other hand, if, in uttering some expression P, they have certain paradigmatic examples or particular definitions or descriptions in mind which they regard as fixing the meaning of P.[117] Some examples may help to make this distinction clear.

Case 1: The mayor of a small town is told that the city's ancient elm trees are being destroyed by Dutch elm disease. He issues an ordinance providing for periodic spraying of all local elm trees at public expense. Later he learns that the types of trees he had long uncritically supposed to be elms are actually beeches. Must an intentionalist hold that what the ordinance actually requires is that *beech* trees be sprayed for Dutch elm disease? No, for the mayor's semantic intentions were almost certainly spare rather than rich; that is, his intention, was simply to refer to those things that are correctly believed to be elm trees. He did not intend to enact his own beliefs about the sense or reference of "elms."[118]

Case 2: A legislature enacts a law imposing strict standards of due care in the handling of toxic substances in, say, 1945. Relying on then-current scientific definitions and evidence, the legislators in 1945 had specific scope beliefs about what substances were toxic. We now have different and better theories about toxins. Should judges committed to enforcing the intended "meaning" of statutes now impose strict liability only on the handling of those substances that the enacting legislators intended to regulate? Surely not. For, again, the enactors' semantic intentions were likely spare rather than rich. Their dominant intent was to impose legal regulations on the handling of those things that are *in fact* toxic. They did not intend to enact into law their own scope beliefs about toxins.[119]

The preceding distinctions permit us to state more precisely how strict intentionalists differ from their moderate counterparts. Fundamentally, strict intentionalists believe that judges should enforce the framers' (actual or counterfactual) scope beliefs either (a) because they believe that this is always, in fact, consistent with the framers' own semantic or interpretive intentions,[120] or (b) because they believe on normative political grounds that judges should restrict themselves to enforcing the framers' scope beliefs, even if it could be shown in particular cases, or generally, that this is inconsistent with the framers' semantic or interpretive intentions.[121] Moderate intentionalists, by contrast, believe that the framers' scope beliefs should be enforced only to the extent that they do not conflict (as, in fact, they sometimes do) with the framers' semantic intentions.

Moderate intentionalists are thus committed to determining, for each constitutional provision, whether the intended meaning was concrete or abstract, rich or spare, temporally indexed or temporally fixed.[122] They are also committed to an often conceptually separable task: determining what we might call the *underlying propositional form* of constitutional provisions. What I mean by this can be illustrated with the aid of the following example.

The Equal Protection Clause of the Fourteenth Amendment states: "[N]or [shall any state] deny to any person within its jurisdiction the equal protection of the laws." For intentionalists, as we have seen,[123] "a thing which is within the intention of the makers of a [law] is as much within the [law] as if it were within the letter; and a thing which is within the letter of a [law] is not within the [law] unless it be within the intention of the makers."[124] Imagine (quite implausibly) that each of the clause's framers understood it as expressing the same proposition, namely that

(EP) No state shall discriminate on the basis of race against any person within its jurisdiction with respect to the fundamental civil rights enumerated in the Civil Rights Act of 1866.[125]

This proposition, then, would express what I term the underlying propositional form of the equal protection guarantee.

Consider a second example. The Establishment Clause of the First Amendment states: "Congress shall make no law respecting an establishment of religion." Imagine that there were two original readings of the clause, namely

(ES) Congress shall make no law according any religious sect or denomination a preferred status

and

(ES*) Congress shall make no law according any religious sect or denomination a preferred status; nor shall it make any law aiding all religions impartially.

Assume, moreover, that a clear majority of the framers favored (ES) over (ES*). Then, given certain plausible intention voting procedures,[126] (ES) states the underlying propositional form of the Establishment Clause.

In practice, as moderate intentionalists generally concede,[127] there may be serious evidential difficulties in determining or reconstructing the underlying propositional form of a given provision. But suppose no such problems beset (ES). Still, interpretive quandaries remain. For example, how exactly are we to construe the key term "religion"? Strict intentionalists will have a ready answer: a religion, for establishment clause purposes, is whatever the framers would originally have counted as such.[128] Moderate intentionalists, on the other hand, must ask a series of further questions related to the framers' semantic intentions. Were these intentions abstract or concrete, rich or spare? If abstract or spare, how exactly should judges attempt to determine the best conception or real referent of "religion"? If concrete or rich, what sorts of paradigmatic examples or particular definitions or conceptions did the framers regard as fixing the meaning of "religion" for establishment clause purposes? Is there any evidence that the clause was "purposely left to gather meaning from experience,"[129] that later generations were expected to read their own "evolving" and hopefully "maturing"[130] conceptions of religious phenomena into the notion of an "establishment of religion"? These are the sorts of difficult historical and philosophical questions moderate intentionalists are committed to answering.

Moderate intentionalism, as I have characterized it, may sound suspiciously like some of the nonoriginalist positions described toward the end of the previous chapter. And in fact, as some commentators have noted,[131] it may be difficult to say whether a particular theorist should be classified as a moderate intentionalist or as a moderate nonoriginalist. Paul Brest has suggested one clear difference: that moderate intentionalists treat original history as binding when it speaks clearly, while nonoriginalists treat historical intentions as at most presumptively binding.[132] But this in fact is wrong on both counts: some nonoriginalists insist that clear original intentions must be enforced,[133] and most intentionalists concede that even clear original intent is not always determinative.[134] Most of the relevant differences, I think, are matters of degree rather than kind. Two such differences seem particularly noteworthy.

First, moderate nonoriginalists generally accord greater weight than do moderate intentionalists to the Court's own prior interpretations of constitutional provisions. As we saw above,[135] there are significant conceptual limits on the extent to which originalists can acquiesce in judicially sanctioned departures from the Constitution's original intent. Moderate nonoriginalists, by contrast, may and generally do accord substantial respect to settled constitutional precedent.

Second, moderate intentionalists generally take a dimmer view than do moderate nonoriginalists of judicial discretion and policy making in constitutional law. The former, accordingly, tend to be quite skeptical of arguments purporting to show that judges have been "delegated" with the Olympian responsibility of discovering and enforcing as fundamental law the best "conceptions" or "real referents" or "aspirational meaning"[136] of the Constitution's abstract language.[137] Where the historical record clearly indicates that the framers *did* intend certain constitutional provisions to be read as broad invitations to judicial freelancing, moderate intentionalists are committed to interpreting those provisions in the sense intended. As a rule, however, such alleged "invitations" tend to be scrutinized for authenticity far more strictly by moderate intentionalists than by advocates of moderate nonoriginalism.

Whose Intentions Count?

This brings us to the final taxonomic task of this chapter: noting the various answers intentionalists have given to the question, Whose original intentions ultimately count for purposes of originalist jurisprudence? The usual suspects are these five:

(a) the *drafters* (i.e., those persons who actively participated in drafting constitutional language);[138]

(b) the *Framers*[139] (i.e., those delegates to the Philadelphia Convention who proposed the original Constitution and those members of Congress who proposed the various amendments);[140]

(c) the *ratifiers* (i.e., those members of the state legislatures and ratifying conventions who ratified the original Constitution and its various amendments);[141]

(d) the *people* of the United States (i.e., those citizens or voters whose agents, the Framers and the ratifiers, proposed and adopted the Constitution);[142]

(e) some *combination* of (a)–(d).[143]

In addition to identifying which of these groups should be counted as the Constitution's framers, intentionalists must also decide whether each member of the selected group should be accorded an "intention vote"[144] or only those members who supported the particular provision at issue.[145] Once the relevant group of intention voters is identified, intentionalists must then settle on an intention-voting procedure (majority rule, plurality rule, etc.) that will determine which of these intentions were actually enacted as law.[146]

These are not questions of merely academic interest; different answers may result in far-reaching differences in constitutional doctrine. For example, some historical studies focusing on the drafters' or Framers' understanding of the Fourteenth Amendment have concluded that the amendment was designed to make all or most of the Bill of Rights binding on the states.[147] By contrast, studies concentrating on the ratifiers' or public's intent have generally concluded that no such effect was intended.[148]

Or consider an example involving the choice of intention-voting procedures. To date, only a few intentionalists have presented an explicit theory of intentionalist voting.[149] One notable exception is University of Connecticut law professor Richard Kay. Kay's theory embodies a kind of near-unanimity rule: all and only those intentions held in common by virtually every intention voter are constitutionalized as binding law.[150] Suppose, then, that two-thirds of the framers of the Fourth Amendment believed that it was an "unreasonable" search and seizure within the meaning of the amendment for law-enforcement officials to break doors in making warrantless felony arrests.[151] One-third believed that it was not. On Kay's near-unanimity rule, since neither of these scope beliefs appears on virtually every "intention ballot," the minority view effectively wins by default: the amendment does not bar such police conduct. On various alternative voting procedures (e.g., majority rule), however, it is the majority view which would prevail and become binding fundamental law.

SUMMARY

This has been a complex discussion, and it may be useful if I summarize its main conclusions. We began by noting that it is difficult to state with precision just what originalism asserts, since commentators have characterized the theory in varying and often inconsistent ways.[152] After examining a number of rival characterizations,[153] we concluded that originalism is most helpfully viewed as a family of related theories, not as a single theory for which a set of necessary and sufficient conditions can usefully be supplied.[154] The most widely discussed form of originalism, we noted,[155] takes the form of a theory of constitutional adjudication. According to this theory, roughly stated, judges deciding constitutional cases should accord binding authority to the original intent of the United States Constitution. It is this general version of originalism which is the focus of this study.

We next saw that there are important differences in the ways proponents of originalism would proceed to fill out this rough characterization of their theory. Some originalists, for example, would require judges to uphold challenged governmental actions unless those actions are clearly and uncontroversially inconsistent with the Constitution's original intent; others would permit judges to strike down challenged state actions whenever a mere preponderance of the evidence indicates that those actions violate original intent.[156] Again, while virtually all originalists have qualified their commitment to original intent with some degree of commitment to the principle of *stare decisis*, we saw that there is a significant difference, in practice, between originalists who attach only slight weight to precedent and those who view respect for past judicial decisions as an important virtue in constitutional adjudication.[157]

We saw, next, that there is a major division between those originalists who view original "intent" as a matter of original textual meaning (original textualists) and those who view it as a matter of originally intended or understood meaning (original intentionalists). Many recent commentators, following Paul Brest's seminal analysis of the varieties of originalism,[158] have distinguished "strict" from "moderate" forms of original intentionalism and original textualism.[159] Much of this chapter has been an attempt to clarify and illustrate the importance of this distinction. After rejecting various common alternative analyses,[160] we concluded that original textualism is best viewed as a kind of literalism. Strict textualists believe that constitutional provisions should be read literally, much like an informed literalist of the day would have read them;[161] moderate textualists, by contrast, permit modest departures from this original literal meaning to avoid inconsistency and absurdity, or to achieve a closer fit with the apparent intentions or purposes of the provisions' framers.[162] The distinction between strict and moderate forms of original intentionalism, we noted,[163] has similarly been widely misunderstood. The most serious misconception, we saw,[164] is that moderate intentionalists believe that judges are free to treat the framers' abstract purposes as surrogates for the plainly intended meaning of constitutional provisions. It was argued that this view is in fact a form of nonoriginalism[165] and that moderate intentionalism is more accurately understood as the view, roughly, that the framers' semantic intentions (their intended meanings) are what ultimately matter in constitutional adjudication.[166] This view, we pointed out,[167] should be distinguished from strict intentionalism, which holds that judges should decide constitutional questions as the framers themselves (would have) intended them to be decided.

Finally, we noted[168] that intentionalists have given importantly different answers to related questions that are fundamental to intentionalist theory: (1) Whose original intentions should ultimately count in originalist jurisprudence? and (2) What voting procedure should originalists adopt to determine which original intentions have been enacted as law?

This completes our typology of originalist theories. Our next task is to determine which form of originalism is most defensible.

3

The Most Defensible Form of Originalism

> It should be a working precept of all jurisprudential criticism and polemics that before launching an attack one should first identify worthy opponents and attribute to them what one considers to be the least vulnerable interpretation of their views that the relevant texts will sustain. Intellectual debate is impoverished when one attacks caricatures; soft targets generally only suit weapons with correspondingly low firepower.
>
> —William Twining[1]

In Chapter 2 we saw that there are many different forms of constitutional originalism and that there are often important differences between these competing versions. The purpose of this chapter is to determine which of these versions is in the end most attractive and defensible. Michael Perry has recently noted[2] that one major reason why the recent debate over originalist jurisprudence has thus far been so unilluminating is that critics of the theory, anxious to portray originalism as a "basket case"[3] that no thoughtful person could seriously entertain,[4] have often ended up attacking straw men that few if any originalists actually accept. For their part, proponents of originalism have generally been content to do little more than restate long-familiar objections against rule by electorally unaccountable "Platonic Guardians"; very few have presented sustained explications and defenses of particular versions of originalism.[5] The result of such tactics, not surprisingly, has been deadlock and continued confusion. A more promising strategy, as Perry has suggested,[6] would be for both sides to seek at least broad agreement on the soundest form of originalism. This would help to clarify and advance the debate in two important ways. First, it would oblige proponents of the theory to proffer and defend answers to certain fundamental questions that have long been squarely posed in the literature but almost never squarely addressed. Second, it would oblige critics of originalism to lay aside the tactics of caricature that have served only to impoverish debate, and to take seriously a theory of constitutional adjudication that, for all its familiar difficulties, is unquestionably one of great power and compelling simplicity" and one "deeply rooted in our history and in our shared principles of political legitimacy.[7] In the following chapters, then, I shall pursue in detail the strategy Perry has recommended and which he himself has pursued on a more modest scale.[8] I shall attempt, that is, to articulate the soundest form of originalism of which I can conceive; I shall then argue that even this most defensible form of theory should be rejected.

ORIGINALISM AND THAYER'S RULE

> Right is weighed by principle; it is not estimated by numbers.
>
> —James Wilson[9]

We saw earlier[10] that some versions of originalism confine judges deciding constitutional cases to enforcing rights that flow more or less uncontroversially from the language or clearly intended meaning of the written Constitution. Taking a cue from Alexander Bickel,[11] I shall refer to such theories as versions of *clear-mistake originalism*. What all theories of this type have in common is the claim that whenever a challenged governmental action is not clearly inconsistent with the original intent of a constitutional provision, courts should defer to the judgments of the representative branches and uphold the constitutionality of the challenged action. There seem to be two principal attractions to such an approach. First, it fits better than do leading alternative theories with a principle that many theorists view as axiomatic in the American political system: the principle that governmental policymaking should be made by officials who are electorally accountable to the people.[12] Second, it provides a ready answer to one of the most common objections to originalism: that the theory provides no guidance to judges in the numerous cases in which appeals to the plain meaning or original history of constitutional language are inconclusive.[13] In these cases, clear-mistake originalists will insist, the duty of judges is clear: they must defer to and enforce whatever practical constructions have been made by the electorally accountable branches of government.

As Thayer convincingly demonstrated in his classic defense of the theory,[14] clear-mistake originalism was widely endorsed (although sometimes, it appears, only in the breach)[15] in the early years of the American constitutional tradition. However by 1893, when Thayer's article appeared, the theory was already in obvious and accelerating decline. In part, as is often claimed,[16] this decline may have been due to an attempt by conservative judges to "usurp" policy making power from elected officials in order to promote their own notions of sound economic and social policy. But it is also important to note that, prior to the 1890s, the Court had seldom been called upon to interpret many of the abstract constitutional expressions ("freedom of speech," "due process of law," "equal protection of the laws") that have since become the major focuses of constitutional litigation. The original intent of these and other abstract constitutional provisions has long been, and remains, a subject of lively historical controversy. As a consequence, those theorists who favor limiting judicially enforceable rights under these provisions to rights that flow more or less uncontroversially from the plain meaning or original history of their language are urging, in effect, that contemporary majorities, acting through their elected representatives, should be the ultimate judges in most cases of the boundaries of majority power and minority freedom. This is a view of constitutional decision making that courts have long rightly rejected as inconsistent with the fundamental design of American constitutional government. Historians now generally agree that the Constitution, as it came from the hands of its eighteenth-century framers, was in many respects a deliberately antimajoritarian document.[17] Responding to perceived democratic excesses during and after the American Revolution, the Constitution's framers sought to dilute the impact of popular opinion by creating an elaborate system of separated and enumerated powers, indirect elections, and checks and balances among the three branches of the national government. An essential feature of this system was the establishment of an independent federal judiciary, insulated from majoritarian pressures and empowered, as Alexander Hamilton said, to

> guard the constitution and the rights of individuals from the effects of those ill humours which the arts of designing men, or the influence of particular conjunctures, sometimes disseminate among the people themselves, and which . . . have a tendency . . . to occasion dangerous innovations in government, and serious oppressions of the minor party in the community.[18]

Judges restricted to enforcing constitutional rights that no reasonable person could deny would not be "bulwarks of a limited constitution against legislative encroachments,"[19] as the framers intended, but would instead be pliant instruments of dominant interest groups and majority will. As Justice Robert Jackson said, "The very purpose of a Bill of Rights was to withdraw certain subjects from the vicissitudes of political controversy, to place them beyond the reach of majorities and officials and to establish them as legal principles to be applied by the courts."[20] Clear-mistake originalism, by leaving the definition of minority rights largely to the vagaries of majoritarian politics, would turn what was meant for bread into stone.[21]

Defenders of the theory might retort that legislatures, over the course of American constitutional history, have proved better protectors of individual liberties and minority rights than have courts. This is not a charge that can lightly be dismissed. Almost half a century ago, the distinguished historian and civil libertarian Henry Steele Commager mordantly observed that the record of judicial review prior to the constitutional revolution of 1937

> discloses not a single case, in a century in a half, where the Supreme Court has protected freedom of speech, press, assembly, or petition against congressional attack. It reveals no instance . . . where the Court has intervened on behalf of the underprivileged—the Negro, the alien, women, children, workers, tenant farmers. It reveals on the contrary that the court has effectively intervened again and again to defeat congressional efforts to free slaves, guarantee civil rights to Negroes, protect workingmen, outlaw child labor, assist hard-pressed farmers, and to democratize the tax system.[22]

During the so-called Lochner era[23] alone, the Court struck down nearly 200 statutes and administrative rules regulating business and protecting employees and consumers.[24] "So wretched a performance," Raoul Berger concludes, "inspires little confidence in the Court as a 'national conscience.' "[25]

The era when courts were apt to read the Fourteenth Amendment as having enacted Herbert Spencer's *Social Statics*,[26] however, is long past and is no more likely to be revived than the era of Jim Crow equal-protection jurisprudence. As Michael Perry has said, "The issue for the present generation of constitutional theorists is not—not principally, at any rate—how noninterpretive review worked in the last half of the nineteenth century or even in the first half of the twentieth century, but whether noninterpretive review has served a salutary, perhaps crucial governmental [policy making] function during the modern period."[27] In our own time one of the most significant facts bearing on this choice is that judges tend to be far more tolerant than the mass public in their attitudes toward minority rights and civil liberties.[28] Because of their relative freedom from political pressures and their institutionalized commitment to principled decision making, courts have a capacity, as Alexander Bickel has said, "to appeal to men's better natures, to call forth their aspirations, which may have been forgotten in the moments hue and cry,"[29] that legislatures often lack. Over the past five decades, for example, legislatures have enacted or declined to repeal laws imposing racial segregation,[30] criminal sterilization,[31] legislative malapportionment,[32] restrictions on marital and family privacy,[33] and gender and other forms of discrimination.[34] Over this same period, state legislatures, attorneys general, and other elected officials have sought to deny or infringe basic rights of fair criminal procedure, including the right to a speedy trial[35] by an impartial jury,[36] rights to compulsory process[37] and cross-examination of witnesses,[38] privileges against self-incrimination[39] and double jeopardy,[40] the right of indigent defendants to free assistance of counsel,[41] and the right to be proved guilty beyond reasonable doubt.[42] In each case, the Court has struck down the state laws or actions in question. Few would now deny that as a result of these Court decisions, we now live in a more just and more morally defensible society. Yet it is doubtful that any of these judicial decisions were clearly legitimate by originalist standards. This highlights both how radical the doctrine of clear-mistake originalism is and how dubious is the claim that legislatures and political majorities are apt, in general, to reach sounder decisions about fundamental minority rights and civil liberties than are judges who have deliberately been insulated from majoritarian pressures for this very purpose.

It should be noted, however, that many legal theorists accept a theory of law that, if true, might be used to support clear-mistake originalism. According to this theory, associated most prominently with H. L. A. Hart,[43] all law, strictly speaking, is clear law. If a law, *L*, does not clearly apply to *x*, then on Hart's view it is either indeterminate whether *L* applies to *x* or it is clear that *L* does not apply to *x*. So-called hard cases, that is, cases in which informed legal observers disagree about whether a law does or does not apply to a given fact situation, are thus cases in which judges must exercise discretion: they must make new law rather than simply apply existing law. This conception of law flows, in part, from a widely accepted theory of language, one that views linguistic meaning as essentially a matter of social convention. According to this view, general terms in legal rules are typically "open-textured": that is, they contain both a "core" of settled meaning and a "penumbra" where their meaning is indeterminate.[44] An object is said to fall within the core meaning of a term if virtually all competent speakers of the language would agree that the object lies within the extension of the term; an object falls within a term's penumbral meaning, on the other hand, if competent speakers would disagree about whether the term applies to that object. Ordinary Fords and Cadillacs, for example, are paradigmatic instances of motor vehicles; they thus fall within the core meaning of "motor vehicle." Motorized wheelchairs, mopeds, and airplanes, on the other hand, are more debatable examples; they thus fall within the penumbral meaning of "motor vehicle." Since it is indeterminate, on this view, whether, say, airplanes are motor vehicles, a judge required to decide whether a statute barring the knowing transportation of stolen motor vehicles across state lines applies to airplanes[45] must make, rather than apply, law. The way in which this widely accepted theory of language and law might be used to support clear-mistake originalism is as follows. Judges, it may be argued, clearly have no legitimate power to nullify the decisions of elected officials unless those decisions are contrary to fundamental law.[46] But the law, on this conception of law and language, extends only to cases that fall within the core of settled meaning of legal language, that is, to those cases to which the language of the law clearly applies.[47] Thus, judges have no legitimate power to strike down the decisions of elected officials unless those decisions are clear violations of constitutional language.[48]

One response to this argument would be to accept the theory of legal meaning that underlies it but to deny that judges may never exercise significant discretion, that is, make law, in reviewing governmental actions for constitutionality. Somewhat surprisingly, this seems to be Robert Bork's view. He writes:

> [M]ost [constitutional] doctrine is merely the judge-made superstructure that implements basic constitutional principles. . . . Where there is a known principle to be explicated the evolution of doctrine is inevitable. Judges given stewardship of a constitutional provision—such as the first amendment—whose core is known but whose outer reach and contours are ill-defined, face the never-ending task of discerning the meaning of the provision from one case to the next.[49]

The view Bork is arguing for here—that judges properly exercise at least a limited lawmaking role in defining the outer boundaries of abstract constitutional provisions, and that courts, rather than legislatures, are the primary "stewards" of such provisions—has long been a widely accepted view among both liberal and conservative constitutional commentators.[50] We have already seen some reasons why such a view is attractive; later we shall notice others.

A more far-reaching response to the foregoing argument would be to reject its underlying assumptions about the nature of law and legal meaning. It might be argued, for example, that it is untrue, in general, that in hard cases judges must make rather than apply law—that typically there are "right answers" in cases in which informed lawyers disagree about which outcome the law requires.[51] Moreover, it might be denied that the meaning of general expressions in legal rules is typically indeterminate with respect to fact situations to which those expressions neither uncontroversially apply nor uncontroversially fail to apply.[52] The first, more general response to this argument raises a set of issues too large to be discussed within the limits of this study. The second response, however, shall be examined at some length in Chapter 4.

ORIGINALISM AND THE VALUE OF PRECEDENT

> It is an inadmissably narrow conception of American constitutional law to confine it to the words of the Constitution and to disregard the gloss which life has written upon them.
>
> —Felix Frankfurter[53]

We noted earlier[54] that originalists disagree over the proper role of precedent in constitutional adjudication. Strong originalists believe that little or no respect should be accorded to past judicial decisions that conflict with the Constitution's original intent; weak originalists, by contrast, believe that fairly substantial respect should be paid to such decisions. Which of these views is more defensible?

In constitutional law, as in law generally, the principle of *stare decisis* serves a number of important values. It promotes the value of liberty by helping to ensure that "government in all its actions is bound by rules fixed and announced beforehand."[55] It promotes the value of fairness by respecting the requirement of formal justice that like cases be treated alike. It serves the values of stability and certainty by enabling individuals to rely on past decisions and to make choices and commit resources based on these expectations. Finally, it promotes the value of efficiency by discouraging the continual relitigation of legal issues and freeing judges from the necessity of continually rethinking such issues *de novo*.[56]

A Court that gave little weight to its own prior decisions would not only disserve these important values, it would also very likely imperil its own institutional capacity to perform effectively its critical role in American government. From the early years of the Marshall Court[57] to the present day, the Court's use of its unenumerated power of judicial review has provoked controversy and, at times, serious threats of reprisal by the political branches. Hostile or anxious Congresses have impeached Supreme Court justices,[58] restricted Court jurisdiction over controversial issues,[59] threatened to withhold funding necessary for the implementation of Court decisions,[60] and canceled whole Supreme Court terms.[61] Strong-willed presidents have attempted (sometimes successfully) to achieve short-term political goals by "packing" or "unpacking" the Court,[62] and have effectively nullified Court decisions by refusing to enforce them.[63] At times, unpopular Court rulings have been substantially evaded or impaired by lax enforcement or outright defiance by state officials[64] or by widespread citizen noncompliance.[65] All this suggests, as Jesse Choper has argued at length,[66] that the Court does not have inexhaustible political capital. Lacking "influence over either the sword or the purse,"[67] and subject in various ways to what Garry Wills[68] has aptly termed the "shoot-out" powers of a sufficiently aroused Congress, the Court must depend upon its own powers of persuasion and its accumulated capital of political and popular prestige. It is thus of great significance that many of the Court's historic decisions, although apparently indefensible on originalist grounds, are now fully integrated and accepted parts of American constitutional doctrine. Many of the Court's landmark decisions on racial discrimination,[69] gender equality,[70] application of fundamental provisions of the Bill of Rights to the States,[71] basic procedural rights of criminal defendants,[72] cruel and unusual punishment,[73] federal implied powers,[74] presidential ascendancy in foreign policy,[75] delegability of legislative and executive powers,[76] paper currency,[77] and federal commerce powers[78] seem to fall into this category. The level of public and congressional commitment to many of these precedents, as evidenced in the 1987 battle over the Supreme Court nomination of Robert Bork, is quite deep.[79] A Court committed to the undoing of these precedents would inevitably arouse intense public and political opposition, badly undermine its own prestige, and risk Court-curbing reprisals that might seriously impair the Court's long-term capacity to perform its basic constitutional functions of protecting individual rights and policing the boundaries of constitutional grants. Of course, if these established precedents were clearly unjust or in obvious ways trenched on fundamental liberties, it could be argued that the Court must adhere to the maxim "*Fiat justitia, ruat coelum.*"[80] But few would claim that the preceding examples suffer from such infirmities.

Finally, an originalist Court that attached little weight to precedent would systematically flout a value that many originalists place at the center of their constitutional jurisprudence: the value of judicial restraint in a system of government committed fundamentally to the ideal of democratic self-rule.[81] The concept of judicial restraint is notoriously contestable, but two values are generally viewed[82] as central to the notion: first, that judges should avoid usurping the policymaking functions of popularly elected bodies and officials by showing appropriate deference to their decisions; and second, that judges should show great respect for controlling precedent. By these criteria, an originalist judge who maintains that original constitutional intent always trumps countervailing precedent would clearly be committed to a program of sweeping judicial activism.

All of this suggests that originalists should attach relatively significant weight to constitutional precedent, particularly to those decisions that are now thoroughly embedded in the fabric of American life and law. This is not to say that originalists should treat the principle of *stare decisis* as an inflexible command. As we have seen,[83] the logic of originalism demands that its adherents view the Constitution itself, rather than any gloss that judges have written upon it, as the ultimate touchstone of constitutionality. Nor, for obvious reasons, would it be wise for originalists to view all past constitutional decisions as irreversible, even if this were consistent with the spirit of their theory. Because "correction through legislative action is practically impossible"[84] when the Supreme Court adopts a mistaken construction of the Constitution, a rigid adherence to prior Court decisions would mean that many of these mistaken rulings would become permanent deformations of constitutional law. In sum, while originalists cannot give controlling or even very great weight to prior holdings inconsistent with original intent, they can and should recognize that in fundamental respects American government and constitutional doctrine have developed in ways that do not comport with original intent, and that now cannot reasonably be judicially overthrown.

TEXT VERSUS INTENT

> There is no surer way to misread any document than to read it literally.
>
> —Learned Hand[85]

Original textualists, as we have seen,[86] hold that judges, in construing constitutional language, should stick close to the literal meaning of that language. Historically, textualists have cited five major advantages of their view over intentionalist approaches to constitutional adjudication.[87] First, textualism reduces the risks of politically unaccountable judicial policy making by prohibiting judges from straying too far from the "plain" or literal import of constitutional language in search of the probable intentions or general purposes of the framers.[88] Second, a textualist approach to constitutional adjudication typically requires judges to engage in less historical research than do intentionalist approaches. This not only saves time and expense,[89] it also promotes a stabler constitutional order by anchoring constitutional doctrine in the comparatively firm ground of literal meaning, rather than on the shifting sands of amateur historical scholarship.[90] Third, textualism is less vulnerable than is intentionalism to the vexing problem of discovering or constructing a single authoritative original intent on the basis of meager historical evidence or in the face of a multiplicity of conflicting and apparently incommensurable individual original intentions.[91] Fourth, textualism respects the requirement, often said to be ingredient in the ideal of the rule of law,[92] that persons subject to the coercive power of the state be given fair notice when that power is likely to be employed.[93] Finally, the constitutional text is superior in authority to the framers' intent, because only the text was submitted to the ratifiers for their approval.[94]

These arguments doubtless have some force. On the other hand, however, there are a host of serious and familiar difficulties with literalist approaches to constitutional interpretation. Two problems are particularly important. First, many constitutional provisions clearly were not intended to be construed with wooden literalness, and become destructive of the framers' purposes and of widely shared notions of political morality and effective governance if interpreted in that way. Second, many constitutional provisions, even if they were originally intended to be read strictly or narrowly, can no longer be read in this way consistently with long standing and widely accepted ideals of individual rights and governmental power. I shall develop these two points in turn.

We noted in Chapter 1 that the original Constitution and Bill of Rights were framed by men committed to the traditional interpretive canon that laws should not be construed literally, so as to defeat the apparent intent of their makers, but "equitably" or "rationally" so as to effect that intent and an outcome consistent with justice and right reason.[95] A number of constitutional clauses and provisions reflect the framers' confidence that courts would continue to adhere to this traditional approach to legal interpretation. Literally construed, for example, the Double Jeopardy Clause of the Fifth Amendment extends only to those criminal prosecutions that place in jeopardy the "life or limb[s]" of defendants. The framers, of course, intended the protection to extend also to prosecutions that threatened the *liberty* of criminal defendants,[96] and courts have ruled accordingly.[97] Similarly, in requiring that "[e]very order, resolution or vote to which the concurrence of the Senate and House of Representatives may be necessary . . . shall be presented to the president of the United States,"[98] the framers clearly did not intend to require that every vote taken prior to the passage of legislation, or every resolution not intended to have the force of law, be submitted to the President, as this "obviously ill-considered provision"[99] literally implies. Again, in mandating that the "citizens of each State shall be entitled to all Privileges and Immunities of Citizens in the several States,"[100] the framers clearly did not intend to bar all preferential treatment, however reasonable or minor, by a state of its own citizens over citizens of other states. Here, as elsewhere, as courts have consistently held,[101] the framers chose sweeping language to express a broad principle that judges were not expected to apply with mechanical literalness. Earlier, we saw that this is also apparently true of the First Amendment "absolutes" forbidding Congress from enacting laws prohibiting the free exercise of religion, or abridging freedom of speech, press, assembly, and petition, and of the Sixth Amendment guarantee of a jury trial in "all criminal prosecutions."[102]

With respect to each of the preceding examples, a strictly literal construction would both disserve the framers' purposes and produce outcomes indefensible on grounds of political principle or policy. There are other constitutional provisions that *were* originally intended, it seems, to be interpreted more or less literally, but which even originalists now generally concede should not now be so interpreted. Thus, while a literal reading of the clause vesting "[a]ll legislative Powers"[103] in the two Houses of Congress would seem to prohibit expansive delegation of lawmaking authority to independent regulatory agencies and executive officials, most originalists would agree that long standing Court decisions[104] sanctioning such delegations should not now be judicially overruled,[105] despite clear evidence of the framers' commitment to the Lockean principle *Delegata potestas non potest delegari.*[106] Similarly, while a literalist approach to the Commerce Clause, which vests Congress with power "[t]o regulate commerce . . . among the several States,"[107] would require a dramatic rollback of current federal regulatory authority, few originalists now press for such a rollback,[108] notwithstanding strong evidence of the framers' commitment to a regime of state-centered federalism.[109]

One important reason for preferring intentionalist over textualist strategies of constitutional adjudication is thus that the former tend to produce outcomes that are morally and politically more defensible than those produced by textualist strategies. This, of course, is exactly as one would expect, given that the original Constitution was drafted and ratified by men who strongly believed that the "spirit" or "reason" of a legal instrument was at least as important as its "letter" in determining the instrument's proper construction.[110]

Intentionalist approaches also tend to be more consistent than texualist alternatives with a conception of judicial responsibility that originalists have traditionally endorsed and that continues to command wide support today: that of judges as subordinate political officials whose task is not to frustrate the declared will of those entrusted with lawmaking authority, but rather to act as "honest agents" of those lawmakers by seeking to ascertain and give effect to their will, at least where this is consistent with a judge's higher allegiance to fundamental law.[111] Widespread acceptance of this "honest" agent conception of judicial responsibility helps to explain why, as noted earlier,[112] "plain meaning" approaches to statutory and constitutional adjudication came under sharp attack in the early decades of this century and are now generally repudiated: it became clear that judges were employing such approaches to frustrate the intended purposes of progressive statutory and constitutional initiatives.[113] Textualists, in effect, seek to replace this currently prevailing honest agent model of judicial responsibility with an older view: one that sees judges and lawmakers as in some respects natural antagonists.[114] Convinced that fairness and predictability are among the preeminent virtues of law, textualists hold that judges should play the role of legislative gadflies, continually goading lawmakers to draft clear, explicit, and detailed legislation if they wish to have their will enforced by courts. So far as statutory interpretation is concerned, there is much to be said for this "flagellant theory"[115] of judging, as British jurists[116] and American admirers of British legal hermeneutics[117] have long maintained. But the attractions of this model in the context of American constitutional adjudication are much less compelling, basically for three reasons. First, of course, the framers are long dead, and hence cannot be goaded into doing anything.[118] Second, it is widely known that many heavily adjudicated constitutional provisions have not been, and are not now, literally construed by courts; thus, a sudden veer toward literal interpretations of these provisions would disserve the values of fairness and predictability rather than advance them. Finally, with constitutions, far more than with statutes, there are often weighty reasons for drafting them in terms of "majestic generalities,"[119] leaving it to later interpreters to adjust these broad, ringing expressions to the mundane demands of *prudentia* in a complex and constantly changing world. Drafting constitutions in this way allows them to have a measure of flexibility in the face of unforeseeable future contingencies.[120] It also makes it easier for constitution makers to reach agreement, since, as noted earlier,[121] it is generally easier to achieve consensus on general principles than it is on issues of detailed application. Finally, as Erwin Chemerinsky has argued at length,[122] this approach serves a vital unifying function by enabling persons with widely differing political views to agree on the basic moral legitimacy of the Constitution, and even to imagine that their own specific conceptions of moral and political ideals are embodied in its general language. Textualism, by requiring literal construction of this general language, tends to undercut at least the first and third of these values in ways that moderate intentionalism, in particular, does not.

We can provisionally conclude, then, that intentionalism is a sounder, more defensible approach to constitutional adjudication than textualism is. There are two ways in which we might find it necessary to modify this provisional conclusion. First, we might find, as many critics have argued,[123] that intentionalism is hopelessly unworkable or even incoherent. If these critics are right, and textualist theories fare better against such criticisms than intentionalist theories do, then some version of textualism might yet prove to be the most defensible form of originalism. Second, we might decide, in the end, that the soundest form of originalism is actually some *mixed* theory—perhaps one that is fundamentally intentionalist, but that nonetheless makes certain concessions to textualism in order to accommodate the latter's historic strengths. Before considering these questions, however, we must first determine which form of intentionalism is most defensible. We begin with the two most general forms of the theory: strict and moderate intentionalism.

STRICT VERSUS MODERATE INTENTIONALISM

Strict intentionalists, we saw,[124] hold either (1) that courts, in deciding constitutional questions, should enforce the framers' specific intent (i.e., their actual beliefs about the proper scope of constitutional language) or (2) that such courts should enforce *both* the framers' specific intent and their counterfactual intentions (i.e., those beliefs about the proper scope of constitutional language the framers would have held if, contrary to fact, they had considered whether a given provision does or does not apply to a given object or state of affairs). A moderate intentionalist, by contrast, holds that courts, in construing constitutional provisions, should seek to discern and enforce those principles or propositions the framers originally believed themselves to be proposing or ratifying as fundamental law.[125] Thus, while strict intentionalists look to the framers' beliefs regarding the *reference* or *extension* of constitutional language, moderate intentionalists look, instead, to the intended *meaning* or *sense* of that language.[126]

Raoul Berger has defended strict intentionalism as the theory of adjudication to which the framers themselves intended courts to adhere.[127] Berger's claim has been challenged by other constitutional historians,[128] but it is clear this is an argument no side can win: the evidence is simply inconclusive.[129] It seems unlikely, in fact, that the framers *had* a considered preference for either strict or moderate intentionalism, since the distinction between these theories remained unclear until comparatively recently.[130] Moreover, even if it could be shown that the framers *did* intend courts to decide constitutional cases by looking to the framers' actual or counterfactual scope beliefs, it would still need to be argued that original interpretive intentions of this sort are binding on courts today. To argue that the framers' interpretive intentions are binding because the framers intended them to be would clearly be question begging.[131] Some independent normative argument is thus needed to support this claim. We shall see later, however, that there are sound reasons for *not* treating the framers' interpretive intentions as authoritative.

Second, it might be argued that strict intentionalism is preferable to moderate intentionalism because only the former is consistent with the attractive theory, discussed above,[132] that courts should be honest agents of their political superiors. The argument might be developed as follows: Strict intentionalism, by requiring judges to decide constitutional cases as the framers themselves would have decided then, clearly respects the requirement that judges seek to effect, rather than to frustrate, the will of those acting constitutionally within the bounds of their lawmaking authority. Moderate intentionalism, by contrast, is inconsistent with this honest-agent model, as the following example reveals. Imagine that it could be shown that a clear majority of the framers of the Equal Protection Clause intended the clause to enact the following principle:

> (EP*) No state shall discriminate against any person when the discrimination reflects only prejudice.[133]

Suppose also that most of the clause's framers clearly believed that laws prohibiting women from serving on juries are not founded simply on prejudice, but instead reflect reasonable beliefs about the ability of women to perform satisfactorily the duties of jurors.[134] Today, of course, such sexist stereotypes are seen be groundless. Moderate intentionalism, accordingly, would require contemporary judges to strike down such laws. To do so, however, would be contrary to the clearly expressed will of the framers, and hence would be inconsistent with the duty of courts to act as honest agents of their political superiors.

This argument assumes that the will of the framers is properly respected in constitutional adjudication only when courts enforce the framers' (actual or counterfactual) scope beliefs, even when it is clear that the framers misunderstood the force of their own principle. It is far from clear, however, why moderate intentionalists should accept this assumption. We noted earlier[135] that if a legislature votes to enact a law regulating the handling of toxic substances, the natural presumption would be that it intended the law to apply to substances that really are toxic, not to those that it would have counted as such. For a court to enforce the mistaken scope beliefs of such a legislature would thus frustrate its collective will, rather than effect it. Similarly, if the framers of the Fourth Amendment[136] intended to prohibit searches and seizures that are, in fact, "unreasonable," courts would not be acting as honest agents of those framers if they were to enforce the latter's mistaken beliefs about which sorts of searches and seizures actually are unreasonable. In short, this strict intentionalist argument assumes precisely the point that many moderate intentionalists deny: that the framers intended their own conceptions about the proper reach of constitutional language to serve as the touchstone of correct constitutional interpretation.

A defender of strict intentionalism might argue, third, that it is generally easier to determine the framers' actual or counterfactual scope beliefs than it is to determine a single canonical "principle" or "meaning" that the framers may have sought to enact in drafting or ratifying constitutional provisions. This is true, it might be argued, for two reasons. First, there is often much better evidence of how the framers expected particular provisions to be applied than there is of any original agreement as to the precise "meaning" such provisions were intended to convey. For example, historians generally agree that the framers of the Equal Protection Clause believed that the clause did not prohibit segregated public education,[137] bans on interracial marriage,[138] or laws denying political rights to women.[139] But there is no agreement as to the specific "principle," if any, the framers collectively intended the clause to enact. Second, even when there is reasonably good evidence of the framers' semantic intentions, that evidence often indicates that the framers disagreed over just what principle they were proposing or ratifying. When that occurs, a moderate intentionalist apparently confronts a much more serious difficulty in "summing" the various competing principles into a single collective "intent" than that faced by his strict intentionalist rival. This is so because beliefs about the specific applications or effects of legal rules are often *commensurable* in ways that semantic intentions are not.

To see this, imagine that half of the framers of a provision, *P*, believed it would apply only to *A* and *B*, and half believed it would apply also to *C*, *D*, and *E*. Imagine further that a strict intentionalist judge is presented with the question: Did the framers "intend" *P* to apply to *C*? The answer will depend on which theory of intention voting the judge chooses to apply. On Kay's near-unanimity theory, examined earlier,[140] the answer will be "no," since by hypothesis the only scope beliefs on which there was unanimity or near-unanimity were those whose objects were *A* and *B*. On, say, a "representative intention" approach,[141] on the other hand, the answer will be "yes," since a mythical "median" or "representative" framer would have held that *P* does apply to *C* if a vote had been taken on that very issue.

Now imagine that a moderate intentionalist comes to the following conclusion regarding the original meaning of the Eighth Amendment's Cruel and Unusual Punishments Clause: roughly a third of the framers intended to enact their own specific conceptions of cruel punishment; another third intended to constitutionalize an "evolutionary" conception of such punishment, so that the clause would prohibit punishments that are generally believed to be cruel at whatever time the interpretive question is asked; and the last third intended to enact a broad concept of cruel punishment, one that prohibits punishments that are in fact cruel, regardless of what the framers themselves or later generations may believe to be cruel. Given the apparent incommensurability of these different semantic intentions, a strict intentionalist might plausibly argue that there is no nonarbitrary and plausible way of aggregating or summing these intentions into single collective intent of the sort that moderate intentionalists seek.

This argument has some force, but it is important that it not be overstated. *Both* strict and moderate intentionalism clearly confront massive evidentiary difficulties.[142] So serious are these difficulties, in fact, that to ask which of these theories enjoys an advantage on this score may sound a bit like the "choice" Woody Allen puts to graduates:

> More than any other time in history, mankind faces a crossroads. One path leads to despair and utter hopelessness. The other, to total extinction. Let us pray that we have the wisdom to choose correctly.[143]

But however that may be, it is doubtful, in fact, that either theory enjoys a clear advantage in terms of the reliability and ease with which it is able to ascertain (or construct) the kinds of historical intentions it seeks. No doubt there are constitutional provisions for which it is relatively easy to identify a number of the framers' specific scope beliefs yet quite difficult to pin down with any confidence some particular "principle" the framers collectively intended to enact. It is perfectly clear, for example, that the framers did not believe that the Eighth Amendment prohibited all forms of capital punishment.[144] Yet it is hotly disputed just what proposition or principle the framers understood the amendment to express.[145] Conversely, however, there are also provisions for which there is no serious doubt about their intended meanings, but little surviving evidence of how the framers expected the provisions to be applied to particular cases. The most obvious examples are provisions involving deliberately vague language, such as the Eighth Amendment ban on "excessive" fines or the Fifth Amendment requirement that private property not be taken for public use without "just" compensation. To suggest that modern-day courts, in deciding how clauses of this sort should apply to contemporary controversies, should perform heroic feats of imaginative transposition with the eighteenth-century framers would obviously be senseless.

Nor is it true that, for practical purposes, strict intentionalism enjoys any real advantage over moderate intentionalism in its ability to construct a single collective original intent from the conflicting and possibly incommensurable intentions of individual framers. Had we full and accurate information about the semantic intentions and actual and counterfactual scope beliefs of the framers, perhaps it would often be easier to "sum" psychological states of the latter sort than it would be those of the former. As things stand, however, sophisticated theories of intention-summing are a bit like jet engines in the Stone Age: there simply is not the wherewithal to put them to practical use. The best that we can usually hope to say with any confidence is that *most* of the framers believed so-and-so. As we shall see later, conclusions of this sort do provide enough historical information to apply a few fairly crude theories of intention-summing. However, none of these theories confers any real advantage on one form of intentionalism over another.

Finally, it might be argued that strict intentionalism has this advantage over moderate intentionalism: that it better affirms those values of stability, clarity, and certainty that originalists have always viewed as among the principal virtues of their theory.[146] Strict intentionalism serves these values by confining judges to a single value-neutral task: discovering and enforcing the specific intentions or conceptions of the framers. Moderate intentionalism, by contrast, is likely to result in less stability and predictability, since in some circumstances it authorizes judges to use their own political judgment in carrying out the framers' abstract, spare, or evolutionary semantic intentions, and it is often difficult to predict how judges might exercise such discretion.

One response to this argument would be to note that in practice no form of originalism can escape the uncertainties inherent in wide-ranging judicial discretion: the historical record is so inconclusive, so full of gaps and ambiguities, that originalist judges of all stripes must continuously make difficult and controversial historical and normative judgments.[147] This *tu quoque*, however, while just, is far from decisive. If certainty and stability are indeed the cardinal virtues of constitutional adjudication, then it must be conceded that strict intentionalism does enjoy a distinct advantage over its moderate rival.

A major strength of moderate intentionalism, however, is precisely that it recognizes the importance of striking a balance between the values of predictability and stability on the one hand, and those of flexibility and adaptability on the other.[148] One of the most common and (as I shall later argue) most damaging objections to originalism is that the theory is too static—that it fails to appreciate the need for constitutional principles to have sufficient elasticity and breadth to cope with the problems and needs of a constantly changing society.[149] Moderate intentionalism enjoys the significant advantage of being able to respond, as strict intentionalism does not, both to originalism's traditional concern with the values of certainty, stability, and judicial restraint, and to the perennial complaint of originalism's critics that the theory is hopelessly at odds with the need to treat the Constitution as a living, flexible document.

A second advantage moderate intentionalism enjoys over strict intentionalism is its capacity to recognize that constitutional provisions, in principle, may signify aspirations and values that transcend the framers' temporally bounded conceptions of the scope of those provisions. Critics of originalism such as Sotirios Barber[150] and Michael Moore[151] have persuasively argued that the Constitution is a more ennobling and inspiring document if seen as signifying real values—real justice, real liberty, and real equality—rather than as signifying merely the historically conditioned conceptions of such values by past generations. Viewing constitutional principles as "aspirational"[152] in this way enables the Constitution to become a "lodestar" for aspirations to "social justice, brotherhood, and human dignity."[153] Less grandly, it permits interpreters to avoid outcomes that are deeply repugnant or even unthinkable to contemporary sensibilities. It is this second consideration, perhaps more than anything else, that accounts for the shift by many prominent originalists during the latter years of the Reagan administration away from strict intentionalism toward forms of moderate intentionalism.[154] These theorists apparently came to realize that politically unimpugnable decisions like *Brown v. Board of Education*[155] and *Reed v. Reed*[156] could not be defended on strict intentionalist premises, but could be colorably defended on recognizably originalist grounds if the notion of original intent could somehow be cut loose from the framers' concrete opinions about the legal effects of their constitutional handiwork.[157] Moderate intentionalism thus seemed an attractive halfway house between two unacceptable extremes: a jurisprudence that constitutionalized the repellent prejudices of former generations on the one hand, and a jurisprudence of open-ended judicial policymaking on the other. In short, by adopting moderate intentionalism, conservatives could admit that the framers had sometimes wrought more wisely than they had known, yet deny that they had wrought half so "wisely" as nonoriginalists often claimed.

It thus appears, on balance, that moderate intentionalism is a more defensible form of originalism than either textualism or strict intentionalism. Later, we shall ask whether it is necessary to modify this conclusion, and if so to what degree. Before turning to that and other matters, however, it is necessary to complete our general account of the most defensible form of originalism. This we do by taking up the question: Whose intentions should ultimately count in originalist adjudication?

WHO ARE THE FRAMERS?

It is useful to divide this question into two: (a) Who are the framers of the original Constitution? and (b) Who are the framers of the twenty-six amendments to the original Constitution? I shall consider the second question first.

Who Framed the Amendments?

For many years, the prevailing originalist view has been that courts, in interpreting a constitutional amendment, should give weight *both* to the intentions of the congressional framers who proposed the amendment and to the intentions of those state legislatures that ratified it.[158] The usual justification for according intention votes to both groups is that the Constitution itself, in Article V, specifies that a proposed amendment becomes law only if passed by a two-thirds majority in both Houses of Congress and ratified by at least three-fourths of the state legislatures.[159] Because, by law, both Congress and the state legislatures are essential actors in the amendment-making process, courts properly look to the intentions of both groups in construing amendments, just as in construing federal statutes, courts rightly look to the intentions of both Houses of Congress and not simply to those of the House that initially proposed or passed the statute.[160]

The leading alternative view is that courts, in interpreting an amendment, should accord binding authority to the "public understanding" of the amendment's meaning, not to the "subjective intentions" of the amendment's framers or ratifiers.[161] In recent years, proponents of this view (call it *public-understanding originalism*) have advanced three arguments in its defense: (1) that public-understanding originalists can largely avoid the problem of summing conflicting subjective intentions which afflicts other intentionalist theories;[162] (2) that laws generally, and constitutional provisions and amendments in particular, are public acts, and hence should be construed as they were originally publicly understood, not in accordance with the private intentions of their framers or ratifiers;[163] and (3) that the framers and ratifiers themselves must have intended that courts treat the original public understanding of constitutional language as controlling.[164] I shall consider these arguments in order.

The first argument rests on the common confusion, noted earlier,[165] between public-understanding originalism and original textualism. The latter looks, as we have seen, to the literal "dictionary" meaning of words; the former to the original understanding of the American people[166] as a whole. We saw that there is good reason to believe that these two sorts of "meanings" sometimes come apart in constitutional contexts. Textualism, it is true, *is* able largely to avoid the problem of summing conflicting intentions.[167] But this is not true of public-understanding originalism. If the object is to determine how the American people as a whole originally understood a given provision, it is necessary to examine *evidence* of what the American people *as a whole* actually thought; it is not enough simply to consult dictionaries or common-law authorities or to invoke patently fictive bromides about the people's "presumptive" knowledge of congressional and state legislative constitutional debates.[168] A public-understanding originalist must determine, for example, whether the term "person" in the Fourteenth Amendment was publicly understood in its customary legal sense, as applying to corporations, or rather in one of its many nontechnical senses, as applying only to natural persons or to some subset of natural persons.[169] Similarly, in asking how the American people as a whole originally understood the expression "bill of attainder,"[170] it is not enough for a public-understanding originalist simply to note that the term had a fixed technical sense in the English common law, and from this conclude without more ado that "informed" members of the public must have known of this sense and understood the constitutional clause prohibiting such bills in light of this common-law meaning. For there is evidence that many "informed" Americans during the founding era understood the expression "bill of attainder" in a broader sense than was then standard among English common lawyers.[171] Again, no dictionary or common-law authority can inform originalist historians about how the American public as a whole originally understood the Fourteenth Amendment's prohibition against any states making or enforcing any law abridging the "privileges or immunities" of citizens of the United States. What little evidence there is suggests that "informed" citizens disagreed about the meaning of the clause, just as their congressional and state representatives disagreed.[172] In short, public-understanding originalists cannot avoid the problem of summing disparate original intentions. Indeed, if anything, this problem is all the more vexing for such theorists, since there are far more intentions to be summed and fewer reliable sources of information are available to support the sorts of conclusions public-understanding originalists are committed to finding.

Something similar may be said of the second argument, which asserts that "secret" intentions, unknown to the public, should not be viewed as enacted into law. This too betrays a confusion between textualism and public-understanding originalism. To oversimplify, textualism deals with the problem of publicly unavailable lawmakers' intentions by the effective, if drastic, expedient of making dictionaries the touchstone of correct interpretation. Public-understanding originalism, however, is unavoidably committed to enforcing constitutional rules whose original meaning was publicly unknowable at the time those rules were adopted. In searching for the original public understanding of, say, the Equal Protection Clause, contemporary public-understanding originalists can ransack modern libraries in search of clues as to how informed citizens of Nevada, Maine,

Illinois, and the other thirty ratifying states originally understood the clause.[173] But in 1867, a typical citizen of Nevada obviously had no reliable access to the public understanding that then prevailed in Maine or in most of the other ratifying states; to him, the "sense of the nation" must have been at least as difficult to discern as it now is for modern historians. If public-understanding originalists are seriously troubled by the prospect of courts enforcing publicly unavailable intentions, the best option (short of a conversion to textualism or to some form of nonoriginalism) would be for them to adopt what I earlier termed[174] an "agency" theory of framers' intent. In particular, since for many amendments, including the entire Bill of Rights, the only minimally informative recorded public deliberations are those of the Congresses that framed the amendments,[175] such theorists might wish to identify the intent of the people with the intent of the congressional Framers, who acted as the former's agents in this regard. But then, of course, for practical purposes public-understanding originalism collapses into the view, which initially looked to be quite different, that the group whose intent ultimately matters for purposes of originalist adjudication is that of the Framers.

The third argument for public-understanding originalism asserts that the Framers and ratifiers of amendments must themselves have intended courts to accord dispositive weight to the original public understanding of those amendments, since in many cases the Framers or ratifiers knew that no adequate records of their own deliberations were being kept,[176] and in some cases took steps to ensure that no such records could be kept.[177] Again, however, if this argument supports any view, it supports textualism rather than public understanding originalism, because the Framers and ratifiers must also have known that there were no reliable ways of determining the *public's* understanding of most amendments either. The inconclusiveness of this argument is also shown by the fact that many of the Founders, including Washington,[178] Jefferson,[179] and Madison,[180] clearly believed that the intent of the Framers or of the ratifiers of the original (unamended) Constitution *was* the ultimate touchstone of correct interpretation of the document, even though there were then no adequate published accounts of these groups' deliberations.[181]

Perhaps the most forceful argument for public understanding originalism involves an appeal to the deeply rooted and attractive notion that American constitutions, both federal and state, owe their status as fundamental law to the fact that the sovereign people themselves have adopted them.[182] The central claim of this argument is that to regard the Framers or ratifiers of constitutional provisions as empowered to determine the *meaning* of these provisions (rather than simply to propose and ratify strings of words) is inconsistent with any sufficiently robust conception of the *people* as the ultimate source of fundamental American law.

Note that this argument does not in any way depend upon the hoary fiction of agency law that *qui facit per alium facit per se.*[183] What is asserted, rather, is that there is a sense in which constitutional amendments are *literally* acts of the people. The argument does not deny that the people have delegated to Congress and to the state legislatures the power to make *syntactic* changes in the Constitution. It *does* deny, however, that the people have delegated to these bodies the power to determine the canonical meaning of constitutional language ratified in their name. Only in this way, it is claimed, is it really possible to vindicate the proud boast that the ultimate source of constitutional grants and limitations is "We the people."

This argument raises a host of difficulties that cannot be explored here. Perhaps the most fundamental question to be asked is whether it really is more attractive to view constitutional amendments as (in this peculiar way) direct acts of the people, rather than simply as acts of legitimate representatives of the people. In a famous passage in *Federalist* 10, Madison noted that one of the important advantages of a representative democracy over direct popular rule is that a usual effect of the former is

> to refine and enlarge the public views, by passing them through the medium of a chosen body of citizens, whose wisdom may best discern the true interests of their country, and whose patriotism and love of justice, will be least likely to sacrifice it, to temporary or partial considerations.[184]

Madison here identifies the basic rationale for vesting constitutional "meaning votes" with representatives of the people rather than with the people themselves. As a rule, the former will be better informed about, and more likely to have given careful consideration to, such matters as the likely effects and underlying purposes of proposed amendments, the "mischiefs" such amendments are designed to remedy, the common-law background of technical legal terms, and the relation of proposed amendments to existing constitutional doctrine and practice. To a degree, to be sure, these advantages may be offset by the familiar gambit of restricting meaning votes to "informed" members of the public. But these "informed" citizens are either acting as (unelected) representatives of the uninformed segments of the public or they are not. If they are, then why should binding authority be accorded to *their* intentions rather than to the intentions of those elected representatives to whom the Constitution expressly entrusts the amendment-making power? If they are not, then what remains of the claim that amendments are literally and directly acts of "the people" themselves?

Originalists, accordingly, should reject the view that the people are the framers of constitutional amendments. An alternative view, we have seen, identifies the framers of amendments with their *congressional Framers*. As defenders of this view have argued,[185] there are clear practical advantages in limiting intention votes to the Framers. Extending such votes to the ratifiers significantly increases the amount of legislative history busy judges must consult. Moreover, finding or constructing a *collective* legislative intent is clearly more difficult when the intentions of twenty or thirty legislative bodies must be considered, rather than simply those of the House and Senate. Finally, there is generally much better evidence of what Congress originally understood an amendment to mean than there is of the ratifiers' original understanding.

This argument is unconvincing, however. If it were sound, it would clearly justify far more sweeping disenfranchisements of intention voters. Limiting intention votes to, say, the House and Senate floor managers of proposed amendments would vastly simplify the task of determining a single canonical original intent. But there is an obvious and compelling objection to any such restriction: the fact that the Constitution expressly requires validly enacted amendments to be assented to by two-thirds of both Houses of Congress. Because the Constitution also expressly requires valid amendments to be ratified by three-fourths of the state legislatures, a similar argument can be made against denying intention votes to these legislative bodies.

A second argument for limiting intention votes to the congressional Framers relies on the speaker's theory of meaning. The argument, in brief, is as follows. The meaning of an utterance is determined by its speaker's intentions. The "speaker" of a constitutional amendment is Congress, since it drafted and adopted the final language of the amendment—language, it should be noted, that the various ratifying bodies have no authority to alter.[186] Thus, the meaning of an amendment is determined by the intentions of the Congress that proposed it for adoption.

This argument, too, is unconvincing. We saw earlier that the traditional view that utterance meaning is always a function of speaker's meaning has come under heavy attack in the twentieth century.[187] But suppose we accept this traditional view *arguendo*. Still, few if any intentionalists have wished to identify the "speaker" of a law with the initial *draftsman* of a law: not even the most doctrinaire (statutory) intentionalist suggests, for example, that the intentions of the executive bureaucrats, interest-group attorneys, or congressional aides who actually draft most congressional bills[188] should be viewed as decisive. What intentionalists have always asserted, rather, is that the intent of the "*maker*" of a law is controlling. The "maker" of a law is standardly understood to be those persons or groups whose assent or acquiescence is required by law to give a proposed measure the force of law.[189] According to this standard view, then, the "maker" of constitutional amendments is both Congress and the ratifying state legislatures, since by the express terms of Article V the assent of both groups is necessary to give proposed amendments the force of law. Thus, unless it can be shown that this standard view is incorrect, and that the sole "maker" of constitutional amendments is Congress, this argument fails.

A stronger case can be made for according intention votes only to the *ratifiers* of constitutional amendments. Article V authorizes Congress to "propose" amendments to the states. Some evidence[190] suggests that the framers understood Congress's role in the amendment-making process to be *solely* that of proposing amendments to the states: the actual authors of amendments were understood to be the state legislatures, acting either as representatives of "the people" of the various states *qua* members of those states,[191] or of "the people" of the United States *qua* members of the United States.[192] If this was indeed the framers' understanding of Congress's role in the amendment process, it would seem to follow that, for originalists, courts must adhere to this original understanding.

This argument fails for two reasons. First, there is, in fact, no conclusive evidence that the framers intended courts, in adjudicating cases arising under constitutional amendments, to accord intention votes only to the state legislatures that ratified those amendments.[193] Second, even if there were such evidence, it would not follow that originalists must hold that courts are bound to conform to such an intention. For as we shall see in the following chapter, originalists both can and should deny that original interpretive intentions of this sort are binding on later interpreters.[194]

In short, the standard view appears to be correct. In searching for the original intent of constitutional amendments, courts rightly focus on the intentions of both the congressional Framers and the state ratifiers.

Who Framed the Original Constitution?

This question is more complex than the question of who framed the amendments, since with the Constitution of 1787 there is no relevant law corresponding to Article V that specifies which groups must assent in order for a provision to acquire the status of fundamental law. Both the proposal and adoption of the Constitution were revolutionary acts, unauthorized by existing law.[195] Aside from public-understanding originalists, few originalists have denied the intention voting credentials of the special state conventions that ratified the Constitution. The members of these conventions were elected by the people, whose "original right to establish, for their future government, such principles as, in their opinion, shall most conduce to their own happiness, is the basis, on which the whole American Fabric has been erected."[196] What is far more problematic is whether intention votes should also be accorded to members of the Philadelphia Convention that framed the original Constitution.

The case for denying intention votes to the Philadelphia Framers is strong. The fifty-five delegates who attended the Convention represented only twelve of the thirteen states.[197] These delegates were appointed by the various state legislatures, rather than chosen in popular elections.[198] Moreover, the Convention clearly exceeded its commission by proposing a fundamentally new form of government rather than simply recommending amendments to the Articles of Confederation.[199] Finally, a number of the most influential members of the Convention explicitly stated that they viewed the preratification Constitution as a mere proposal, "nothing but a dead letter," as Madison declared in the House of Representatives in 1796, "until life and validity were breathed into it by the voice of the people, speaking through the several state conventions."[200]

However, originalists have strong reasons for resisting the denial of intention votes to the Philadelphia Framers. One of the most serious and widely urged objections to originalism is that gaps in the historical record often make it impossible to recover the framers' intentions.[201] This objection becomes all but unanswerable if only the intentions of the ratifiers are viewed as authoritative, for the surviving records of the state ratification debates are seriously deficient both in terms of completeness and reliability. Fortunately for originalists, however, a reasonable case can be made for according intention votes to both the Framers and the ratifiers of the original Constitution.

First, appeals to the Framers' intent can be defended on grounds of precedent. Over at least the last century and a half, courts have recurrently treated the intentions of the Philadelphia Framers as dispositive of constitutional issues.[202] Appeals to the Framers' intent have thus figured centrally in the *ratio decidendi* of a huge number of constitutional decisions. Given the virtues of precedential constraint discussed earlier, originalists can plausibly argue that this long standard practice should not be abandoned.

Second, even though the Framers were not directly elected by popular vote, they may still be viewed as legitimate representatives of the people, having been appointed by the state legislatures at the request of Congress.[203] Those chosen to attend the Federal Convention were all prominent and respected public figures in their respective states,[204] and many were men of national and even international reputation. Reflective of this public esteem is the fact that more than a third of the thirty-nine signers of the Constitution were later elected to serve in the First Congress.[205]

Finally, the fact that the Framers themselves may have meant their own intentions not be treated as authoritative is scarcely decisive. Alleged interpretive intentions of this sort, as I shall later argue,[206] should not be viewed as binding on later interpreters. As a preview of that fuller discussion, we may note here that this is a particularly clear example of why originalists are well advised *not* to treat original interpretive intentions as binding. We have just seen that unless the Philadelphia Framers are included among the framers, originalism has no adequate response to the powerful objection that the theory is unworkable, because not enough evidence survives to permit reasonably confident reconstructions of the framers' intent. Originalists thus have a good reason to accept the proposition that

> (1) The substantive intentions of the Philadelphia Framers are binding on subsequent judicial interpreters.

Some originalists have also wished to assert

> (2) Both the framers' substantive and interpretive intentions are binding on subsequent judicial interpreters.

To do so, however, is risky. For a fair amount of evidence suggests that

> (3) One of the framers' interpretive intentions was that the Philadelphia Framers' substantive intentions should not be binding on subsequent judicial interpreters.

That is to say, there is a fair amount of evidence that (1)–(3) form a contingently self-defeating set.[207] To avoid this difficulty, originalists should either seek to disprove (3) (a formidable undertaking) or, better, reject (2). What they emphatically should not do is reject (1), for that claim, I have argued, is central to any minimally defensible originalist theory.

In sum, the most defensible form of originalism accords binding authority to the intentions of both the Framers and the ratifiers of constitutional provisions. To complete our examination of the soundest form of originalism, we must address four additional questions: (1) Should originalists treat the framers' interpretive (as well as substantive) intentions as binding? (2) Which theory of intention-summing should originalists adopt? (3) What should originalists do if, in certain cases, it proves impossible to discover (or construct) any coherent original intent? and

(4) What should originalists do in cases in which, although the original meaning of relevant constitutional provisions is not in dispute, those provisions yield no determinate answer to a particular constitutional controversy? These questions will be taken up in the following chapter.

Except for these remaining issues, this concludes our investigation of the most defensible form of originalism. To summarize the principal conclusions of the present chapter: We saw, first, that originalists should reject all forms of clear-mistake originalism (the view, roughly, that courts should strike down acts of the representative branches only if those acts are clearly or uncontroversially inconsistent with the original intent of some constitutional norm.) Next, we concluded that originalists should accord relatively significant weight to prior Supreme Court decisions, particularly to those decisions that have become thoroughly embedded and accepted parts of American life and law. Third, we determined (provisionally) that the soundest form of originalism is some form of moderate intentionalism (the view, roughly, that courts deciding constitutional issues should accord binding authority to the semantic intentions of the framers.) Finally, we saw that the most defensible form of moderate intentionalism will accord binding authority to the semantic intentions of both the Framers and the ratifiers of constitutional provisions.

4

Three Misconceived Objections to Originalism

In this chapter I examine and rebut three common but misconceived objections to originalism. The first objection asserts that originalism "self-destructs," since the framers intended their substantive intentions not to be treated as authoritative for purposes of constitutional adjudication. The second claims that recent work in philosophical semantics has undermined certain central assumptions of conventional originalist theories. The third asserts that originalism rests crucially on a legal fiction: the fiction that it is generally possible to combine or aggregate the varying intentions of individual framers into a single coherent collective intent. I shall take up these objections in order.

THE CLAIM THAT ORIGINALISM IS SELF-REFUTING

In an influential 1985 essay,[1] H. Jefferson Powell argued that the framers of the Constitution did not intend their own understanding of constitutional language to be binding on future interpreters. Since that essay appeared, a number of constitutional scholars, including such prominent theorists as Ronald Dworkin[2] and Mark Tushnet,[3] have suggested that Powell's work poses serious trouble for originalism.[4] Their argument is simple: If originalism requires judges to enforce the original intentions of the framers, but the framers themselves intended their intentions not to be treated as authoritative, then originalism is committed to mutually inconsistent propositions and so self-destructs as a theory of constitutional adjudication.

There are two ways in which an originalist might attempt to derail this argument. The first would be to challenge Powell's historical thesis that the framers affirmatively intended courts to employ nonoriginalist modes of constitutional interpretation. A number of constitutional historians have attempted such rebuttals.[5] My own research, as reported above,[6] generally supports their conclusions. It is doubtful that the framers collectively intended judges to employ any particular theory of constitutional interpretation. But if they did, there can be little doubt that this interpretive theory was some variety of originalism. For during the founding era and indeed for much of the succeeding century, originalism was not simply the dominant theory of constitutional hermeneutics; with unimportant exceptions it was the only such theory.[7]

A second way of responding to the charge that originalism is self-defeating is to argue that originalists are not committed to treating *all* of the framers' intentions as binding. In particular, it can be argued that originalists are not committed to treating the framers' *interpretive* intentions as binding. It is this second response that I shall develop and defend here.

We saw in Chapter 2 that one form of originalism, original textualism, is not even *prima facie* committed to the claim that the interpretive intentions of the framers are binding. Thus, the objection that originalism *per se* is self-defeating is clearly indefensible. What remains to be considered, then, is the more modest claim that *intentionalist* varieties of originalism are self-defeating.[8]

How, exactly should we construe this objection? Perhaps the argument is this:

(1) Intentionalists hold that judges should treat all of the framers' original intentions as binding.

However, as Powell has shown,

(2) One of the framers' original intentions was that judges should not treat the framers' original intentions as binding.

Hence, by obvious steps,

(3) Intentionalists are committed *both* to the claim that judges should treat the framers' original intentions as binding *and* to the claim that they should not.

Our discussion in Chapter 2 of the main varieties of intentionalism enables us to see straightaway why this argument fails. No intentionalist claims that *all* of the framers' original intentions are binding, at least as the notion of "intention" is ordinarily understood. In common usage, "[a] man's intention is what he aims at or chooses"[9] in performing some action. In this broad sense, it is plain that there are many sorts of original intentions that no intentionalist views as binding. We saw earlier, for example, that intentionalists do not regard the highly abstract purposes stated in the Constitution's Preamble as giving rise to judicially enforceable duties.[10] This is also true of those original purposes that we might term *nonjuridical intentions*: intentions the framers believed that the Constitution would achieve but which were not understood as giving rise to any legal duties. Thus, the founders clearly intended that George Washington would be the first president.[11] But no one would suggest that this intention imposed any sort of duty on voters or presidential electors to vote for Washington in the first presidential election. Similarly, there is abundant evidence that the framers intended members of the Electoral College to be citizens of "superior discernment, virtue, and information,"[12] who would "exercise an independent and nonpartisan judgment as to the men best qualified for the Nation's highest offices."[13] But no intentionalist would claim that this original purpose imposes on voters a constitutional duty (much less a judicially enforceable duty) to elect presidential electors of "superior discernment." This is true *a fortiori* of those nonjuridical intentions that Michael Moore terms "institutionally inappropriate"[14] intentions. Thus, it may be true, to take a famous example, that one of the framers' intentions in drafting and ratifying the Constitution was to further their own personal and class financial interests.[15] But no one would contend that this (alleged) intention, considered abstractly, is one that courts are or ever were bound to enforce.

A far more plausible form of the objection is this:

> (1*) Intentionalists hold that judges should treat as binding both (a) the framers' original interpretive intentions and (b) a specified subclass of the framers' original substantive intentions.

But, as Powell has demonstrated,

> (2*) One of the framers' original interpretive intentions was that judges should not treat *any* of the framers' original substantive intentions as binding.

Therefore, by obvious steps,

(3*) Intentionalists are committed *both* to the claim that judges should treat some of the framers' original substantive intentions as binding *and* to the claim that they should not.

Some leading intentionalists, including Raoul Berger[16] and Robert Bork,[17] do apparently hold that (at least some of) the framers' interpretive intentions are binding. Other prominent intentionalists, however, including Richard Kay[18] and Earl Maltz,[19] expressly deny that such intentions need or should be viewed as authoritative. Thus, even if it can be shown that the framers intended judges to employ nonoriginalist modes of constitutional interpretation, the most that follows is that *some* forms of intentionalism are self-defeating. What needs to be determined, then, is whether the soundest form of originalism does or does not accord binding authority to the framers' interpretive intentions. I shall argue that it does not.

As we have seen, the central worry for originalists here is not that historians might someday produce convincing evidence that the framers positively intended judges to adopt some nonoriginalist methodology. The available evidence indicates quite clearly that while the framers disagreed about which form of originalism judges should adopt, there was general agreement that nonoriginalist modes of adjudication were improper.[20] The major concern, instead, is that by embracing interpretive intent, originalists may be driven to adopt positions that seriously weaken the overall plausibility and appeal of their theory.

For example, substantial evidence exists that the framers both hoped and expected courts would strike down laws that seriously trenched on natural rights, whether those rights were expressly or impliedly embodied in the written Constitution.[21] This doctrine, while not formally inconsistent with originalism, is clearly inconsistent with many of the core values that make originalist theories attractive, including stability, certainty, and judicial restraint. Thus, by embracing interpretive intent, originalists risk being committed to a position they clearly wish to avoid.

Moreover, as we saw earlier,[22] a strong case can also be made that one of the framers' interpretive intentions was that the intent of the Philadelphia Framers should be accorded little or no weight in determining the canonical meaning of constitutional rules. This again, however, is not an interpretive intention that originalists can happily embrace. For, as we noted, if the Framers are not accorded intention votes, it becomes all but impossible to reach reasonably confident historical conclusions about the framers' intent.

Again, a strong historical case can be made that the framers intended courts to adopt some version of clear-mistake originalism.[23] As we have seen, however, clear-mistake originalism is not an attractive form of originalism, in part because it provides insufficient protections against majoritarian infringements of minority rights. Here again originalists who embrace interpretive intent are playing a dangerous game of historical roulette, gambling that further research will not demonstrate that they are committed to an indefensible form of the theory.

These risks might be worth taking if there were some clear theoretical advantage to be gained by insisting that the framers' interpretive intentions are binding. But it is hard to see what this might be. Nonoriginalists are likely to be unimpressed by the "argument" that judges should accord binding authority to the framers' intent because the framers intended they should. Perhaps it could be argued, as an intramural issue among originalists, that it is somehow more attractive on normative political grounds to view judges as having a *legal* duty to employ some particular originalist methodology rather than simply a political or moral duty.[24] However, the practical difference between these two views is obscure. (Federal judges, for example, need not commit *legal* offenses to be removed from office.)[25] Whatever added attraction there may be in treating the framers' interpretive intentions as binding appears to be too slight to justify the considerable risks this view also involves.

In short, the common objection that originalism is self-defeating has very limited force. Even if it is conceded, *arguendo,* that the framers intended judges to be nonoriginalists, the objection shows at most that some forms of intentionalism (namely, those that regard the framers' interpretive intentions as binding) are self-defeating. The argument has no force against more defensible forms of originalism.[26]

CONCEPTUALISM AND THE CAUSAL THEORY OF REFERENCE

A second and more formidable objection to originalism is that the theory, at least as traditionally conceived, is inconsistent with various recent developments in philosophical semantics. The most influential version of this objection is Ronald Dworkin's claim that the framers intended to enact abstract "concepts" rather than specific "conceptions."[27] A more recent form of the objection, advanced by David Brink[28] and Michael Moore,[29] is that originalism is inconsistent with the recently introduced but now widely accepted "causal" theory of reference. I shall examine Dworkin's version of the argument rather briefly, since it has been extensively discussed in the literature. I shall discuss the second form of the objection at greater length.

Dworkin's Concept–Conception Distinction

Dworkin's claim that the framers, in enacting the Constitution's grand generalities and abstract phrases, intended to enact broad concepts rather than specific conceptions[30] has proved enormously attractive to liberal constitutional theorists,[31] for fairly obvious reasons. For at least three decades prior to Dworkin's introduction of the concept/conception distinction, liberal and mainstream constitutional scholars had generally agreed, in Justice Frankfurter's much-quoted words, that "[g]reat concepts like 'Commerce . . . among the several States,' 'due process of law,' 'liberty,' 'property,' were purposely left to gather meaning from experience."[32] At the time, such claims were widely understood to mean that the framers had *delegated* to judges the task of subtly *changing* the meaning of the constitution's "great concepts" to accord with evolving standards of morality and contemporary needs.[33] This was naturally an attractive view to many post-New Deal liberals, but it was also vulnerable to two rather obvious lines of attack. First, the notion that unelected and largely unaccountable judges were authorized, in effect, to amend the constitution by interpretation naturally gave rise to concerns about judicial tyranny and the erosion of cherished liberties.[34] Second, the claim that the framers had delegated to judges the task of giving specific content to the evolving meaning of the Constitution's grand generalities left liberal judicial activists open to the charge that there was no genuinely principled difference between their preferred approach to constitutional adjudication and the approach of conservative judicial activists during the Lochner era.[35]

Dworkin's claim that the framers intended to constitutionalize broad "concepts" was attractive to liberal constitutional theorists at least in part because it provided them with plausible responses to these common objections while preserving the basic attractions of the older delegation model. Against the charge that judicial amendment of the Constitution is illegitimate, such theorists could now retort that it is actually *conservatives* who are committed to such judicial amendment, since the Constitution, properly understood, requires judges to seek out and enforce the best conceptions of the abstract concepts the framers had enacted.[36] And against the claim that there is no principled difference between liberal and conservative judicial activism, liberals could argue that the reactionary outcomes produced by the latter were not simply ill-advised exercises of authorized judicial discretion, but were instead flatly *mistaken* interpretations of constitutional principles, since they rested on indefensible conceptions of the abstract concepts embodied in those principles.[37]

Suppose we give a name to the view that the framers intended to enact abstract concepts: call it *conceptualism*.[38] Commentators have disagreed whether originalists can consistently endorse conceptualism.[39] More precisely, they have disagreed whether someone who holds *both* that the framers' semantic intentions should be enforced *and* that these semantic intentions were highly abstract should be counted as an originalist. The dispute is largely academic, since virtually everyone who claims that the framers enacted abstract concepts also claims that the framers' intent is often trumped by evolving precedent, values, or needs.[40] In principle, however, anyone who asserts that the framers' original semantic intentions are binding should be counted as an originalist. Consequently, I shall treat Dworkin's argument that the framers intended to enact broad concepts not as an objection to originalism *per se*, but rather as a challenge to various forms of originalism as conventionally understood and applied.

Conceptualism, in the sense defined, is essentially a historical claim. Surprisingly, however, no defender of the view has produced sustained historical arguments in its behalf. Instead, what one typically finds, at best, are brief defenses of one or both of two claims: first, that the framers' choice of abstract language ("due process of law," "equal protection of the law") strongly suggests that they intended to enact general concepts and abstract principles rather than specific conceptions;[41] and second, that it is unreasonable to impute to the framers an intention to enact concrete conceptions and principles, given their aspiration to produce "a constitution intended to endure for ages to come, and, consequently, to be adapted to the various *crises* of human affairs."[42]

Neither of these arguments is convincing. In fact, the historical record is clear that the framers often employed abstract language to express quite concrete or specific conceptions or rules. Two examples should serve to make the point.

Since the early years of this century,[43] the Due Process Clause of the Fifth Amendment has been interpreted by the Court as barring federal laws and practices that are "arbitrary, capricious, or unreasonable,"[44] that violate norms "implicit in the concept of ordered liberty,"[45] or that trench on values "so rooted in the traditions and conscience of our people as to be ranked as fundamental."[46] Construed in any of these ways, the clause does indeed express an abstract or vague standard, the correct application of which is often bound to be controversial. But there is general agreement among constitutional historians and commentators that the clause, as originally understood, prohibited only governmental deprivations that resulted when a person, entitled by law to various fundamental *procedural* protections ("due" service of process, trial by jury, grand jury indictment, and so forth), was denied those protections.[47] Thus, while the language of the Fifth Amendment Due Process Clause may be abstract, its original meaning, as Charles Curtis has said,

> was as fixed and definite as the common law could make a phrase. It had been chiseled into the law so incisively that any lawyer, and a few others, could read and understand. It meant a procedural process, which could be easily ascertained from almost any law book.[48]

Something similar may be said of the First Amendment Free Speech Clause.[49] Today, courts read the clause as expressing a relatively abstract principle: the principle, roughly, that government may not directly restrict expression unless that expression poses a "clear and present danger"[50] or falls within one or more "well-defined and narrowly limited classes of speech," such as perjury, incitement, or libel, "the prevention of which [has] never [been] thought to raise any Constitutional problem."[51] Read in this way, the clause certainly does require judges to make difficult and inevitably controversial decisions in search of a correct "balance" between competing public and private interests. There is persuasive evidence, however, that the intended meaning of the clause was not nearly so abstract or difficult to apply. Currently, there appear to be two leading views of the clause's original meaning. According to the first view, whose most illustrious defender was James Madison, the clause "was meant as a positive denial to Congress of any power whatever on the subject"[52] of speech and press.[53] According to the second, whose supporters included John Marshall,[54] the clause was intended only to enact the traditional common-law conception of freedom of expression, which prohibited government from instituting any system of licensing or prior restraint, but did not bar subsequent prosecution or civil action for speech deemed harmful to "the security or welfare of the government, or the safety, character and property of the individual."[55] On either reading, the clause articulates not an invitation for present-day judges to search out and enforce the most defensible "conception" of the proper limits of governmental power over speech, but rather a clear and reasonably determinate standard that judges can apply without, as John Hart Ely derisively remarks, needing to keep up with the *New York Review of Books*.[56]

Such examples could easily be multiplied. In fact, as one leading liberal nonoriginalist has said,[57] evidence is "wholly lacking" that the framers of *any* constitutional provision intended to constitutionalize broad "concepts" in Dworkin's sense of the term. This should not be surprising since, as Mark Tushnet has noted,[58] conceptualism "relies on modern theories of law [and language] that were quite foreign, indeed probably would have been incomprehensible, to the framers of the Bill of Rights and the fourteenth amendment." Moreover, even if the framers did grasp the gist of the modern distinction between abstract concepts and specific conceptions, their well-documented suspicion of judicial activism and discretion[59] makes it quite unlikely that they would have sanctioned the sort of freewheeling judicial interpretation Dworkin's view implies.

Originalism and the Causal Theory of Reference

We turn now to a different, though related, argument against conventional varieties of originalism: that these theories implicitly rely upon various traditional assumptions about linguistic meaning that causal theorists of reference have recently shown to be false. To understand this objection we need to look briefly at traditional theories of meaning and their alleged failings.

As Stephen Schwartz explains,[60] traditional theories of meaning (often lumped together under the label "description theories" or "descriptivism") assert three basic claims:

> (1) Each meaningful term has some set of identifying properties or descriptions associated with it; this set constitutes the *sense* or *meaning* of the term.
>
> (2) The sense or meaning of a term, in the sense specified, determines the *extension* or *reference* of the term.
>
> (3) Analytic truths are based on the meanings of terms.[61]

On this view, then, the *meaning* of a word is a set of criteria that speakers use to apply the word, and a word *refers* to all and only those things that satisfy those criteria. So, for example, the meaning of the proper name "Richard Nixon" is given by some definite description (e.g., "the man elected president in 1968") or by some cluster of such descriptions. "Nixon" refers to whoever satisfies all (or, in some versions of the theory, most)[62] of these associated descriptions. Likewise, the meaning of "tiger" would be something along the lines of "large carnivorous quadrupedal feline, tawny yellow in color with blackish transverse stripes and [a] white belly."[63] "Tiger" refers to whatever things these criteria, or most of them, uniquely apply to.

Beginning in the early 1970s, several philosophers of language, most notably Saul Kripke,[64] Keith Donnellan,[65] Hilary Putnam,[66] and David Kaplan,[67] argued that this traditional theory was wrong, at least for certain classes of terms, including proper names and natural kind terms. A wide array of arguments were deployed against the orthodox theory.[68] Here I shall focus on just three of these objections.

First, it was argued that the traditional theory produces unwanted trivialities.[69] If the name "Richard Nixon," for example, just means "the man elected president in 1968," the sentence "Nixon was elected president in 1968" is semantically equivalent to the trivial sentence "The man elected president in 1968 was elected president in 1968." But that is clearly false.

Second, it was claimed that the older semantics produces counterintuitive modal consequences.[70] Suppose, for example, that the meaning of "Shakespeare" is given by the description "the English playwright who wrote *Hamlet*." In that case, the sentence "Shakespeare wrote *Hamlet*" states a necessary—indeed an analytic—truth. But that is surely false. It is certainly conceivable that we could discover that someone other than Shakespeare, say Francis Bacon, had actually written the play.

Finally, it was argued that the traditional semantics implies, falsely, that most theoretical disagreements are merely verbal rather than real.[71] Recall that on the traditional view, if speakers associate different properties or descriptions with a term, it follows that they *mean* different things by the expression. So, for example, when Einsteinians first challenged the established Newtonian theory of mass,[72] the two sides were not really disagreeing about the real nature of mass. Rather, Newtonians meant one thing by the term "mass," Einsteinians another, and thus the two sides were simply talking past one another. Similarly, most moral and theological disputes, on this view, are really "only about the meaning of a sound,"[73] not genuine disagreements, since close inspection reveals that the contending camps employ different criteria for deciding when their respective claims are true. But this view of theoretical disagreement, as causal theorists pointed out, is implausible. In practice, we do not suppose that disputants are referring to different things—and hence simply talking past one another—if they associate different (and non-coextensive) properties with different terms. Most informed observers would agree, for example, that Newtonians and Einsteinians really were disagreeing about the nature of mass, even though they conceived of that nature in importantly different ways. Thus, the traditional semantical theory is false.

The alternative theory, or "picture,"[74] causal theorists proposed now apparently constitutes the new orthodoxy.[75] On this view, there are at least some classes of terms that do not achieve reference through any mediating "sense" or "meaning." Instead, these terms refer directly to the objects in their extension. That extension is fixed not by any intervening descriptions or concepts, but rather by a causal or historical chain linking present and past uses of a term. A standard way in which a term might be connected to a referent is as follows: A name is given to an individual in an initial act of ostensive "baptism" or "dubbing": "I shall call him 'Aristotle.'" The name is then handed down from speaker to speaker. As long as succeeding speakers intend to use the name as earlier speakers have, the initial reference is preserved. In the case of Aristotle, it is plausible to suppose that these referential links have been preserved. Thus, when I use the name "Aristotle" I succeed in referring to the Greek philosopher who bore that name, even if, in fact, most of the descriptions standardly associated with the name are false.

Defenders of the causal theory have argued that it applies to various other classes of terms in addition to proper names.[76] Most causal theorists extend it, for instance, to natural kind terms such as "water," "gold," and "tiger." Consider this last term. According to traditional description theories, "tiger" conventionally refers to whatever creatures uniquely instantiate a set of stereotypical phenomenal properties, roughly corresponding to the description quoted above: "large carnivorous quadrupedal feline, tawny yellow in color with blackish transverse stripes and [a] white belly." Plainly, this will not do as a *definition* of "tiger": a three-legged or albino tiger is not a metaphysical impossibility.[77] More pointedly, as Kripke notes,[78] it is conceivable that we should one day discover (perhaps on a trip to Alpha Centuari) creatures that look externally exactly like tigers but that have a radically different internal makeup. Kripke argues forcefully—and his intuitions seem to be widely shared[79]—that such creatures would not be tigers. He takes this to show that the traditional account of how natural kind terms achieve reference is mistaken. Instead, such terms refer by means of a causal network. Earlier speakers "baptized" what they took to be paradigm specimens of tigers, and the term "tiger" now refers, via reference-preserving causal or historical links, to whatever creatures have the same *underlying nature* as the initial paradigms. Something similar may be said of the term "gold." *Pace* Locke,[80] the reference of "gold" is not determined by any set of uniquely applicable conventional criteria (being a shiny, yellow, malleable, fusible metal, for example). Rather, the term refers to tokens of the same *kind* of substance that earlier speakers called "gold." We now know that the relevant kind-criterion in this case is microstructural: "gold" designates the element with the atomic number 79. This, of course, was a relatively recent empirical discovery. But this new scientific understanding of the "essence" of gold does not mean that the meaning of "gold" has shifted over time. Rather, historically remote speakers of our language meant by "gold" exactly what we mean, namely, that substance that has the same underlying nature as paradigm samples of gold.

How do these developments in semantics bear on the controversy over originalism? According to Brink and Moore, in the following way. The most defensible form of originalism, as we have seen, accords binding authority to the framers' semantic intentions. Defenders of this view have typically assumed that such intentions are capable of providing significant constraints against judicial discretion and policy making. They have assumed, that is to say, that the fundamental value choices for purposes of constitutional adjudication have already been made by the framers. Judges need rarely if ever *make* significant constitutional value choices; they need only *discover* them. Their proper role, in brief, is that of dispassionate constitutional historian, not moral philosopher.[81]

Brink and Moore, relying on the work of Putnam and other causal theorists, argue that this view of the framers' semantic intentions is fundamentally mistaken. They note that the framers, as believers in natural law, were moral realists who believed that there are *moral* (as well as natural) kinds that exist independently of our conventions and beliefs. This suggests that we may properly extend to normative constitutional terms like "fair," "cruel," and "good" the same semantic analysis that causal theorists have applied to such natural kind terms as "water" and "gold." In barring the infliction of "cruel" punishments, for example, the framers presumably meant to bar punishments that are, in fact, cruel, not those that they or anyone else may have believed to be cruel. They did not, that is, intend to enact their own (or their age's) beliefs about the correct *application* of the abstract language they wrote into fundamental law. Rather, they intended simply to use that language correctly (that is, causally). Thus, the conventional originalist assumption that the meaning of constitutional language is discoverable through disinterested historical inquiry is misconceived. In fact, once we are satisfied that the framers' semantic intentions were indeed spare, historical questions become largely irrelevant. Because the meaning of the Constitution's grand clauses is given by the way the world is, not by anyone's moral or linguistic conventions, judges must look to substantive moral and political theory, not history, to discover the most defensible account of that meaning.

The claim that the original meaning of constitutional language is to be determined causally rather than descriptionally I shall term *constitutional realism (realism,* for short). Taking a cue from Brink,[82] we can distinguish two forms of realism. *Conventionalist realism* looks to the textual or conventional meaning of constitutional words and holds that such words should be interpreted causally even if the framers' semantic intentions regarding those words were clearly rich rather than spare. *Intentionalist realism*, by contrast, looks to the intended meaning of constitutional language and asserts that such language should be construed causally precisely because its framers' semantic intentions were spare rather than rich. Since, as I argued earlier,[83] textualist approaches to originalist constitutional interpretation are less defensible than intentionalist approaches, I shall discuss only the second (intentionalist) form of constitutional realism here.

Like its close cousin, conceptualism, realism gives rise to vexing questions of classification. Perhaps the most important of these for our purposes is whether realism is or is not consistent with moderate originalism. A few paragraphs back, I suggested that conceptualism and moderate originalism should be viewed as consistent in theory but not in practice. The same relationship holds, I believe, between realism and moderate originalism. In practice, virtually all self-identified originalists strongly resist the suggestion that the framers' semantic intentions were highly abstract or spare.[84] This is hardly surprising, since both realism and conceptualism produce outcomes that conflict sharply with such core originalist values as predictability and judicial restraint.[85] Nevertheless, since realism is not formally inconsistent with moderate originalism, I shall treat it as an objection to originalist theories *as conventionally understood and practiced,* not as an objection to originalism *per se.*

Constitutional realism might be criticized on any number of grounds. The most far-reaching criticism, of course, would reject the causal theory wholesale.[86] Since, however, I believe that the causal theory, suitably qualified, is true, this is not an objection I shall advance.

Nor, as a moral realist, do I find persuasive the charge that the causal theory is inapplicable to moral or, more generally, normative terms.[87] There are, to be sure, significant differences between normative terms on the one hand and proper names and natural kind terms on the other.[88] Nevertheless, I agree with Moore and Brink that none of these differences present an insuperable obstacle to extending the causal theory to at least many uses of normative language.

The real problem, rather, is with the claim that the *framers'* semantic intentions were spare. Put simply, there is little or no direct evidence that this is true and much indirect evidence that it is false.

No realist, so far as I know, has offered any *direct* evidence that the framers' semantic intentions were spare. Instead, they appeal to various bits of indirect evidence: the fact that the framers often deliberately preferred abstract to concrete language; that they were presumably wise enough to appreciate both the defeasibility of their own particular conceptions of broad constitutional standards and the folly of attempting to "freeze" any particular historical conceptions into a charter of government "intended to endure for ages to come;"[89] and that, as causal theorists have argued, the causal theory is "presupposed by the intentions with which we speak in everyday life."[90] There is, however, far more convincing evidence, both direct and indirect, that the framers' semantic intentions were at least generally rich rather than spare.

An extended discussion of the direct evidence for this claim is obviously impossible within the limits of this study. Over the course of this essay we have noted a few fragments of this considerable body of evidence. Hamilton's remarks on the "precise technical import"[91] of the Fifth Amendment Due Process Clause and Marshall's claim that the term "liberty of the press" has a "definite and appropriate [common-law] signification, completely understood"[92] are but two examples. On the other hand, I know of no direct evidence that clearly supports a realist reading of the framers' intent.

There is also persuasive indirect evidence against the realist thesis. One bit of such evidence, curiously overlooked in the literature, is the enormous prestige in late eighteenth-century America of the semantical theory of John Locke.[93] Widely regarded by the framers' generation as the Newton of the mind,[94] Locke developed in detail a thoroughly descriptivist theory of language. Conventional groupings of things into various species or kinds, including *moral kinds*,[95] he held, are the "workmanship of the understanding"[96] rather than of nature. Thus, the reference of a term like "gold" is not fixed by any supposed microstructural "real essence"[97] of those things commonly called "gold." Instead, "gold" refers to whatever things fall under the "nominal essence"[98] of gold, i.e., a particular abstract *idea* of various phenomenal properties, the possession of which is conventionally regarded as necessary and sufficient for a thing to be classed as gold. This view reflects Locke's central semantic thesis that "words in their primary or immediate signification stand for nothing but the *ideas* in the mind of him that uses them."[99] Since ordinarily we have no idea of "the unknown constitution of [substances], whereon their discoverable qualities depend,"[100] Locke believed that these supposed "real essences" cannot be what determines the reference of our substance terms.

It might be objected that this appeal to Locke misconceives the extent to which a person's actual semantic intentions are open to conscious inspection. Perhaps the framers, if asked, would have endorsed something like a Lockean view of language. Even so, Moore and Brink might argue, this would not settle the issue of whether their semantic intentions were in fact rich or spare. Speakers' semantic intentions, like their motivations, are simply not that transparent. To determine a person's "deeper semantic intentions"[101] it is often necessary to ask fairly deep counterfactual questions of the sort that Kripke and Putnam ask with respect to typical uses of natural kind terms like "gold" and "tiger."[102]

There are familiar problems of manipulability and uncertainty that afflict counterfactual approaches to determining historical intent.[103] But suppose we set aside these difficulties and concede that it is appropriate, in seeking to determine the framers' "deeper" semantic intentions, to ask what the framers would have said if they had reflected on the sorts of considerations Kripke and Putnam take to show that speakers' meanings are typically spare. Even so, I believe that a convincing case can be made that the framers' semantic intentions were at least typically rich rather than spare.

One obvious problem for the realist thesis is that so much of constitutional language consists of technical or quasi-technical terms drawn from the common law. Terms like "bill of attainder," "ex post facto law," "letters of marque and reprisal," "corruption of blood," "presentment," "felony," "equity," "grand jury," "admiralty," "due process of law," "liberty"[104] "establishment of religion," and "freedom of the press" all had technical and more or less settled common-law meanings. In some cases, it is true, the framers appear to have understood common-law terms in ways that differed somewhat from their established technical meanings.[105] But even in these cases, the evidence is clear that the new meaning closely tracked the old. These technical terms, as causal theorists have themselves emphasized,[106] are paradigmatic examples of words to which the causal theory does not apply.

Moreover, as we saw in the preceding chapter,[107] the framers often used nontechnical terms in ways that differed from their ordinary or literal senses. Thus, the framers plainly intended that the term "person" as used in the Fugitive Slave Clause should extend to black slaves.[108] Just as clearly, however, they did not intend that slaves should be deemed "persons" within the meaning of the Fifth Amendment Due Process Clause.[109] Again, historians have generally agreed that Justice Curtis was correct in his brilliant dissent in *Dred Scott*[110] that at least many free blacks were originally considered to be "citizens" within the meaning of the Diversity of Citizenship Clause[111] (authorizing federal courts to hear suits "between citizens of different States"). At the same time, however, it is difficult to deny Chief Justice Taney's claim in his majority opinion in that case[112] that free blacks were not originally considered "citizens" for purposes of the Privileges and Immunities Clause,[113] since such a reading would have invalidated dozens of laws in both northern and southern states discriminating against out-of-state free black sojourners and settlers.[114] Such examples show clearly that Moore is wrong in claiming that "people do not have semantic intentions different from the *right* way to apply a word," and thus that "[s]emantic intentions . . . drop out entirely as helpful tools in interpretation."[115] In fact, as I earlier argued at length,[116] the Constitution is replete with expressions that the framers understood more expansively or restrictively than their literal meaning would suggest.

Finally, it bears repeating in this context that the founders were deeply suspicious of judicial lawmaking and discretion.[117] We noted earlier that this suspicion deepened during the first half of the nineteenth century,[118] culminating in the furious public and congressional reaction[119] to the Court's activist proslavery decision in *Dred Scott*. Not until relatively late in that century, with the rise of the doctrine of substantive due process, does one begin to find significant support for the notion of an activist judiciary. Given the framers' clearly expressed distrust of judicial policy making and discretion, it is simply incredible that they would have endorsed the activist view of constitutional adjudication implicit in contemporary constitutional realism.

Is this to say that an originalist judge ought *never* to adopt a realist interpretation of the framers' semantic intentions? That is a stronger claim than I should wish to defend. Consider the following adaptation of an example used by Moore.[120] The president lies stricken by an assassin's bullet. Doctors certify that, although his heartbeat and respiration are artificially sustained, he has suffered total and irreversible brain death. Declaring the president to be "dead" within the meaning of the Twenty-fifth Amendment, the vice-president immediately announces that he has assumed the powers and duties of the presidency. Several days later, pursuant to Section 4 of that amendment, the (former) vice-president, together with other principal officers of the executive branch, transmit to the president pro tempore of the Senate and the Speaker of the House of Representatives their written declaration that the president is unable to discharge the powers and duties of his office."[121] Later, suit is filed in federal court turning on the issue of whether the new (acting) president was in fact president in the days prior to his written declaration to Congress that the (former) president was unable to discharge his duties. To decide the case the court must determine whether the (former) president was dead during that period or merely disabled.

Should the court be much influenced by the fact that, at the time the amendment was ratified (1967), the standard legal definition of 'death' was the irreversible cessation of circulatory and respiratory functions?[122] Probably not. Here it does seem plausible to say that "[m]ost ordinary speakers intend by their use of the word "death" to name a natural kind of event whose nature it is the business of science to reveal as we learn more about it,"[123] and that the amendment's framers shared these realist linguistic intentions. By adopting this reading of the amendment, the court would be free to apply the now widely accepted definition of death proposed by the President's Commission for the Study of Ethical Problems in Medicine and Biomedical and Behavioral Research (1981), and now adopted in most states, according to which any person "who has sustained . . . irreversible cessation of the entire brain, including the brain stem, is dead."[124] This reading, of course, would support the claim of the new president that he did indeed become president at the moment the former president suffered irreversible brain death.

Thus, I do not assert that the framers' semantic intentions were always rich rather than spare. What I claim, rather, is this: (1) that there is convincing evidence that the framers' semantic intentions were often rich and (2) that there is no adequate basis for concluding that *any* of the Constitution's heavily litigated normative phrases ("due process of law," "equal protection of the laws," "cruel and unusual punishments," "freedom of speech," etc.) were intended by their framers to be open-ended invitations to judges to seek out and enforce the best contemporary understandings of the abstract real moral qualities these phrases allegedly name. If these claims are correct, it follows that the strong versions of constitutional realism endorsed by Brink and Moore are mistaken.

THE PROBLEM OF "SUMMING" DISPARATE INTENTIONS

> The second case whereby the statute shall be taken is *ex mente legislatorum*, for that is chiefe to be considered, which, althoughe it varie in so muche that in maner so manie heades as there were, so many wittes; so many statute makers, so many minds; yet, notwithstandinge, certen notes there are by which a man maie know what it was.
>
> —Anonymous Author of *A Discourse Upon Statutes (c. 1560)*[125]

I turn now to consider one of the most common arguments against originalism, namely, that the whole notion of a collective original intent is largely a fiction since it is seldom, if ever, possible to "sum" the varying intentions of individual framers into a single coherent shared or representative intent. I shall consider different versions of this objection and argue that none of them are convincing.

The most radical form of the argument, often urged by legal realists in the 1930s and 1940s,[126] is what Moore terms the "group mind objection."[127] According to this view, all talk of legislative "intent" is irremediably senseless, since mental states can properly be attributed only to individuals, not to collectivities. As Moore notes,[128] this argument is largely an *ignoratio elenchi* because few if any originalists do assume that a collective body has a mind. Instead, what originalists typically claim is that it is possible "to paraphrase [talk of] the intent of the legislature into talk of the intentions of individual legislators in some combination."[129]

But are such paraphrases really possible? Many recent critics of originalism have argued that they are not.[130] Significantly, their point is not—or at least not fundamentally—that there are hopelessly difficult *evidential* problems in recovering the framers' intent. Rather, their claim is that even if we had an ideally complete accounting of each of the framers' intentions, it still would be impossible in most cases to discover or construct a coherent collective intent. In the following few paragraphs I sketch what I take to be the most defensible form of this argument.

Intention-voting theories can be grouped into two basic types.[131] *Constructive* theories, as the label suggests, attempt to *construct* a collective intent by aggregating varying individual intentions into "a composite thrust of many individual intents, no one of which need wholly coincide with the composite."[132] In previous chapters we noted two theories of this type: Kay's near-unanimity theory, which identifies the collective intent of the framers with the set of more or less specific intentions held in common by (nearly) all of the framers,[133] and a "representative intention" theory, which identifies the framers' collective intent with the intentions an average or median framer (would have) held.[134]

Nonconstructive intention-voting theories, by contrast, aim not to *construct* a collective intent but to *discover* one. Two versions of such theories have been discussed in the literature. The first is the so-called *agency* (or *delegation*) model of framers' intent, which views the framers as having "delegated" their intention votes to certain agents—normally the drafters or sponsors of constitutional provisions—whose individual intentions are thus identifiable, for interpretive purposes, with the collective intent of the framers.[135] The second version, generally known as the *majoritarian* or *majority intention* model, views the framers as having constitutionalized a particular reading *R* of a provision *P* just in case *R* was (or would have been) the reading of *P* favored by a majority of the framers (or, alternatively, by the requisite majorities or supermajorities necessary to propose and ratify *P*).[136]

None of these various theories, according to the present objection, is satisfactory. It is true that some type of constructive theory might work tolerably well with strict intentionalist theories. As Daniel Farber notes, strict intentionalists tend to conceive of original intent as a "kind of multiple choice examination to be administered to the framers in which all the questions look like this: 'Constitutional provision *X* covers fact-pattern *T*. True of false?'"[137] On this picture of original intent, it may often make sense to attempt to identify a set of actual or counterfactual scope beliefs shared by a majority or supermajority of the framers (or held by a mythical "representative" framer). But we have seen that strict intentionalism is a less defensible form of originalism than is moderate intentionalism. The latter seeks to determine, not the framers' scope beliefs, but rather the legal principles or propositions the framers understood themselves to be enacting. And as we saw above,[138] the whole notion of constructing a "composite thrust" with respect to differing and perhaps incommensurable principles or propositions is fraught with seemingly insuperable difficulties.

Nonconstructive theories fare no better. Agency theories, to be sure, have some plausibility in originalist *statutory* interpretation. This is so for two reasons. First, only a small fraction of today's voluminous statutory law is actually read by more than a handful of legislators.[139] Accordingly, there usually will be no shared original understanding of specific statutory provisions outside a small circle of interested lawmakers. Second, and relatedly, there is a well-established convention in American legal practice that official committee reports and floor statements by bill sponsors and managers are to be regarded as specially privileged for interpretive purposes.[140]

Neither of these conditions holds in the field of constitutional law, however. Framers of constitutional provisions do presumably give more or less careful consideration to the meaning of those provisions. Accordingly, there may often be real, rather than merely imputed, collective intent in constitutional contexts. Moreover, there is no convention in constitutional law authorizing judges to treat a few select framers as agents for the hundreds or thousands of others whose assent is necessary for a provision to become law.[141]

Finally, no majoritarian approach will work. Recall that for a provision to have become part of the original Constitution, it needed the support of majorities in (a) at least half of the state delegations present at the Constitutional Convention and (b) at least nine state ratifying conventions.[142] Each of the twenty-six amendments, with the exception of the twenty-first,[143] became law only when backed by (a) at least two-thirds of the members of each house of Congress and (b) majorities or supermajorities[144] in three-fourths of the state legislatures. It is plausible to say that "an intention can become binding—only become an institutional intention—when it is shared by at least the same number and distribution"[145] of framers as is needed to enact a constitutional provision into law. This requirement may often be met with respect to the general aims or purposes of particular provisions. But history makes clear that there was frequently no strong consensus on the specific principle or proposition expressed by a given provision.[146] Thus, a majoritarian approach will often yield the conclusion that there was no original collective intent of the sort originalists seek. Accordingly, there is no plausible theory of intention voting to which originalists can appeal.

This argument is unconvincing. It is possible for originalists to develop a coherent and more or less plausible theory of intention voting. In the remainder of this chapter I present and defend such a theory.

The central features of my suggested account are these:

(1) If the available evidence suggests that a particular reading *R* of a provision *P* was shared by majorities in at least half of those

bodies that framed and ratified *P*, then *R* is the originally intended reading of *P*.

(2) If the available evidence suggests that there was no reading shared by the requisite number of framers (as specified in (1)), interpreters should adopt that original reading of *P* that comports best with the general purposes of *P* and the basic structure and aims of the Constitution as a whole.

This account has three main virtues. First, it is consistent with the basic political principle that constitutional norms should be adequately grounded in the consent of the governed. Second, it ensures that all (or nearly all) constitutional provisions will *have* an original intent, either actual or constructed. Finally, it effectively channels judicial discretion without eliminating it altogether.

I turn now to consider three possible objections to this account.

First Objection: Mere Majorities Are Not Enough

One salient feature of the foregoing account is that it rejects the common view that an intention can become an "institutional" intention only if it is shared by at least the same number and distribution of the framers as is necessary to enact a constitutional text. The basis for this view is seldom made clear. But presumably it is thought that any other intention-voting schema would violate the spirit of Articles V and VII[147] of the Federal Constitution, which require (or did require) supermajorities for the adoption of constitutional provisions.

This view fails to consider, however, the very different purposes served by Articles V and VII, on the one hand, and a theory of intention voting on the other. Article VII's nine-state ratification requirement was mainly intended to guarantee that enough states agreed on the soundness of the proposed Constitution so as to give the resulting new nation a reasonable chance of success.[148] Article V, as Madison noted, was meant to provide a set of amendatory procedures that would guard "equally against that extreme facility which would render the constitution too mutable; and that extreme difficulty which might perpetuate its discovered faults."[149] A theory of constitutional intention voting, on the other hand, is designed primarily to ensure that it is the *framers'* values that ultimately count in constitutional interpretation, not those of later interpreters. This end is likely to be frustrated by the strict requirement that an original reading of (say) an amendment be shared by majorities or supermajorities in *both* houses of Congress and, standardly, by *both* legislative assemblies in at least three-fourths of the states. In principle, that would mean that a single state legislative assembly could defeat an interpretation favored by every member of Congress and every member of every other ratifying legislature. My account rightly precludes such an absurdity.

Second Objection: Too Much Discretion Is Accorded Judges

Some originalists might object that my theory provides inadequate safeguards against the imposition of a judge's own values. This is so, it might be said, because there is rarely an adequate basis for concluding that a particular reading was actually shared by the requisite majorities. As we have seen, there is often little or no direct evidence of what the vast majority of the framers understood a given provision to mean. This means that part (2) of my account would do most of the work. But the test proposed there (namely, whether a particular reading comports better than alternative original readings with the general purposes of a given provision and the basic structure and aims of the Constitution as a whole) is so vague that judges, in practice, will be free to read into the Constitution whatever values they choose.

This objection misconceives the role of historical evidence in originalist adjudication. Unlike nonjudicial constitutional historians, an originalist judge can rarely afford the luxury of indecision. Like Pascal's wagerer,[150] such a judge must often leap beyond the evidence, because the choice to suspend judgment is itself typically a choice of great significance. As Robert Bork expresses the point: "[Originalists] must not expect too much of the search for original understanding in any legal context. The result of the search is never perfection; it is simply the best we can do; and the best we can do must be regarded as good enough—or we must abandon the enterprise of law and, most especially, that of judicial review."[151] Thus, the fact that there is often scant historical evidence supporting the existence of a shared original understanding is not fatal to the originalist enterprise.

In some cases, of course, the available evidence may be just hopelessly inconclusive or, alternatively, strongly support the conclusion that there was no shared intent. When that proves to be the case, originalists can respond in a variety of ways. My suggestion—that they adopt that original reading that coheres best with both the underlying purposes of the provision at issue and the basic structure and aims of the Constitution as a whole—is one traditional response.[152] Other possibilities include deferring to whatever interpretations the representative branches have placed on the provision;[153] declaring the provision to have no judicially enforceable meaning;[154] appealing to prior judicial interpretations of the provision; or reverting to a strict intentionalist approach. My reasons for preferring the approach I suggest to any of these alternatives should be clear from earlier discussions and need not be recapitulated here. Some originalists may find that my approach creates an unacceptable risk that judges will read their own "personal" values into the constitutional text.[155] If so, such theorists are free to adopt some alternative approach that reduces this risk. The central point remains, however, that it *is* possible to develop a coherent theory of intention voting that comports with originalism's core values and concerns.[156]

Third Objection: The Need for Supplementary Rules

Finally, it might be objected that my theory of intention voting is incomplete in important ways. This objection requires us to consider two questions postponed from Chapter 3: (1) What should an originalist do if her historical research indicates that the framers' *had* no consistent collective intent? (2) What should an originalist do if the framers' intent yields no answer to a current constitutional problem? I shall consider these questions in turn.

On any plausible theory of intention voting it may sometimes be found that the framers had no coherent collective intent. *National Mutual Insurance Co. v. Tidewater Transfer Co.*[157] provides a striking illustration of how, in principle, this can happen. The question presented there was whether Congress may authorize federal courts to hear suits between residents of the District of Columbia and citizens of a state. Seven justices concluded that Congress does not have this power under Article III, section 2, which extends the judicial power of the United States to controversies "between citizens of different States." Six justices found that Congress does not have this power under Article I, section 8, which, among other things, empowers Congress to "exercise exclusive Legislation" over the District of Columbia. All nine justices agreed that if neither Article I nor Article III confers such power, then no such power exists. Nonetheless, five justices held that Congress does have this power![158]

Assuming, purely for argument's sake, that this voting pattern accurately represents the framers' views, it clearly presents a problem for my theory of intention voting. But not just for my theory. As public choice theorists have demonstrated, there is *no* method of collective choice that can satisfy both a consistency requirement and four other seemingly unexceptionable conditions of fair voting.[159] Originalists, accordingly, must develop some way of handling inconsistencies in the original understanding.

One reply might be that at this point originalism simply breaks down; judges may legitimately look to contemporary values to resolve incoherencies in the original understanding. But this capitulation may be a bit premature. As an alternative, originalists might turn to either more abstract or more concrete original intentions. At a very concrete level they might ask: How would the framers *themselves* have resolved this inconsistency if given an opportunity to do so? The problem with this kind of *Gedankenexperiment,* as Paul Brest notes, is that it is all too easy to find oneself in a "fantasy world"[160] more of one's own making than of the framers'. It seems better, then, to move up the ladder of abstraction and see if the inconsistencies in question can be resolved by appealing to the framers' general purposes and the basic structural features of their constitutional design. If this inquiry still fails to produce a defensible solution,[161] then, and only then, should originalists look to non-original values.

Lastly, we turn to the problem of "gaps" in the original understanding. What should an originalist do if she concludes that the framers had no relevant original intent with respect to a particular constitutional problem?

Richard Kay argues that this is a pseudoproblem. "Implicit in the Constitution," he claims, "are [two] 'back-up' rules which [taken together] cover all things not provided for in explicit rules."[162] The first such rule is that "any action of the federal government not traceable to the enumerated institutions and powers is an exercise of power not granted to it and is contrary to the Constitution."[163] The second rule is that any action of a state government consistent with express constitutional limitations on state power is constitutionally permissible.[164] In tandem, these back-up rules imply that there "are no omitted cases."[165]

This argument rests on a confusion. Consider just a few of the problems associated with a single constitutional clause: Article V's requirement that "on the Application of the Legislatures of two-thirds of the several States, [Congress] shall call a Convention for proposing Amendments." If a state petitioned for such a convention a century ago and never formally rescinded that call, should Congress still count that state as a valid applicant? If one state calls for a convention to consider, say, a balanced-budget amendment and another to consider an abortion amendment, should both be counted in a single group? May Congress limit the types of issues a convention may consider? If not, are there any legal safeguards against the danger of a "runaway" convention? May Congress establish procedural rules for the conduct of such a convention? If so, is this power plenary or limited? Could Congress, for example, require that all proposed amendments be approved by at least three-fourths of the states (or delegates) present?[166] Attempts to answer these and a host of related questions by appeals to the original understanding have largely proved fruitless;[167] if the framers *had* any collective intent on these matters (which is unlikely), it is now past recovery. Do Kay's "back-up" rules, then, provide the needed answers? They do only if these questions can somehow be rephrased as questions about federal and state power. Thus, instead of asking, for example, whether Congress may establish convention procedures, one asks: Is it within Congress's enumerated powers to establish such procedures? But to that question the proper answer is: It is only if Article V, properly construed, confers such a power. But that is just what we wanted to know in the first place.[168]

Originalists have long recognized that the original understanding may sometimes have gaps[169] or be inconsistent.[170] They have also generally conceded that original intent is not an inviolable standard but is sometimes rightly subordinated to firmly entrenched precedent or compelling national interests.[171] In other words, they have generally acknowledged, at least implicitly, the need for what I earlier called supplementary rules:[172] rules designed to provide guidance to judges when the original understanding is inconsistent, undiscoverable, inapplicable, or trumped by other legal and political values. Just what these supplementary rules should be is a question, obviously, on which there may be much disagreement, and one too large to be addressed within the limits of this study. Enough has been said, however, to indicate that in principle originalists *can* develop both a theory of intention voting and a set of supplementary rules adequate for their purposes. Accordingly, we may conclude that this third objection, like the two previous ones examined in this chapter, is unsuccessful.

5

The Case Against Originalism

> [W]e study the day before yesterday, in order that yesterday may not paralyze today, and today may not paralyze tomorrow.
>
> —F.W. Maitland[1]

> It is of course dangerous that judges be philosophers—almost as dangerous as if they were not.
>
> —Paul Freund[2]

We have now completed the painstaking but necessary task of sorting through the many competing forms of originalism and determining which of these forms is most defensible. The upshot of this investigation has been that there is a version of originalism—call it *sophisticated originalism*[3]—that does enjoy clear advantages over its competitors. This theory, as we have seen, is resistant to a number of objections standardly advanced against originalism, including those major objections examined in the preceding chapter. The question we must now consider is whether even this soundest form of originalism is in the end defensible.

THE ENDURING APPEAL OF ORIGINALISM

In earlier chapters we looked, in passing, at all of the main arguments for originalism. Before turning to a critical examination of the theory, it may be useful to review briefly some these arguments.

Some common arguments for originalism, we saw, are wholly spurious. This is true, for example, of all arguments resting on the claim that originalism is the only theory consistent with the ordinary meanings of "law," "meaning," or "interpretation."[4] As recent debates in law and other disciplines have made clear, these terms have no single, canonical meaning. Rather, they are used in a variety of senses (or perhaps express broad "concepts") spacious enough to accommodate both originalist and nonoriginalist theories of adjudication.

Another standard argument for originalism is that it accords with "the values inherent in 'inflexibility'—the values of stability and clarity."[5] This claim, as I shall later argue in detail, is doubly mistaken. In one sense, originalism affords *too little* stability, both because it gives insufficient weight to precedent and because historical conclusions about the original understanding are subject to rapid and significant change as historical fashions come and go. And in another sense, originalism affords *too much* stability, since it sets in granite readings of constitutional language that may be ill suited to the problems and needs of later generations.

Perhaps the most common argument for originalism is its consistency with what is often said to be the "master norm" of the American political tradition, the principle of majority rule.[6]

The limitations of this appeal to majoritarianism have often been noticed. Critics have pointed out, for example, that the process by which the Constitution was framed and ratified was not particularly democratic;[7] that respect for the principle of majority rule has always been balanced in our political tradition by a respect for minority and individual rights;[8] and that originalism may often require judges to *frustrate* the will of contemporary majorities.[9] These points are all well taken, but their force should not be overstated. It cannot plausibly be denied that the principle of democratic self-government is among the core values of our political system. Nor can it be denied that originalism comports better with democratic values than do most nonoriginalist theories.[10] This is so for two reasons. First, originalist interpretations, if sound, have some colorable claim to be grounded in the consent of the governed—a claim nonoriginalist interpretations often (at least) cannot make. Second, there is broad agreement that many key constitutional provisions—the two Due Process Clauses, the Equal Protection Clause, the Cruel and Unusual Punishments Clause, among others—were originally understood to impose relatively narrow limitations on the will of political majorities. Nonoriginalists, by contrast, tend to read these and other provisions far more expansively, as imposing fairly substantial constraints on governmental power. Thus, there is doubtless some merit in the originalist claim that their view is supported by widely shared democratic values.

The main reason for originalism's enduring attraction, however, has nothing specifically to do with democratic values. Originalist modes of interpretation, after all, dominated Western jurisprudence long before modern democratic regimes ever appeared on the scene.[11] Moreover, in our own constitutional tradition, originalism seems historically to have enjoyed at least as much support in jurisdictions in which judges are electorally accountable as it has in jurisdictions in which they are not.[12] These facts suggest that the major source of originalism's appeal lies in what Thomas Grey terms "deeply rooted . . . shared principles of political legitimacy."[13] One such principle is that officials charged with *interpreting or enforcing* the law should not usurp the authority of those charged with *making* it.

Two related concerns should be noted here. First, there is a widely shared concern that it would be dangerous to permit government officials, whether electorally accountable or not, to flout the will of the framers as formally expressed in a constitutional provision by adopting a construction of the provision that clearly was not intended. This was a worry frequently emphasized by the Founders, who knew well, as Washington reminded the nation in his Farewell Address, that "change by usurpation . . . is the customary weapon by which free governments are destroyed."[14] The Founders' generation was clearly most alert to the danger of *elected* officials rendering the Constitution "a blank paper by construction;"[15] the judiciary was widely viewed as the "least dangerous"[16] branch. In our time, of course, the focus has largely shifted to the risks, real or imagined, of judicial "usurpation" of legislative prerogatives. And although some of these risks, as critics have persuasively argued,[17] are frankly overblown,[18] the fundamental worry persists that vesting nine essentially unaccountable "Platonic Guardians"[19] with the power to "update" the Constitution poses long-term threats both to cherished liberties and to critical governmental structures and powers.

Second, and more generally, there is a sense that it is simply *wrong,* as a rule, for political subordinates to supersede or thwart the policy making authority of their lawful superiors, even when effective political controls exist to ensure that such actions pose little risk. Thus, even though most state judges are electorally accountable, few historically have considered themselves free, even when backed by clear popular majorities, to depart from the obviously intended meaning of state constitutional provisions.[20] Plainly, this cannot be explained by any supposed commitment to majority rule. Instead, what we see here is a commitment to what Henry Monaghan has called the "*grundnorm*" of American politics: the principle that "the body politic can at a specific point in time definitively order relationships, and that such an ordering is binding on all organs of government until changed by amendment."[21] On this view, it is the *framers* who possess ultimate lawmaking authority in the constitutional realm, not judges or other officials acting in their ordinary legal or political capacities. And as subordinate officers in the constitutional hierarchy, judges along with other government officials have a duty not to undermine or usurp the lawmaking authority of the framers but to respect it, until "the people have by some solemn and authoritative act annulled or changed the established form."[22]

I suspect that the enduring appeal of something like the preceding view of political and legal authority is what ultimately explains why, for most of our nation's history, originalism was not simply the dominant theory of constitutional construction, but really the only such theory.[23] In attempting to block this argument, nonoriginalists have employed two basic strategies. First, they have sought to show that the ultimate lawmaking authority of the framers is actually *consistent* with nonoriginalism. To this end, they have argued that the framers deliberately "delegated" later generations of judges with extensive lawmaking powers, or that the framers enacted broad "concepts" or had "spare" semantic intentions. None of these claims, as we saw in the preceding chapter, is borne out by the historical record. This leaves only the second and more radical strategy: to *deny* the ultimate lawmaking authority of the framers. This response is summed up in Justice Holmes's oft-quoted dictum that "the present has a right to govern itself."[24] On this view, law "is a tool for arranging *today's* social relations and expressing *today's* social values; and we fully expect our laws, no matter when enacted, to speak to us *today*."[25] Advocates of this present-oriented approach argue that the original understanding of constitutional provisions is often unresponsive to current values and needs, and that it is sometimes entirely proper for judges to "update" such provisions to fit changing circumstances the framers could not have foreseen. Later in this chapter I shall defend a modest version of this present-oriented view. First, however, I shall discuss two related difficulties that afflict even the soundest form of originalism.

THE PROBLEM OF STABILITY

> [W]ise constitutional interpreters do not rest absolute positions on the shifting sands of historical opinion.
>
> —H. Jefferson Powell[26]

The burden of much of the preceding argument has been to show that originalism is not the "basket case"[27] critics often allege it to be. On the contrary, in its most defensible form originalism is an attractive, coherent, and basically workable theory, rooted in widely shared notions of political legitimacy. Its weaknesses, as Michael Perry has said, are "comparative" rather than "intrinsic":[28] it lacks certain strengths available to moderate forms of nonoriginalism.

One of these strengths is stability, an important component, as we have seen,[29] of the ideal of the rule of law. In principle, nonoriginalists are able to promote the virtue of long-term stability and continuity by adopting a comparatively robust principle of precedential constraint. Originalists, however, are open to the objection that their theory, consistently applied, would result in rapid, dramatic, and often unpredictable shifts in constitutional doctrine.

The most obvious reason for this, discussed in greater detail below,[30] is that originalism would require an "extraordinarily radical purge"[31] of established doctrine to correct two centuries of deflections from the original understanding. In response, originalists often retort that their theory would actually *foster* stability in the long run, since it would provide judges with a common "neutral" standard for constitutional judgment.[32] But this response fails for the following reason.

Originalism requires judges to play a role for which they are usually untrained: that of constitutional historian. To perform this role responsibly, judges must defer, as a rule, to the judgments of those who are historians by trade. But this deference has costs; for constitutional history is an exceptionally fluid and contested field of historical inquiry. By treating history as decisive, originalism becomes hostage to changing historiographic fashions, and "original intent" becomes a recipe for weather-vane jurisprudence.

Consider a few examples, beginning with the Eighth Amendment. For a century following its adoption in 1791, it was generally agreed that the amendment was originally understood to prohibit only barbarous and torturous punishments of the sort that had been common in Tudor and Stuart England.[33] Then, in 1892, in an impressively documented dissent in *O'Neil v. Vermont,*[34] Justice Stephen J. Field argued that this standard reading was mistaken: the framers, in fact, had intended to prohibit disproportionately severe punishments as well as those that were barbarous or torturous.[35] Less than two decades later, Field's view prevailed on the Court,[36] and for many years it remained the accepted account of the framers' intent.[37] Finally, however, in 1969, an unknown young scholar named Anthony Grannuci powerfully argued that the older view was substantially correct after all[38]—a conclusion that later studies have tended to confirm.[39]

Or consider the endlessly mooted question of whether the Fourteenth Amendment was intended to "incorporate," i.e., make applicable to the states, the Federal Bill of Rights. For roughly eighty years following the amendment's ratification in 1868, courts and historians split on the issue, the former consistently opposing full incorporation[40] and the latter, in the main, supporting it.[41] Then, in 1947, the advantage swung in favor of the incorporationists, as three members of the Court joined Justice Black's elaborately researched appendix to his dissent in *Adamson v. California*,[42] urging that full incorporation had indeed been intended by the framers. This was followed two years later by a trenchant, point-by-point critique of Black's argument by Stanford historian Charles Fairman.[43] Historians and commentators have generally found Fairman's case against incorporationism to be persuasive.[44] But it has never lacked for respected critics.[45] And with the publication, in 1986, of Michael Kent Curtis's important book, *No State Shall Abridge*,[46] which vigorously challenges Fairman's analysis, many scholars regard the incorporation issue as once again an open question.[47]

Finally, consider the First Amendment Establishment Clause. For most of our constitutional history, the prevailing view was that the clause had originally been understood to enact roughly the following principle: the federal government may not enact any law establishing a national church or religious creed, nor may it favor or promote any religious denomination or sect at the expense of others.[48] The clause, that is, was not originally understood to require governmental neutrality between religion and irreligion; it permitted federal aid to religious organizations or groups so long as that aid was provided on an equal and impartial basis and for the sake of legitimate federal ends.[49] Then, in 1947, in the landmark case of *Everson v. Board of Education*,[50] the Court abruptly abandoned this traditional "nonpreferentialist" reading of the clause. It held, instead, that the framers had intended to erect a "wall of separation"[51] between church and state, a wall that prohibited any direct government support for religious causes or organizations.[52] Following *Everson*, this "separationist" interpretation enjoyed widespread acceptance, both on and off the Court, for many years.[53] Beginning in the mid-1970s, however, a vigorous defense of the older nonpreferentialist reading of the clause was mounted by conservative scholars.[54] These revisionists, in turn, were challenged by liberal counterrevisionists in the mid-1980s.[55] And thus the debate continues, with no clear winner yet in sight.

Such examples could be multiplied at considerable length, but the general point should already be clear: originalism, consistently applied, is a prescription for a shifting, unpredictable, and incoherent constitutional jurisprudence. This would be true even if judges were professional historians, which they assuredly are not. And this lack of professional training and expertise, for obvious reasons, exacerbates the problem.

Because judges (and their clerks) are lawyers rather than professional historians, they routinely botch history when they set their hands to it.[56] What often results, as Alexander Bickel notes, is a kind of "ping-pong"[57] between judicial historical assertion and, later, serious historical scholarship that refutes it. Judges then typically react by preferring the stability and predictability of settled law to the vagaries of further law-office history.[58] For originalists, however, such a reaction is indefensible; what ultimately matters, in their view, is getting history right. And so the anchor must be weighed and the sails hoisted yet again, with no assurance that the next bit of amateur historical scholarship will be any better than the first, or that even the most creditable scholarship will not be rendered obsolete by the next issue of the *American Journal of Legal History*.

Now admittedly I have overstated the problem in one important respect: sophisticated originalists, as we have seen,[59] do accord *some* weight to precedent; and this unquestionably provides some basis for continuity and stability. As we shall see in the following section, however, this appeal to precedent is not an adequate solution to the problem.

THE PROBLEM OF PRECEDENT

One of the most damaging charges against Robert Bork during his 1987 Senate confirmation fight was that his elevation to the Court would place at risk decades of judicially mandated gains in the areas of civil rights and civil liberties.[60] This criticism was the central theme of Senator Edward Kennedy's notorious "Robert Bork's America" speech on the Senate floor:

> Robert Bork's America is a land in which women would be forced into back-alley abortions, blacks would sit at segregated lunch counters, rogue police could break down citizens' doors in midnight raids, schoolchildren could not be taught about evolution, writers and artists could be censored at the whim of government, and the doors of the federal courts would be shut on the fingers of millions of citizens for whom the judiciary is often the only protector of the individual rights that are the heart of our democracy.[61]

Bork's supporters were naturally infuriated by Kennedy's speech.[62] But the charges—delivered prior to Bork's "confirmation conversion" on the importance of adhering to settled precedent in constitutional adjudication[63]—were not wholly unfounded. We have seen that any originalist who asserts that original intent always trumps conflicting precedent is thereby committed to a long list of extremely unattractive propositions. Such a theorist must concede, for example, that the Constitution permits states to execute pre-adolescent children;[64] to punish offenders by branding, earcropping, or other forms of bodily mutilation;[65] to treat prison inmates as "slaves of the state;"[66] to ban interracial marriages;[67] to sterilize repetitive offenders;[68] to bar married couples from using contraceptives;[69] to prohibit religious minorities from voting or holding political office;[70] to deny indigent criminal defendants free legal assistance;[71] to impose long prison sentences for consensual homosexual activity;[72] and to deny equal rights to women.[73] Likewise, such a theorist must hold that the federal government is not constitutionally barred from discriminating against women, blacks, or other minorities;[74] that the government has no power to make paper currency legal tender;[75] that much of the modern administrative and welfare state must be dismantled;[76] that modern notions of expansive presidential powers, particularly in the field of foreign policy, must be abandoned;[77] and that decisions recognizing broad federal powers to regulate interstate commerce must be reversed.[78]

The fact that "strong" originalism of this sort would result in the kind of constitutional Armageddon just described is an obvious *reductio* of the theory. We saw earlier, however, that originalists both can and should accord significant respect to precedent in constitutional adjudication.[79] And in this way, it might be suggested, originalists can avoid the charge that their theory demands a sweeping and patently unacceptable repudiation of current doctrine.

We have also seen, however, that there are limits on the extent to which an originalist can consistently permit precedent to trump original intent.[80] In this respect, the controversy over original intent falls into a common pattern. Often it is possible for one theory to make limited concessions to its opponent; but at some point concessions shade off into capitulation, and the integrity of the theory is lost. It is here, I suggest, that even the soundest form of originalism reaches the limits of its plausibility. For the theory can be made defensible only if it concedes so much to its opponent that it ceases to be, in any meaningful sense, originalist.

We should begin by recalling that many once-controversial constitutional issues are now, as Henry Monaghan notes, "so far settled that they are simply off the agenda."[81] As examples, Monaghan cites the legitimacy of the later legal-tender decisions, the unconstitutionality of state-sponsored segregation and gross political malapportionment, and the legitimacy of the profound structural transformations effected by the New Deal.[82] The fierce controversies out of which these bedrock principles emerged are now "old, unhappy, far-off things, and battles long ago,"[83] which no judge, as even Robert Bork admits,[84] would now dream of rekindling.

A notch below these off-the-agenda matters is a set of doctrines now contested by almost no one except some of the more doctrinaire members of the New Right. A partial list includes the doctrine that the Fourteenth Amendment incorporates at least most of the Bill of Rights;[85] the doctrine that the Due Process Clauses protect more than merely procedural rights;[86] the principle that the Constitution protects certain fundamental "unenumerated" rights, including a right to decisional "privacy;"[87] the doctrine that the Equal Protection Clause prohibits state-sponsored gender discrimination (absent important or compelling governmental interests);[88] and the doctrine that the Eighth Amendment Cruel and Unusual Punishments Clause does not merely prohibit punishments regarded as cruel in the founding generation.[89] Each of these holdings is now so firmly embedded in our constitutional structure, and enjoys such wide and deep public and professional support, that it cannot reasonably be argued that they should now be judicially overthrown.

Finally, there are constitutional precedents that are now more or less up for grabs between their originalist critics and their nonoriginalist defenders. Into this category fall all doctrines for which a plausible case can be made both (1) that they violate the original understanding and (2) that they should be repudiated on that account. Examples of this last category are bound to be controversial. But the usual suspects include the Fourth Amendment exclusionary rule,[90] the Fifth Amendment Miranda rule,[91] current abortion[92] and obscenity[93] doctrine, and many of the leading principles of current establishment clause[94] and Eighth Amendment jurisprudence.[95]

This short list is not, of course, intended to be exhaustive. But no plausible expansion of it can alter the fact that the items falling under the first two categories, taken together, are more fundamental, doctrinally, than those falling under the third. Not that issues like abortion, capital punishment, and the like are not vital matters of public concern; they clearly are. But they belong to the branches of constitutional doctrine, not to the trunk or roots. And because constitutional doctrine is now so pervasively nonoriginalist, no originalist, properly so-called, can rest content with simply pruning a few offensive branches; he must lay his axe to the roots. But this, I have argued, is precisely what cannot justifiably be done.

Consider an analogy drawn from another area of jurisprudence: the theory of punishment. Philosophers of law have long recognized that retributivist and utilitarian approaches to the justification of legal punishment need not be viewed as irreconcilable opposites; various "mixed" or "impure" forms of the theories are possible.[96] Thus, a retributivist need not hold, for example, that the severity of a punishment must be strictly proportionate to the moral gravity of an offense; she can hold, instead, that moral desert merely sets an upper and a lower bound to permissible punishments, and that within this range the precise degree of punishment is properly determined by considerations of social utility.[97] This kind of mixed retributivist theory is perfectly coherent so long as the range in which utilitarian considerations are permitted to operate is comparatively narrow. But if that range is defined very broadly, then the notion of moral desert is subordinated to that of utility, and the theory ceases to be a form of retributivism at all.

Likewise, any "originalist" theory that fails to attack the roots of the current constitutional order effectively subordinates original intent to precedent, and thus ceases to be a genuine form of originalism at all. Originalists, by definition, are committed to the primacy of original intent. But stones that the Constitution's builders rejected have now become foundation stones of a constitutional order very different from, and in many ways far grander than, that which the framers envisioned. And to that earlier vision we cannot and should not now seek to return.

THE NEED FOR A LIVING CONSTITUTION

> Time works changes, brings into existence new conditions and purposes. Therefore a principle to be vital must be capable of wider application than the mischief which gave it birth. This is peculiarly true of constitutions. They are not ephemeral enactments, designed to meet passing occasions. They are, to use the words of Chief Justice Marshall, "designed to approach immortality as nearly as human institutions can approach it." The future is their care and provision for events of good and bad tendency of which no prophecy can be made. In the application of a constitution, therefore, our contemplation cannot be only of what has been but of what may be.
>
> — United States Supreme Court (1910)[98]

All originalists agree that, *as an original matter,* courts are bound to adhere to the original understanding. They agree, that is, that departures from original intent can be justified, if at all, only if such departures are required by controlling precedent or practical construction. In this final section, I argue that this claim is indefensible. There are limits on the extent to which the framers may rightly govern us from their graves.

We saw earlier that the most forceful argument for originalism turns on a certain conception of political hierarchy, namely, that it is the *framers* who possess ultimate constitutional authority, subject only to the formal amendatory power reserved to the people's representatives under Article

V.[99] It is now time to look more closely at this picture of constitutional hierarchy.

The basic problem with the picture was noted two centuries ago by Noah Webster. "[T]he very attempt to make *perpetual* constitutions," he wrote, "is the assumption of a right to control the opinions of future generations; and to legislate for those over whom we have as little authority as we have over a nation in Asia."[100] Given the fact that the Constitution was adopted by a relatively small number of "propertied, white males who had no strong incentives to attend to the concerns and interests of the impoverished, the nonwhites, or nonmales who were alive then,"[101] it is hard enough to explain how the framers acquired legitimate political authority over many members of their own generation. But the problem is even more acute with respect to future generations. None of *us* were parties to the original constitutional compact. Why, then, should we feel bound to subordinate *our* conceptions of sound governance, *our* notions of fundamental values and rights, to those held by men who have been dead now for over a century?

Originalists are apt to reply that we are not in fact "bound" by the framers' handiwork: we are free to amend the Constitution any time we choose. But this argument is largely a sham. Of the more than nine thousand constitutional amendments that have been introduced in Congress,[102] only twenty-six have been adopted—fifteen since the close of the eighteenth century. For good or ill, the unvarnished truth is that Article V is now "very nearly a dead letter."[103] So the question remains: By what right do the dead govern the living?

The answer is, by no right, unless we, the living, in some way confer such authority upon them. "As a *document*," Edward Corwin pointed out, "the Constitution came from its framers, . . . but as a *law* the Constitution comes from and derives all its force from the people of the United States of this day and hour."[104] Corwin inferred from this that "the proper point of view from which to approach the task of interpreting the Constitution is that of regarding it as a living statute, palpitating with the purpose of the hour, re-enacted with every waking breath of the American people, whose primitive right to determine their institutions is its sole claim to validity as a law and as a matrix of laws under our system."[105] But this "palpitation theory" goes too far in the opposite direction. For the whole point of our written Constitution is to preserve from "the moment's hue and cry"[106] those human rights and other principles to which our polity has historically been committed.

Corwin is clearly correct to this extent, however: political authority must ultimately be grounded in the attitudes and interests of *contemporary* citizens and officials, not in any political bargains struck by past generations.[107] The Founders apparently recognized this, and concluded from it that popular majorities could alter or abolish *any* existing government and constitution, *even in ways not expressly provided for by positive law*.[108] Whether this radical inference is sound political theory I leave for others to decide. Here I insist only on the far more modest claim that the right of the living to govern themselves extends at least this far: that courts may sometimes be justified in rejecting the original understanding when this understanding clearly is no longer responsive to contemporary values and needs.

I must be careful not to be misunderstood. I am not, of course, suggesting that judges should be free to declare that presidential elections should occur every two years or that the United States should adopt a parliamentary system of government.[109] Obviously there should be powerful constraints on the capacity of any official, appointed or otherwise, to "amend" the Constitution by ignoring its plain commands. Nor am I suggesting that courts should depart from the original understanding for trivial or insubstantial reasons. The arguments supporting originalism, while not compelling, do in my view establish a fairly strong presumption in favor of adhering to original intent. Still, it is clear that some play in the joints must be allowed if a constitution written to reflect the values and problems of a predominantly rural, agrarian, Anglo-Saxon, slaveholding society is to serve the often very different values and problems of our urbanized, pluralist, postindustrial nation today.

The need for some measure of flexibility in constitutional adjudication is due in part to a fortunate miscalculation by the Philadelphia Framers. Contrary to Chief Justice Marshall's oft-quoted dictum that the Constitution "was intended to endure for ages to come,"[110] the men who drafted the 1787 Constitution had little faith that their intensely controversial proposal would serve the needs of remote generations,[111] much less that it would become, in a remarkably short time, the central icon of America's civil religion.[112] For this reason, they wrote into the Constitution (in Article V) an amendment procedure they believed made the process of formal amendment relatively easy.

Here, as elsewhere, the Framers' prescience failed: Article V has become almost an impassable barrier to formal constitutional change. Most observers would agree, however, that this is not, in general, a cause for regret. As Joseph Long noted many decades ago, it is fortunate that the Federal Constitution has

> escaped the fate that has befallen the constitutions of the states. Not only are they subject to constant change, but they have long since ceased to be constitutions in a true sense. Instead of embodying broad general propositions

> of fundamental permanent law, they now exhibit the prolixity of a code and consist largely of mere legislation. No one now entertains any particular respect for a state constitution. It has little more dignity than an ordinary act of the legislature.[113]

Thus, it is precisely because the Constitution speaks in terms of broad principles and majestic generalities, rather than descending into regulatory specifics, that it has been able to serve for more than two centuries as a powerful unifying symbol of our nation[114] and as a "lodestar for our aspirations"[115] as a people.

In order to play this vital unifying and aspirational role, however, it is essential that the Constitution not be read as locked in an eighteenth-century deep-freeze. Evolution by interpretation, as well as by occasional formal amendment, is inevitable if a constitution is to continue to speak to the future with the same relevance and moral force with which it spoke to the past. For only in this way can a short and basically unchanging written charter of government remain responsive to continually evolving conditions and needs.

An example may help to make this point clear. Consider the great early case of the *Genesee Chief*.[116] The issue presented there was the constitutionality of an 1845 federal law extending national admiralty jurisdiction to the Great Lakes and their connecting navigable rivers. Drafted by one of the nation's foremost authorities on admiralty law, Supreme Court Justice Joseph Story,[117] the statute was a response to decades of mounting pressure from western states eager to enjoy the commercial advantages of federal admiralty jurisdiction over the vast network of interior waterways. But while the benefits of the law were clear, there was a major constitutional hurdle: courts had consistently held that the constitutional grant of federal admiralty power was originally understood to extend only to the high seas and to waters within the ebb and flow of the tide.[118] By what authority, then, could Congress extend the judicial power of the United States over matters originally understood to be reserved to the states?

Chief Justice Taney, speaking for the Court in upholding the statute, declined to rest the decision on the ground apparently favored by the Congress that enacted the law: the federal power to regulate commerce between the states.[119] As appellant's counsel had urged in oral argument, to sustain the law on this ground would mean that Congress "could extend the jurisdiction of the federal courts to every case of contract or tort, growing out of the extensive trade and commerce, now carried on, by land and water, among the States of the Union; and thus draw within the cognizance of these courts one half of the litigation of the country."[120] This, in an age of lingering and indeed growing states' rights sentiment, was an almost unthinkable invasion of traditional state prerogatives. Equally unthinkable in that age of formalist jurisprudence was a bold declaration that the Court was making new law for a new day. So Taney did what courts have often done in similar cases: he tortured history to arrive at a result he favored on other grounds.[121]

This drew an impassioned protest from Justice Daniel, the lone dissenter in the case. Daniel pointed out that Taney's appeal to history was a fraud: no one could seriously contend that the framers had intended federal *admiralty* jurisdiction to extend to inland freshwater lakes and rivers.[122] The true ground of the decision, he noted, was the audacious proposition that the Constitution may "be changed, not by amendment in the modes provided, but according to the opinions of the judiciary, entertained upon their views of expediency and necessity."[123] Though he recognized that many would regard his views as "contracted" and "unfitted to the day in which we live,"[124] Justice Daniel preferred to adhere to the traditional rule that the Constitution should be construed in accordance with the plain "meaning of its terms, and by what is believed to have been the understanding of those by whom it has been formed."[125]

I have focused on this (by now) obscure decision because it is perhaps as clear a case as can be found of a justifiable departure from original intent. This is so for a combination of reasons. First, there was nothing "countermajoritarian" about the decision: the Court simply stamped its *imprimatur* on an act of Congress that had long been clamored for by the states. Second, there was no reasonable prospect that the outcome could have been achieved by means of formal amendment. With the specter of civil war looming on the horizon, there was understandably little enthusiasm for a ratification struggle over an issue touching on states' rights. Third, the need for constitutional change was clear. Under the old tidewater rule, western commerce had been stunted by a patchwork of conflicting and hopelessly inefficient laws and procedures that often spelled ruin for shipowners whose vessels were involved in accidents or collisions.[126] A decision striking down the federal law[127] would necessarily have resulted in "great public inconvenience,"[128] as Chief Justice Taney remarked. Finally, the statute, though clearly inconsistent with the original understanding of the Admiralty Clause, was nevertheless fully consistent with the clause's broader purposes, which were (1) to foster "the safety and convenience of commerce, and the speedy decision of controversies, where delay would often be ruin,"[129] and (2) to promote international comity by vesting jurisdiction of disputes involving foreign and possibly hostile vessels in national rather than state courts.[130] Thus, the Court's decision was substantially in accord with what we earlier saw to be traditional principles of legal interpretation, including such time-honored maxims as *ratio legis est anima legis*[131] ("the reason of law is the soul of law") and *cessante ratione legis, cessat et ipsa lex* ("the reason of the law ceasing, the law itself also ceases").[132]

In short, a powerful case can be made for the soundness of the Court's nonoriginalist holding in the *Genesee Chief.* In response, originalists are likely to offer a version of the slippery slope argument: the danger of judges skiing to the bottom of the nonoriginalist slope is so great that they should never be permitted to get on the slope at all.

We saw earlier, however, that "the danger of some wildly erratic judge with the bit in his teeth, charging down some morally outrageous path"[133] is largely an originalist myth. The real danger for much of our constitutional history was rather that the Court would refuse to read the Constitution as a living document. Had this happened, then instead of serving, as it has, as "the proponent and protector of the values which are the premises, goals, needs, and ambitions of our culture, as they have been expressed in our living constitution,"[134] the Court would have become a force of reaction, increasingly out of touch with contemporary problems and needs, until either the Court or the Constitution or both were repudiated as inconsistent with the demands of practical governance and the interests and aspirations of the living.

Historically, and particularly in recent decades, Americans have looked to courts to "stand against any winds that blow as havens of refuge for those who might otherwise suffer because they are helpless, weak, outnumbered, or because they are non-conforming victims of prejudice and public excitement."[135] We as a people reflect with pride on the great human rights cases of the last half-century, which testify to our continuing commitment to the lofty ideals on which our nation was founded. It is thus instructive and somewhat dismaying to recall that "virtually all of constitutional doctrine regarding human rights fashioned by the Supreme Court in this century must be adjudged illegitimate"[136] on originalist premises.

The acid test of originalism, as indeed of any theory of constitutional adjudication, is its capacity to justify what is now almost universally regarded as the Supreme Court's finest hour: its decision in *Brown v. Board of Education*[137] that white America could no longer humiliate and degrade blacks by maintaining segregated public schools. As a candidate for a legitimate departure from original intent, *Brown* has many of the same attractions we earlier saw to be possessed by the *Genesee Chief.* First, there was almost no possibility that desegregation could have been achieved through either federal legislation or constitutional amendment.[138] During the 1950s and 1960s, southern senators and representatives dominated Congress through their control of key committees, and it is certain that they would have blocked any attempt to end segregation through ordinary legislation or formal amendment. Second, *Brown* was not in any deep sense a countermajoritarian decision. As Justice Robert Jackson noted in 1954, public opinion had undergone a "profound change"[139] in the years following the Second World War on the permissibility of state-sanctioned racial segregation. This change was reflected in the "great wave of enthusiasm"[140] with which *Brown* was initially received, everywhere except in the deep South. Finally, as a matter of political morality, the decision in *Brown* was so clearly correct, so clearly a matter of "Simple Justice,"[141] that scruples about the legitimacy of the decision as a product of judicial "activism" no longer have any real purchase.

Recognizing the unassailability of *Brown,* originalists have often sought to justify the decision by claiming that the original understanding of the Equal Protection Clause was broad enough to reach the issue of segregated public education.[142] Appealing mostly to the broad language of clause ("equal protection of the laws"), they have argued that it was originally intended as a sweeping prohibition of unequal treatment of the races by the states.[143] And since, as the Court properly held, separate educational facilities are "inherently unequal,"[144] the holding in *Brown* was correct in their view as a matter of original intent.

This reading of history, however, will simply not bear scrutiny. There is simply no convincing way to explain away the fact that twenty-four of the thirty-seven states in the country had either required or permitted segregated schools at the time the Fourteenth Amendment was adopted, or the fact that Congress itself had authorized segregated schools in the District of Columbia from 1864 onward.[145] Nor can it reasonably be claimed that the framers of the clause meant to enact a broad principle of equality under the law when it was clearly understood at the time that a *further* amendment (the fifteenth) was needed even to guarantee blacks a right so fundamental as the right to vote.[146]

As Robert Bork states, "The role of a judge committed to the philosophy of original understanding is not to '*choose* a level of abstraction'"[147] in seeking and applying the original understanding of a constitutional provision. Rather, it is to find "the level of generality that interpretation of the words, structure, and history of the Constitution fairly supports."[148] By this standard, it is impossible for originalists to produce a convincing rationale for the most triumphant and revered decision in the Court's history: *Brown v. Board of Education. Brown* is thus a cliff over which nonoriginalists may push their originalist opponents.

In sum, even sophisticated originalism, the soundest and most attractive form of originalism, is ultimately indefensible. Although sophisticated originalism is able to avoid many of the objections commonly leveled against other forms of the theory, it remains vulnerable to three standard criticisms: (1) that it would produce excessive instability and discontinuity in constitutional doctrine; (2) that it accords insufficient weight to the value of adhering to deeply entrenched and widely accepted nonoriginalist precedent; and (3) that it fails to recognize that there may be times when the Court is justified in departing from original intent in order to make good on those larger purposes and aspirations that have linked Americans from the founding generation to our own.

6

Back to Cardozo

A few hints, a few suggestions, the rest must be trusted to the artist.

—Benjamin Cardozo[1]

The main aim of this book has been to clarify and advance an important debate in American politics and law over the proper role of original intent in constitutional adjudication. The major conclusion for which I have argued has been a negative one: that originalism is not a defensible theory of what that role should be. Merely negative conclusions, however, are always more or less unsatisfying. Accordingly, in this brief concluding chapter I wish to sketch in broad strokes a positive account of how courts should interpret the Constitution.

The view defended here owes much to the broadly pragmatic theory of adjudication presented in Benjamin Cardozo's 1921 classic, *The Nature of the Judicial Process*. The central feature of that approach is a rejection of all neat, formulaic theories of judicial decision making in favor of what Cardozo termed a "wise eclecticism"[2] in the use of widely accepted judicial methods and tools. As the title of this chapter suggests, I shall argue that judges and constitutional theorists would do well to return to the kind of broadly pragmatic approach Cardozo proposed.

The Nature of the Judicial Process is among the most influential and widely cited books on the process of appellate judging ever written by an American jurist.[3] Cardozo's main focus in the book, as in two subsequent works on judicial method,[4] is on the process of common-law adjudication. But the basic problems confronting judges in common-law cases do not "differ in kind or measure,"[5] he believes, from those judges face in other areas of the law.[6] As applied to constitutional adjudication, Cardozo's broadly pragmatic[7] approach involves three central themes: (1) a rejection of "foundationalist" interpretive theories in favor of a more ad hoc, eclectic approach that emphasizes the complexity and situatedness of constitutional decisionmaking; (2) a claim that, in constitutional law as in law generally, judges must give due weight to considerations of institutional competence and to such rule-of-law virtues as stability and predictability; and (3) an insistence, rooted in what Cardozo saw as the core democratic aspirations of American society, that in the relatively few cases in which a judge may be warranted in making new law for a new day, his task is "to objectify in law, not [his] own aspirations and convictions and philosophies, but the aspirations and convictions and philosophies of the men and women of [his] time."[8] I shall discuss each of these themes in turn.

AGAINST FOUNDATIONALISM

Cardozo, like others in the legal realist movement, was deeply skeptical of attempts to construct anything like a mechanical procedure for deciding cases based on either a single privileged factor (text, intent, social utility, etc.) or on a small number of rank-ordered general principles. Against all such "foundationalist"[9] theories of adjudication, Cardozo argued, as Holmes had earlier, that judicial decisions often rightly turn on some "judgment or intuition more subtle than any articulate general principle."[10]

Drawing on his own experience as a distinguished state appellate judge, Cardozo identified four "methods" commonly employed by judges in extending the law in new directions: logic or analogy (the "method of philosophy"), legal history (the "method of evolution"), legal custom (the "method of tradition"), and social welfare and the mores of the day (the "method of sociology").[11] None of these methods, he argued, could be invoked as a kind of "sovereign talisman"[12] that consistently trumps the others.

All forms of privileged-factor foundationalism, Cardozo believed, succumb to the false lure of an *elegantia juris*; by privileging form over substance, simplicity over context-sensitive judgment, such theories inevitably sacrifice that "social welfare"[13] which it is the "final cause"[14] of the law to promote. Any theory that authorizes judges to resort only to arguments based on history, custom, or analogy is bound to conflict with this highest end, since it would bind the present to the outmoded values and solutions of the past. On the other hand, to permit judges to dispense individualized "justice" by relying exclusively on direct appeals to political morality or social policy would also be inconsistent with the welfare of society, since it would undermine those rule-of-law virtues on which that welfare depends. In short, Cardozo argued, no form of privileged-factor theory can accommodate the commonsense insight, implicit in our legal practice, that "[s]omewhere between worship of the past and exaltation of the present, the path of safety will be found."[15]

Similar problems afflict foundationalist theories that recognize the legitimacy of a plurality of judicial "methods," but insist that these methods can be weighted or in some other way rank ordered to permit relatively simple solutions in cases where the methods point in different directions. Like privileged-factor theories, rank-ordered theories inevitably fail to respond to our sense of the complexity of many legal problems. Judgments about which method ought to prevail in a given case often rightly depend upon "intuitions of convenience too subtle to be formulated, too imponderable to be valued, too volatile to be localized or even fully apprehended"[16] by those charged with making them. By blocking appeals to these sorts of context-sensitive intuitions, rigid preset formulas and rankings tend to generate decisions that are insufficiently responsive to the changing needs of our society and to our shared aspirations for justice through law.

The force of Cardozo's critique of foundationalist theories can be more easily appreciated if we abandon his rather badly named fourfold typology of methods and speak instead in more contemporary idioms. In constitutional law, for example, it is possible to identify at least five kinds of arguments that are almost universally accepted as legitimate in constitutional adjudication and debate.[17] These include arguments based on appeals to (1) the constitutional text, (2) the intent of the framers, (3) the general purposes or structural features underlying individual provisions or the Constitution as a whole, (4) prior judicial decisions and practical constructions, and (5) principles of political morality or social policy. A constitutional foundationalist is typically one who asserts either (a) that only one of these common modes of argument is in fact legitimate or (b) that two or more are legitimate, and that they can be rank ordered or weighted to produce a kind of algorithm for deciding constitutional questions.

In light of our previous discussion of the value of precedential constraint in constitutional law, it is easy to see why no form of privileged-factor theory can possibly succeed. We saw earlier[18] that any plausible theory of constitutional adjudication must give significant weight to arguments from precedent. Yet it is clear that appeals to precedent cannot sensibly be viewed as the *only* legitimate forms of argument in constitutional interpretation. This would not only spell the end of our living Constitution by freezing current constitutional doctrine in place, it would also provide no way for courts to settle disputes on issues related to the many important constitutional provisions that have never been judicially interpreted.[19]

The only plausible forms of constitutional foundationalism are thus those that recognize the legitimacy of a plurality of modes of constitutional argument (including arguments from precedent) and then provide priority rules for weighing those different kinds of argument against one another. Aside from various forms of originalism, such theories are surprisingly rare. There is now broad agreement among constitutional lawyers, both liberal and conservative, that the sheer complexity of many constitutional issues—the wide range of competing and often seemingly incommensurable values, interests, and principles that these issues involve—makes it impossible to address them successfully armed with any simple, formulaic decision procedure. To this extent, at least, it can indeed be said that "[w]e are all legal realists now."[20] So successful were the realists in spreading "the gospel that there is no gospel that will save us from the pain of choosing at every step,"[21] that for more than half a century the Court has never seriously considered officially subscribing to any grand, overarching theory of constitutional interpretation, foundationalist or otherwise.[22] Instead, the Court has generally been content to follow Cardozo's modest advice that in a difficult case a judge must "balance all his ingredients, his philosophy, his logic, his analogies, his history, his customs, his sense of right, and all the rest, and adding a little here and taking out a little there, must determine, as wisely as he can, which weight shall tip the scales."[23] This kind of eclectic, relatively untheoretical, "common-law" approach to constitutional adjudication has always had its critics.[24] In the next two sections, I shall consider the most persistent criticism of this approach: that it gives judges too much leeway to decide cases according to their own personal preferences or political convictions.

PRAGMATISM AND THE RULE OF LAW

Unlike some other legal pragmatists of his day[25] and ours,[26] Cardozo believed strongly that there are and ought to be significant constraints on the power of judges to write their own moral and political ideals into law. The most potent of these constraints, in his view, derived from two sources: (1) the requirement that judges respect the institutional limits on their policy making authority imposed by our American system of limited and separated powers and (2) the need for judges to give due weight to the rule-of-law values of consistency, certainty, and stability in those relatively narrow areas in which they are free to exercise significant policy making authority.

For Cardozo, it was axiomatic that "courts are creatures of the state and its power, and [that] while their life as courts continues, they must obey the law of their creator."[27] It follows that if authoritative legal materials are clear, a judge's sole task is to apply the law as it is given to him.[28] Though judges may have the *power* to ignore clear statutory and constitutional commands, they have no *authority* to do so.[29] By right, they may legislate only "interstitially," that is, between the gaps of settled law.[30] Only in those controversial, "hard" cases in which applicable legal standards are silent, unclear, or inconsistent may judges make new law rather than apply existing legal standards.

Hard cases, as Cardozo rightly insisted, are relatively uncommon in most areas of the law.[31] It might be argued, however, that they are frequent among those constitutional cases decided by the Supreme Court. As Frederick Schauer notes, unless a case "is considered at least slightly difficult for some reason,"[32] the Court will simply refuse to hear it. So even if judges are authorized to legislate only in hard cases, it remains unclear what meaningful limits there are on the authority of a pragmatist-minded Supreme Court to impose its own moral or political agenda from the bench.

Cardozo offers one solution to this problem which we have already seen reason to reject. Like Justice Holmes,[33] Cardozo believed that courts should sustain the constitutionality of statutes "unless they are so plainly arbitrary and oppressive that right-minded men and women could not reasonably regard them otherwise."[34] By this standard, there will be relatively "few cases in which [legislatures have] gone beyond the lines that mark the limits of discretion."[35] Consequently, the great majority of constitutional cases, including those decided by the Supreme Court, will indeed be easy cases.

Cardozo is here invoking a version of "Thayer's Rule." That rule, it will be recalled,[36] permits judges to strike down challenged governmental actions only if those actions plainly and uncontroversially exceed constitutional limitations. We saw earlier[37] why courts should reject this crude method of curbing judicial discretion: it would transform judges into pliant instruments of majority oppression. There may be some room for a "presumption of constitutionality" in cases that do not implicate fundamental rights and liberties.[38] But it would be a mistake for courts to abandon their traditional constitutional role of "stand[ing] against any winds that blow as havens of refuge for those who might otherwise suffer because they are helpless, weak, outnumbered, or because they are non-conforming victims of prejudice and public excitement."[39] Thayer's Rule would require courts to do just that.

Cardozo is on much stronger ground in suggesting a second limit on the power of judges to write their own personal predilections into law: the requirement that judges give due weight to the crucial importance that values such as certainty and consistency play in a well-ordered legal system.

One of the most striking features of contemporary constitutional decision making is the extent to which that decision making is dominated by concerns about the nature, application, and elaboration of precedent.[40] This is doubtless one reason why Cardozo believed that problems besetting judges in constitutional cases are not fundamentally different from those they face in deciding common-law disputes. In both sorts of cases, what judges do, first and foremost, is apply, elaborate, broaden, narrow, distinguish, and occasionally overrule *judicially fashioned* rules of law. Cardozo wisely cautioned against making a "fetich"[41] [*sic*] of doctrinal consistency; like Holmes, he found it "revolting to have no better reason for a rule of law than that so it was laid down in the time of Henry IV."[42] But he also wisely reminded us that "[a]dherence to precedent must . . . be the rule rather than the exception if litigants are to have faith in the even-handed administration of justice in the courts."[43]

Critics of legal pragmatism commonly misunderstand it as being committed to a kind of crude instrumentalism. Ronald Dworkin, for example, has characterized legal pragmatism as the view that judges should "make whatever decisions seem to them best for the community's future, not counting any form of consistency with the past as valuable for its own sake."[44] Even a cursory reading of Cardozo's extrajudicial writings shows how misleading this characterization of legal pragmatism is. As Daniel Farber notes, what legal pragmatists are essentially committed to "is solving legal problems using every tool that comes to hand, including precedent, tradition, legal text, and social policy."[45] Pragmatists see law as a servant of human needs and believe that these needs can best be served by allowing judges to make full use of the "wealth of weapons in the legal armory"[46] to arrive at whatever results seem most reasonable overall. But as Cardozo convincingly argues, pragmatists both can and should recognize that it is often "paramount public policy . . . not lightly to sacrifice certainty and uniformity and order and coherence"[47] for slight gains in justice or utility.

CONVENTIONAL VALUES AND REFLECTIVE EQUILIBRIUM

> When Justices interpret the Constitution, they speak for their community, not for themselves alone. The act of interpretation must be understood with

full consciousness that it is, in a very real sense, the community's interpretation that is sought.

—Justice William Brennan[48]

I have argued that in deciding hard constitutional cases judges should employ an eclectic, "common-law" approach that requires them to weigh a range of potentially competing considerations, including arguments from text, intent, precedent, purpose, and political morality, and determine which of these considerations should prevail in the case at hand. One standard objection to such an approach—that it amounts to an open-ended invitation to judges to smuggle their own personal preferences into law—is somewhat blunted by Cardozo's sound admonition that judges must accord appropriate weight to considerations of institutional competence and to the value of certainty and consistency in law. But stronger medicine than this is clearly needed if legal pragmatism is not to be a prescription for rule by philosopher-kings. The solution Cardozo proposed was to require judges "to regulate [their] estimate of values by objective rather than subjective standards, by the thought and will of the community rather than by [their] own idiosyncrasies of conduct and belief."[49]

Under current and long standing constitutional doctrine, judges are often required to make difficult and unavoidably controversial moral and political judgments. To cite just a few of the better-known examples: Under currently accepted equal-protection, free-speech, and free-exercise standards, judges must decide whether challenged governmental actions serve "important" or "compelling" state interests.[50] One strand of contemporary free-speech doctrine (now under attack by Court conservatives)[51] requires courts to "balance" competing private and governmental interests in cases where a state regulation has merely an incidental suppressive impact on speech or expressive conduct.[52] Current Eighth Amendment jurisprudence prohibits the intentional infliction of "wanton or unnecessary" pain or "grossly disproportionate" punishment on prison inmates.[53] And long-recognized due process principles require judges to determine whether governmental actions violate norms "implicit in the concept of ordered liberty"[54] or trench on values "so rooted in the traditions and conscience of our people as to be ranked as fundamental."[55] Thus a critical question is: What method(s) should courts use in deciding such moral and political questions?

Courts have consistently—and rightly—declined repeated invitations from "grand" constitutional theorists to endorse officially one or another "deep-structure"[56] theory of moral reasoning, such as utilitarianism, Kantianism, or contractarianism.[57] In performing a task as delicate as that of judicial review, courts must often seek to discover or to develop an "overlapping consensus"[58] among persons of fundamentally differing moral, political, and religious views. Available deep-structure theories are simply too controversial and enjoy too little social support to serve this consensus-building function.

Rather than invoking some deep-structure theory, judges have generally relied either on their own personal moral convictions or on what they believe to be widely shared community norms. There are a number of reasons why it is preferable that judges enforce communal rather than merely personal moral standards. First, "given the way in which courts are structured, the legitimacy of the judicial establishment of legal rules depends in large part on the employment of a process of reasoning that begins with social morality rather than with those standards the court thinks best."[59] Second, reliance on widely shared conventional norms promotes the values of consistency and predictability by enabling lawyers and judges to replicate patterns of judicial reasoning in similar cases.[60] Finally, requiring judges to eschew merely personal moral standards alleviates (although it does not eliminate) a familiar problem with judicial lawmaking: how can it be fair to the losing party in a legal dispute to resolve the dispute by applying a legal rule that is announced only after the dispute arose? Confining judges to the enforcement of norms that have substantial social support eases this "retroactivity dilemma"[61] "by ensuring that decisions are rooted in standards that the disputants either knew or had reason to know at the time of their transaction, albeit standards that had perhaps not previously been officially recognized as legal rules."[62]

All of this is familiar ground to legal theorists. Indeed, as Joseph Raz notes, most legal systems in the world take it as a general principle that judges may "act only on those values and opinions which have the support of some important segment of the population."[63] But it is one thing to say that courts should look to conventional morality in deciding common-law or statutory cases; it is quite another to say that this also applies to constitutional decision making. We saw earlier[64] that one of the principal justifications for investing electorally unaccountable judges with the power of judicial review is to protect minority rights against majority tyranny. But if this is the case, John Hart Ely pointedly asks, what sense does it make "to employ the value judgments of the *majority* as the vehicle for protecting minorities from the value judgments of the majority"?[65]

In reply, it might be said that courts can, and often do, invoke broad *national* standards to protect minority rights against overbearing *local* majorities.[66] But this response obviously doesn't go very deep: it provides no comfort for minorities who suffer from widespread or pervasive hostility and prejudice. Ely's challenge is thus a fundamental one for anyone who, like Cardozo, believes that courts should look to conventional values in deciding constitutional cases. Fortunately, Cardozo suggests ways in which that challenge can be met.

First, Cardozo reminds us that "[i]t is the theory of our polity that beneath the transitory flux the judge may be expected to discern the deeper principle, and to rescue it from submergence in what is passing and particular."[67] The function of judges, in other words, is not to act as a mere reflex of popular passions and opinion; they have been insulated from majoritarian pressures precisely in order that they might preserve *fundamental and enduring* national values "against the assaults of opportunism, the expediency of the passing hour, the erosion of small encroachments, the scorn and derision of those who have no patience with general principles."[68] Since it is often the case that minority rights are invaded at times when long-cherished national ideals "have been forgotten in the moment's hue and cry,"[69] courts can and should act to protect those rights by preferring deep conventional values over transient majority preferences.

Second, when courts do look to currently prevailing conventional norms, "the thought to be appraised and heeded is not the hasty or unconsidered impressions of the crowd . . . the whim or humor of the hour."[70] Rather, courts are to look to the stable underlying moral convictions of "those sections of the crowd whose impressions have ripened into genuine opinion."[71]

Cardozo's point here is that courts properly apply certain modest "filtering" devices to community norms in order to screen out various features that would not survive more exacting scrutiny. Although Cardozo himself does not develop this point in detail, it is important for our purposes to do so, for, as Ronald Dworkin notes, "the belief that prejudices, personal aversions and rationalizations do not justify restricting another's freedom itself occupies a critical and fundamental position in our popular morality."[72]

Conventional morality consists of both particular moral judgments and general moral principles. Even if it were otherwise desirable to do so, it would be impossible for courts coherently to enforce conventional morality as such. This is because conventional morality embodies inconsistencies on at least two different levels: certain particular moral judgments conflict with certain general principles, and various general principles conflict with one another. Thus, before conventional morality can be applied to constitutional disputes, some means must be found to eliminate these inconsistencies.

The most plausible solution is to seek what John Rawls calls a "reflective equilibrium"[73] between particular judgments and general principles. One begins with the set of initial moral judgments that command wide popular support. These judgments are then filtered to eliminate those that are held with little confidence or that have been made under the influence of passion, prejudice, obvious factual error, or other conditions that often result in errors of judgment. Those beliefs that survive this filtering process are a community's "considered" moral judgments. One then tests alternative sets of widely shared general principles in order to find that set that best explains, supports, and systematizes these considered moral judgments. As this process of testing proceeds, discrepancies are likely to appear. By going back and forth between judgments and principles, sometimes modifying the former, sometimes the latter, one can eventually arrive at a state in which the community's specific judgments and general principles, duly pruned and adjusted, fit together in a coherent whole. This is what Rawls calls a state of reflective equilibrium.[74]

Needless to say, it would be wholly unrealistic to expect busy judges to carry this search for reflective equilibrium very far in the process of deciding ordinary cases. The model of community norms in reflective equilibrium is thus very much a regulative rather than a working ideal. But judges certainly can perform some of the initial filtering operations needed to arrive at society's considered moral judgments. As Dworkin notes,[75] this is not a means of substituting elitist values for popular ones, but is itself a requirement of popular morality. By excluding those specific moral judgments that their authors themselves would reject upon due examination, we respect the requirement of popular morality that individual liberty not be restricted on the basis of mere prejudice or unreasoned hostility.

An Illustrative Case: Thompson v. Oklahoma

Before concluding, it may be helpful to consider how the broadly pragmatic theory I have sketched might work in an actual case. A good case for this purpose is *Thompson v. Oklahoma*,[76] decided by the Supreme Court in 1988, in which the Court addressed the following question: Does the execution of a person who was fifteen years old at the time of his offense violate the Eighth Amendment prohibition against the infliction of "cruel and unusual punishments"?

Pragmatists, as we have seen, support an eclectic, "common-law" approach to constitutional decision making. According to the particular version of pragmatism set forth above, judges should decide hard constitutional cases by considering a range of potentially competing considerations, including arguments based on appeals to the constitutional text, the intent of the framers, the general purposes or structural features underlying individual provisions or the Constitution as a whole, precedent, and principles of political morality or social policy. The question we must address is thus: How do these various considerations bear on the issue presented in *Thompson*?

There were three opinions in *Thompson*: a plurality opinion by Justice Stevens, a concurrence by Justice O'Connor, and a dissent by Justice Scalia. None of these opinions suggested that the *text* of the Eighth Amendment pointed to a clear outcome in the case.[77] In ordinary usage, the execution of a person who was fifteen at the time of his crime would certainly appear to be "unusual": no one that young had been executed in the United States since 1948.[78] But it is plainly open to dispute whether such an execution would or would not be "cruel." Similarly, none of the justices suggested that arguments based on appeals to the *framers' intentions or broad purposes* were particularly compelling here. As Justice Scalia noted, "The evidence is unusually clear and unequivocal"[79] that the Eighth Amendment was not originally understood to prohibit capital punishment for crimes committed by persons under the age of sixteen. But even Justice Scalia—a professed originalist[80]—conceded that changed circumstances now make it impossible to return to the framers' understanding of "cruel and unusual punishments."[81]

Most of the disagreements in *Thompson* properly focused on issues of *precedent* and *political morality*. The most fundamental disagreement turned on whether the Court should retain or substantially modify its traditional three-part test of Eighth Amendment claims. According to that test, a punishment is unconstitutional if:

> (1) it is a form of punishment originally understood by the framers to be cruel and unusual;[82] or
>
> (2) a demonstrable societal consensus exists that the punishment offends civilized standards of decency;[83] or
>
> (3) the punishment (a) is "grossly out of proportion to the severity of the crime,"[84] (b) "makes no measurable contribution to acceptable goals of punishment and hence is nothing more than the purposeless and needless imposition of pain and suffering,"[85] or (c) is "imposed under sentencing procedures that create a substantial risk that the punishment will be inflicted in an arbitrary and capricious manner."[86]

In *Thompson*, the Court was divided along the following lines. Four members of the Court, Justices Stevens, Brennan, Marshall, and Blackmun, applying the traditional Eighth Amendment analysis, concluded that the amendment prohibits the execution of a person who was fifteen or younger at the time of his or her offense, since such a punishment both (a) is inconsistent with contemporary standards of decency and (b) fails to contribute measurably to either of the two social purposes that purportedly are served by the death penalty, namely retribution and deterrence.[87] Justice O'Connor, concurring in the judgment and also accepting the traditional analysis, found the plurality's argument for (a) plausible but not conclusive and its argument for (b) unconvincing.[88] Preferring to decide the case on narrower grounds than that adopted by the plurality, she concluded those states may not execute persons under age sixteen at the time of their offense under capital punishment statutes that specify no minimum age at which commission of a capital crime may lead to the offender's execution.[89] Justice Scalia, joined by Justice White and Chief Justice Rehnquist, filed a dissenting opinion, arguing that the Eighth Amendment prohibits only those punishments that offend either parts (1) or (2) of the traditional analysis.[90] Finding that both parts of the test were satisfied, the dissent voted to uphold the death sentence of the petitioner. The Court's ninth member, Justice Kennedy, had only recently joined the Court, and took no part in the consideration or decision of the case.

Which of these views best comports with the broadly pragmatic approach set forth above? I shall argue that the holding favored by the plurality was correct—although not precisely for the reasons they offered.

We may begin by considering the dissent's bold contention that the Court should forthrightly repudiate the entire third part of the traditional Eighth Amendment analysis. Scalia offers two arguments for this dramatic revision of long standing Eighth Amendment doctrine, each surprisingly brief and undeveloped. The first argument focuses on the language of the Eighth Amendment—the fact that it bars cruel *and unusual* punishments. The second is a stock conservative alarum against the hazards of replacing "judges of the law with a committee of philosopher-kings." I shall argue that neither of these arguments succeeds.

Justice Scalia's first argument consists of a single sentence: "On its face, the phrase 'cruel and unusual punishments' limits the evolving standards appropriate for our consideration to those entertained by the society rather than those dictated by our personal consciences."[91] Elsewhere he adds a "punishment is either 'cruel and unusual' [i.e., society has set its face against it] or it is not."[92]

This second assertion, like all tautologies, seems pretty unassailable. But what are we to make of the first claim? Those familiar with Justice Scalia's jurisprudence will recognize at once that it flows from his strong commitment to textualism[93]—the doctrine that judges, in interpreting legal texts, should stick close to the "plain" or literal meanings of those texts.[94]

This is a view of legal interpretation that, in constitutional law at least, the Court has consistently rejected for at least five decades,[95] and probably longer.[96] But what is puzzling here is that in this case the "plain" language of the amendment clearly does not support Scalia's reading. "On its face," what the Amendment prohibits are punishments that are cruel, i.e., really cruel, not merely conventionally believed to be such, "and unusual," i.e., rarely if ever imposed.[97] By no stretch does the "plain meaning" of the text require judges to uphold punishments that are both grossly disproportionate and imposed on only a tiny fraction of otherwise indistinguishable offenders.

Scalia's second argument for abandoning part (3) of the traditional Eighth Amendment test is that it is inconsistent with due judicial deference to the judgments of elected officials. I quote from Justice Scalia's fuller statement of this argument in a later Eighth Amendment case, *Stanford v. Kentucky*:

> By reaching a decision supported neither by constitutional text nor by the demonstrable current standards of our citizens, the dissent displays a failure to appreciate that "those institutions which the Constitution is supposed to limit" include the Court itself. To say, as the dissent says, that "it is for *us* ultimately to judge whether the Eighth Amendment permits imposition of the death penalty—and to mean that as the dissent means it, *i.e.*, that it is for *us* to judge, not on the basis of what we perceive the Eighth Amendment originally prohibited, or on the basis of what we perceive the society through its democratic processes now overwhelmingly disapproves, but on the basis of what we think "proportionate" and "measurably contributory to acceptable goals of punishment"—to say and mean that, is to replace judges of the law with a committee of philosopher-kings.[98]

Implicit in this quotation is a vision of constitutional adjudication that can only be described as contraconstitutional. As Justice Brennan notes in his dissent in *Stanford*, "Justice Scalia's approach would largely return the task of defining the contours of the Eighth Amendment to political majorities."[99] But "[t]he very purpose of the Bill of Rights was to withdraw certain subjects from the vicissitudes of political controversy, to place them beyond the reach of majorities and officials and to establish them as legal principles to be applied by the courts."[100] If applied generally to the Constitution's "majestic generalities,"[101] it would undermine the Court's historical role as a protector of minority and individual rights against majoritarian oppression.

The importance of the protections embraced in part (3) of the traditional Eighth Amendment test is nowhere more evident than in the burgeoning field of prisoners' rights law. For most of our constitutional history, courts took a "hands off" approach toward prisons, viewing prisoners as virtual slaves of the state who had lost most of their rights upon conviction.[102] Beginning in the mid-1960s, following the court's decision in *Cooper v. Pete*[103] that inmates have the right to sue prison officials under section 1983 of the Civil Rights Act of 1871, courts began to take a more activist stance toward prison conditions and prisoners' rights. The resulting changes, both in terms of prison conditions and prison-related adjudication, have been dramatic. Whole prison systems have been fundamentally restructured under judicial supervision.[104] Forty-three states are currently under court orders because of prison overcrowding or other abuses.[105] And inmate suits against prison officials, once a mere trickle, have become a virtual flood.[106] As a result, prisoners' rights jurisprudence is now clearly the highest impact area of Eighth Amendment law.

Justice Scalia's proposed two-part test of Eighth Amendment claims is clearly incapable of explaining or justifying this large and important body of prison-reform case law.[107] Scalia's literalist view is that no punishment is barred by the Eighth Amendment unless it is both cruel *and* unusual. But cruel and inhumane treatment of prisoners was the norm prior to the demise of the "hands off" doctrine. Moreover, unless a punishment was originally understood to be prohibited by the Eighth Amendment, Scalia would invalidate it only if there is clear evidence that society now "overwhelmingly disapproves"[108] of it, as evidenced "in the operative acts (laws and application of laws) that the people have approved."[109] By this exacting standard, judicial intervention in prison affairs will rarely if ever be justified, since elected officials and prison administrators have consistently resisted efforts to remedy scandalous conditions in America's prisons and jails.[110]

In sum, Justice Scalia does not meet the substantial burden of proof rightly imposed on those who would overturn precedent as firmly established as is part (3) of the traditional Eighth Amendment test. Consequently, we must determine whether that test does not or does permit the execution of persons who were fifteen or younger at the time of their offense.

Part (1) of the traditional test, it will be recalled, prohibits punishments that fall within the original understanding of the Cruel and Unusual Punishments Clause. We noted earlier that "the evidence is unusually clear and unequivocal" that capital punishment for crimes committed at age fifteen or younger was not originally believed to be barred by the clause. Thus, the first prong of the traditional analysis is clearly satisfied in the present case.

A much tougher question is whether the execution of a fifteen-year-old is prohibited by part (2) of the analysis, the so-called evolving standards test. In assessing whether a particular punishment is consistent with evolving standards of decency, the Court has repeatedly emphasized that its judgments "should not be, or appear to be, merely the subjective views of individual Justices."[111] To avoid this risk, the Court has relied heavily on objective indicia of public attitudes toward challenged forms of punishment, most notably legislative enactments and the decisions of sentencing juries.[112] At the time *Thompson* was decided, the relevant statistics indicated that (1) the last execution in the United States for a crime committed under the age of sixteen was in 1948;[113] (2) over one recent five-year period, only five fifteen-year-olds (and no offenders younger than fifteen) were sentenced to death;[114] (3) fourteen states (including the District of Columbia) did not authorize capital punishment at all;[115] (4) nineteen states authorized capital punishment and set no minimum age at which the penalty might be imposed;[116] (5) eighteen states authorized capital punishment but established a minimum age for its imposition, ranging from sixteen to eighteen.[117]

These statistics are clearly subject to varying interpretations. Thus the dissent in *Thompson,* emphasizing the fact that the death penalty could theoretically be imposed in nineteen states as well as under federal law,[118] found no basis for discerning "with the requisite degree of certainty, a constitutional consensus in this society that no person can ever be executed for a crime committed under the age of 16."[119] The plurality, preferring to spotlight the fact that every legislature that has expressly set a minimum age for capital punishment has set that age at sixteen or above,[120] concluded that the requisite degree of consensus does exist.[121] Justice O'Connor, characteristically,[122] urged a more cautious conclusion: that the evidence supporting such a consensus, while strong, is not yet so compelling that the Court would be justified in declaring a blanket constitutional ban on the execution of any fifteen-year-old offender on the basis of the evolving-standards test.[123]

These disagreements underscore a familiar theme of recent jurisprudence: that judgments about purportedly "neutral" sources of legal values (framers' intent, "plain" meaning, etc.) often prove to be no less contestable and value-laden than judgments that attempt to grapple directly with the normative implications of interpretive choices.[124] In this case, Justice O'Connor's conclusion of "probable but not proven" appears to be the one best supported by the available evidence.

We therefore turn to part (3) of the traditional Eighth Amendment analysis. As we have seen, this requires judges to determine whether a given sanction constitutes grossly excessive punishment, makes no measurable contribution to acceptable penological goals, or is authorized under sentencing procedures that create a substantial risk of arbitrary and capricious outcomes.

Of these three tests, the second has long been the most controversial. First articulated at a time when it was widely believed both that retribution was not an acceptable penological goal[125] and that capital punishment was not a significantly better deterrent to crime than less extreme sanctions,[126] the measurable-contribution principle was vigorously criticized from its inception as inviting judicial policy making in areas best reserved for legislative judgment.[127] Today, now that each of these once-popular beliefs is widely contested,[128] it may well be doubted whether the measurable-contribution principle has any legitimate place in Eighth Amendment jurisprudence.

Such concerns, while valid, should not be overstated. The measurable-contribution principle has long played an important role in the field of prisoners' rights law.[129] Nevertheless, I agree that the principle should play a limited role in the constitutional review of sentencing decisions. In particular, courts should not be quick to second-guess legislative judgments about the comparative deterrent value of various punishments. This is a point on which Justice Stevens' plurality opinion in *Thompson* can rightly be faulted. Stevens concludes that the execution of fifteen-year-old offenders does not measurably contribute to the goal of deterrence.[130] However, he cites no direct criminological evidence for this claim. Moreover, the sorts of reasons he does cite (e.g., the small number of juvenile executions in this century and the unlikelihood that many fifteen-year-old offenders actually engage in the kind of cost-benefit analysis the deterrence rationale presumes) tend to show, at best, that fifteen-year-olds would not be significantly deterred by such executions. But of course a legislature might reasonably determine that a few highly publicized juvenile executions would deter a number of older would-be offenders. And I can see no reason why this should not be considered an "acceptable" penological goal.

A stronger challenge to the constitutionality of executing fifteen-year-olds focuses on whether current capital sentencing procedures serve to ensure that the death penalty for such youthful offenders will not be imposed in an arbitrary and unpredictable fashion. As the nation's foremost authority on juvenile death sentences has argued, the imposition of the death penalty on fifteen-year-olds would seem to be "a prime example of an arbitrary, capricious, and freakish punishment."[131] Department of Justice statistics indicate that during one recent five-year period, 82,094 arrests were made for willful criminal homicide.[132] Of these, only 1,393 of those convicted were sentenced to death.[133] And of this number, only five were younger than sixteen at the time of the offense.[134] These constituted a microscopic 0.3 percent of the 1,861 persons arrested for willful homicide who were under the age of sixteen.[135]

Significantly, challenges based on the arbitrariness of juvenile capital sentences were not put forward in any of the opinions in *Thompson*. Presumably, this was because a majority of the Court had ruled just the previous term in *McCleskey v. Kemp*[136] that such challenges could succeed only if it could be shown that a particular sentencing procedure fails to "focus discretion 'on the particularized nature of the crime and the particularized characteristics of the individual defendant.'"[137] No such proof was attempted in *Thompson*.

In a powerful dissenting opinion in *McCleskey*, Justice Brennan convincingly argued that this "focused discretion" ruling was a wholly unwarranted departure from controlling precedent.[138] Earlier cases had made clear that the crucial question was not whether a given capital sentencing scheme fails to adequately "focus" discretion on particularized considerations, but whether it creates a *substantial risk* that a sanction "unique in its severity and irrevocability"[139] will be imposed in an arbitrary or discriminatory manner.[140] For reasons of precedential constraint, however, the Court correctly did not reopen that *McCleskey* debate in its decision in *Thompson*.

Finally, under the traditional analysis we must determine whether the execution of a person for a crime committed at age fifteen or younger is grossly disproportionate to the gravity of the offense committed.

In assessing the "gravity" of an offense for purposes of proportionality analysis, the Court has traditionally considered both the seriousness of the harm inflicted and the degree of the offender's culpability.[141] For our purposes, the critical question is whether a person under sixteen years of age is capable of acting with the degree of culpability that can warrant the ultimate punishment.

We saw earlier that judges, in addressing normative questions of this sort, should seek solutions that exist in reflective equilibrium with the community's considered moral judgments. Since it is the community's *considered* judgments that are sought, the views of respected professional organizations with special expertise are particularly relevant. Strikingly, one finds a strong consensus among such organizations that the death penalty even for sixteen- and seventeen-year-olds is morally unacceptable.[142] Striking, also, is the fact that capital punishment for juveniles has in practice been abolished throughout the developed world. Worldwide, according to Amnesty International statistics, only eight juvenile executions have taken place since 1979.[143] Three of those occurred in the United States. The other five were carried out in Bangladesh, Rwanda, Pakistan, and Barbados.[144]

In this country, there has long been broad agreement that less culpability should ordinarily attach to a crime committed by a juvenile than to a comparable crime committed by an adult. This is reflected in a wide range of legislative enactments bottomed on the recognition that "'minors often lack the experience, perspective, and judgment' expected of adults."[145] Thus, all states impose special disabilities on juveniles with respect to voting, jury service, marriage, operation of a motor vehicle, and many other activities believed to require a level of maturation and responsibility juveniles typically lack.[146] Moreover, all states have established a juvenile justice system premised on the assumption that most young offenders should not be held to the same standards of accountability as their adult counterparts.[147]

These popularly held beliefs about the limited capacities of juveniles for informed, responsible decision making are reinforced by an impressive body of socioscientific evidence. That evidence reveals adolescents to be "more vulnerable, more impulsive, and less self-disciplined than adults";[148] less able "to control their conduct and to think in long-range terms";[149] more impressionable and subject to peer pressure;[150] more prone to risk taking, bravado, and a false sense of their own "omnipotence and immortality";[151] and less able to grasp and employ moral concepts and patterns of reasoning characteristically featured in adult ethical decision making.[152]

In addition, there is substantial evidence that adolescents sentenced to death typically suffer from "a battery of psychological, emotional, and other problems"[153] widely recognized to diminish an agent's capacity for responsible choice. In one recent study, for example, all fourteen adolescent death-row inmates studied were found to suffer from serious psychiatric disorders, ranging from psychosis to severe paranoia. Nine were diagnosed as suffering from neurological disorders. Only two had IQ scores above ninety. And all but two had been physically or sexually abused, or both.[154]

Taken together, the foregoing considerations strongly support the proposition that death is an excessively harsh punishment for fifteen-year-old offenders. They probably do not prove, however, that "*all* fifteen-year-olds are incapable of the moral culpability that would justify the imposition of capital punishment."[155] And that, according to Justice O'Connor, is what must be shown if the proportionality argument is to succeed.

This contention runs counter to some of the deepest currents of the American legal tradition and the Court's capital punishment jurisprudence. One of the bedrock principles of our legal system is that the awesome punitive powers of the state must be hedged about with safeguards against their abuse. Thus, we invest those brought to the bar of criminal justice with a presumption of innocence[156] and require their accusers to prove beyond a reasonable doubt the guilt of the accused.[157] Likewise, we shield the accused with rights to be judged by their peers,[158] to have the effective assistance of counsel,[159] and to be tried in accordance with fundamentally fair procedures.[160] These familiar features of our acquittal-prone system of criminal justice are thought to be essential both to guard against the risk of individual injustice and to "command the respect and confidence of the community in . . . the moral force of the criminal law."[161] These same considerations apply with equal force when the state stands, not in the role of accuser, but in that of final judge of life and death. As the Court has recognized, our constitutional aspirations impose a "high requirement of reliability on the determination that death is the appropriate punishment in a particular case."[162] In cases where the defendant is fifteen or younger, the risk of an unwarranted sentence of death is so high that no sentencer should be entrusted with such awesome responsibility.

In sum, on broadly pragmatic principles, the execution of persons who were fifteen or younger at the time of their offense violates the Eighth Amendment's prohibition of grossly disproportionate punishments. The plurality in *Thompson* was accordingly correct in holding that, regardless of whether a demonstrable societal consensus now exists that such executions are morally unacceptable, capital punishment for such youthful offenders is not constitutionally permissible.

CONCLUSION

The aim of this chapter has been to sketch, in broad outline, a defensible nonoriginalist theory of constitutional adjudication. The central thesis for which I have argued is that courts and constitutional commentators would do well to return to the kind of broadly pragmatic approach to constitutional interpretation proposed more than half a century ago by Benjamin Cardozo. That approach has two major attractions. First, unlike most competing theories, Cardozo's theory accords closely with actual judicial practice.[163] Second, Cardozo's theory offers an attractive middle way between the jurisprudence of the right, which cloaks reaction under the banners of "original intent" and "judicial restraint," and the jurisprudence of the left, which urges judges boldly to accomplish through open-ended judicial lawmaking leftist political goals that could not possibly be achieved at the polls. For those who seek such a middle way through the thickets of constitutional interpretation, I can suggest no surer general guide than Benjamin Cardozo.

Notes

PREFACE

1. Michael J. Perry, *The Constitution, the Courts, and Human Rights: An Inquiry Into the Legitimacy of Constitutional Policymaking by the Judiciary* (New Haven, Conn.: Yale University Press, 1982), p. 91.

2. Roe v. Wade, 410 U.S. 113 (1973).

3. See, e.g., Mapp v. Ohio, 367 U.S. 643 (1961) (applying the exclusionary rule to state criminal proceedings); Robinson v. California, 370 U.S. 660 (1962) ("incorporating" Eighth Amendment prohibition of cruel and unusual punishments into Fourteenth Amendment prohibition of state deprivation of life, liberty, or property without due process of law); Gideon v. Wainwright, 372 U.S. 335 (1963) (requiring free court-appointed legal counsel for indigent defendants in felony cases); Malloy v. Hogan, 378 U.S. 1 (1964) (incorporating Fifth Amendment right against compulsory self-incrimination); Pointer v. Texas, 380 U.S. 400 (1965) (incorporating Sixth Amendment right to confront witnesses); Parker v. Gladden, 385 U.S. 363 (1966) (incorporating Sixth Amendment right to an impartial jury); Miranda v. Arizona, 384 U.S. 436 (1966) (requiring police to inform persons suspected or accused of a crime of their legal rights prior to in-custody interrogation); Klopfer v. North Carolina, 386 U.S. 213 (1967) (incorporating Sixth Amendment guarantee of speedy trial); Washington v. Texas, 388 U.S. 14 (1967) (incorporating Sixth Amendment right to compulsory process); Duncan v. Louisiana, 391 U.S. 145 (1968) (incorporating Sixth Amendment right to jury trial in non-petty criminal cases); Benton v. Maryland, 395 U.S. 784 (1969) (incorporating Fifth Amendment right against double jeopardy).

4. See, e.g., Engel v. Vitale, 370 U.S. 421 (1962) (barring recitation of state-sponsored prayer in public schools); Abington School District v. Schempp, 374 U.S. 204 (1963) (overturning state law requiring daily Bible readings in public schools); Epperson v. Arkansas, 393 U.S. 97 (1968) (invalidating state law making it a crime to teach the theory of human evolution in public schools);

Lemon v. Kurtzman, 403 U.S. 602 (1971) (prohibiting use of public funds to pay salaries of parochial school teachers teaching secular subjects); Committee for Public Education v. Nyquist, 413 U.S. 756 (1973) (invalidating state programs involving maintenance and repair grants to parochial schools, tuition reimbursements to low-income families, and tax benefits to parents with children in parochial schools); Meek v. Pittenger, 421 U.S. 349 (1975) (barring public provision of assorted instructional materials, auxiliary services, and equipment to private schools); Stone v. Graham, 449 U.S. 39 (1980) (prohibiting posting of Ten Commandments in public school classrooms); Wallace v. Jaffree, 472 U.S. 38 (1985) (invalidating state "moment-of-silence" statute); Grand Rapids School District v. Ball, 473 U.S. 373 (1985) (proscribing use of public funds to pay teachers providing remedial or enrichment instruction in parochial schools); Edwards v. Aguillard, 482 U.S. 578 (1987) (striking down state law mandating equal treatment for evolution and creationism in public schools).

5. See, e.g., Roth v. United States, 354 U.S. 476 (1957) (rejecting earlier, more inclusive judicial standards of obscenity in favor of a narrower test focusing on whether, to the average person applying contemporary community standards, the dominant theme of the material taken as a whole appeals to prurient interest); Stanley v. Georgia, 394 U.S. 557 (1969) (holding that mere private possession of obscene materials cannot constitutionally be made a crime); Cohen v. California, 403 U.S. 15 (1971) (reversing a conviction for wearing a jacket inscribed with the words "Fuck the Draft"); Miller v. California, 413 U.S. 15 (1973) (modifying and generally narrowing the *Roth* test of obscenity).

6. See, e.g., Furman v. Georgia, 408 U.S. 238 (1972) (holding that capital punishment, as then administered in most states, constituted cruel and unusual punishment); Woodson v. North Carolina, 428 U.S. 280 (1976) (striking down state law mandating imposition of death penalty for first-degree and felony murder); Coker v. Georgia, 433 U.S. 584 (1977) (concluding that death as a penalty for rape of an adult woman is grossly excessive punishment and thus prohibited by the Eighth Amendment); Enmund v. Florida, 458 U.S. 782 (1982) (holding that capital punishment for felony murder *simpliciter* violates Eighth Amendment).

7. See, generally, Clifford M. Lytle, *The Warren Court and Its Critics* (Tucson, Ariz.: University of Arizona Press, 1968).

8. See, e.g., Lino Graglia, *Disaster by Decree: The Supreme Court Decisions on Race and the Schools* (Ithaca, N.Y.: Cornell University Press, 1976); Raoul Berger, *Government by Judiciary: The Transformation of the Fourteenth Amendment* (Cambridge, Mass.: Harvard University Press, 1977), pp. 117–33.

9. See, e.g., Christopher Wolfe, *The Rise of Modern Judicial Review: From Constitutional Interpretation to Judge-Made Law* (New York: Basic Books, 1986), pp. 304–7; Trimble v. Gordon, 430 U.S. 762, 777 (1977) (Rehnquist, J., dissenting) (criticizing, on originalist grounds, application of Equal Protection Clause "[e]xcept in the area of the law in which its Framers obviously meant it to apply—classifications based on race or on national origin").

10. See, e.g., Raoul Berger, *Federalism: The Founders' Design* (Norman, Okla.: University of Oklahoma Press, 1987); Bernard Siegan, *The Supreme Court's*

Constitution: An Enquiry into Judicial Review and Its Impact on Society (New Brunswick, N.J.: Transaction Books, 1987), pp. 7–18; Edwin Meese III, "Toward a Jurisprudence of Original Intent," *Benchmark* 2 (1986), pp. 2–3.

11. See, e.g., Berger, *Government by Judiciary*, pp. 134–56; Meese, "Toward a Jurisprudence of Original Intent," p. 5.

12. Richard A. Epstein, *Takings: Private Property and the Power of Eminent Domain* (Cambridge, Mass.: Harvard University Press, 1985), p. x.

13. See ibid. For a similar but less extreme view, see Bernard Siegan, *Economic Liberties and the Constitution* (Chicago: University of Chicago Press, 1980).

14. Article-length discussions of the originalism by philosophers include Samuel Freeman, "Original Meaning, Democratic Interpretation, and the Constitution," *Philosophy and Public Affairs* 21 (1992), pp 1–42; David Couzens Hoy, "A Hermeneutical Critique of the Originalism/Nonoriginalism Distinction," *Northern Kentucky Law Review* 15 (1988), pp. 479–98; David O. Brink, "Legal Theory, Legal Interpretation, and Judicial Review," *Philosophy and Public Affairs,* 17 (1988), pp. 105–48; David Lyons, "Constitutional Interpretation and Original Meaning," *Social Philosophy and Policy* 4 (1986), pp. 76–101; Ronald Dworkin, *Taking Rights Seriously* (Cambridge, Mass.: Harvard University Press, 1977), pp. 131–49; *A Matter of Principle* (Cambridge, Mass.: Harvard University Press, 1985), pp. 33–71; *Law's Empire* (Cambridge, Mass.: Harvard University Press, 1986), pp. 355–79; Stephen Munzer and James Nickel, "Does the Constitution Mean What It Always Meant?" *Columbia Law Review* 77 (1977), pp. 62–77.

15. I am thinking here primarily of various areas of applied ethics: medical, business, and environmental ethics, the morality of capital punishment, nuclear deterrence, and anti-drug legislation, to name just a few. In law, interdisciplinary symposia are becoming increasingly common. Two such symposia that are specially noteworthy for the purposes of this study are "Symposium: Law and Literature," *Texas Law Review* 60 (1982), pp. 373–586; and "Interpretation Symposium," *Southern California Law Review* 58 (1985), pp. 1–725.

CHAPTER 1

1. Home Building and Loan Association v. Blaisdell, 290 U.S. 398, 453 (1934) (Sutherland, J., dissenting).

2. See pp. 10–12.

3. See, e.g., Matthew Bacon, *A New Abridgment of the Law*, 7th ed., 8 vols. (London: A. Strahan, 1832; 1st ed. 1736), VII, p. 487 ("Such a Construction ought to be put upon a Statute as may best assure the Intention which the Makers of it had in View"); Thomas Rutherforth, *Institutes of Natural Law*, 2d American ed., 2 vols. (Baltimore: W. and J. Neal, 1832, 1st ed. 1754–56), II, p. 405 ("The end which interpretation aims at, is to find out what was the intention of the writer"); Sir William Blackstone, *Commentaries on the Laws of England,* ed. by Thomas M. Cooley, 2 vols. (Chicago: Callaghan & Co., 1879; 1st ed. 1766–69), I, p. 58 ("The fairest and most rational method to interpret

the will of the legislator is by exploring his intentions at the time when the law was made, by signs the most natural and probable") (emphasis omitted); Hugo Grotius, *De Jure Belli ac Pacis*, trans. by F. W. Kelsey et al., 2 vols. (Oxford: Oxford University Press, 1925; 1st ed. 1625), II, p. 409 ("The measure of correct interpretation is the inference of intent from the most probable implications"); Samuel von Pufendorf, *On the Law of Nature and Nations*, trans. by Basil Kennett et al. (Oxford, 1710; 1st ed. 1672), p. 420 ("The true End and Design of Interpretation is, to gather the Intent of the Man from most probable signs") (emphasis omitted); Emmerich de Vattel, *The Law of Nations*, trans. by Charles G. Fenwick, 2 vols. (Washington, D.C.: Carnegie Institute of Washington, 1916; 1st ed. 1758), II, p. 201 ("The sole object of a lawful interpretation is to discover the intention of the maker or makers").

4. Aristotle, *Nicomachean Ethics*, in *The Basic Works of Aristotle,* ed. by Richard McKeon (New York: Random House, 1941), p. 1020 (1137b). For a comprehensive discussion of Aristotle's views on *epieikeia*, see Max Hamburger, *Morals and Law: The Growth of Aristotle's Legal Theory* (New York: Biblo & Tannen, 1971), pp. 89–105.

5. Lawrence J. Riley, *The History, Nature, and Use of Epikeia in Moral Theology* (Washington D.C.: Catholic University Press of America, 1948), p. 137.

6. St. Thomas Aquinas, *Summa Theologica,* 3 vols. (New York: Benzinger Bros., 1947), II–II, q. 120, a. 1.

7. See, e.g., Eyston v. Studd, 2 Plowd. 459, 467, 75 Eng. Rep. 688, 699 (1574) ("And Equity, . . . larges or diminishes the letter according to its discretion").

8. 64 Vt. 197, 22 A. 588 (1891).

9. Ibid., pp. 200–201 (quoting Bacon, *A New Abridgment,* VII, p. 459). Bacon, in turn, is quoting, with slight changes, Plowden's note to Eyston v. Studd, 2 Plowd. 459, 467, 75 Eng. Rep. 688, 699 (1574).

10. See William W. Crosskey, *Politics and the Constitution in the History of the United States,* 2 vols. (Chicago: University of Chicago Press, 1953), I, p. 364; Joseph Story, *Commentaries on the Constitution of the United States,* 3d ed. 2 vols. (Boston: Little, Brown, 1858), I, pp. 283–85.

11. See Christopher St. Germain, *Doctor and Student* (London: S. Sweet, 1915; 1st ed. 1523), pp. 45–46.

12. For a discussion of Plowden's views on legal construction, see Frank Horack, "Statutory Interpretation—Light from Plowden's Reports," *Kentucky Law Journal* 19 (1931), pp. 211–25.

13. See, generally, C. K. Allen, *Law in the Making*, 6th ed. (Oxford: Clarendon Press, 1958), pp. 389–93; Stephen A. Siege, "The Aristotelian Basis of English Law, 1450–1800," *New York University Law Review* 56 (1981), pp. 18–59.

14. 17 U.S. (4 Wheat.) 316 (1819).

15. Gerald Gunther, ed., *John Marshall's Defense of McCulloch v. Maryland* (Stanford, Calif.: Stanford University Press, 1969), pp. 168–69.

16. Rutgers v. Waddington, Mayor's Court of New York City (1784), reprinted in Julius Goebel, Jr., and Joseph H. Smith, ed., *The Law Practice of*

Alexander Hamilton: Documents and Commentary, 5 vols. (New York: Columbia University Press, 1964–1981), I, Chap. 3.

17. Ibid., p. 357. Citing Plowden, Hamilton adds: "Statutes [are] to be construed according to the intention of the Legislature; which intention is to be ascertained by supposing the framers of the law wise and honest and well acquainted with all the merits of the case to be determined upon; and under this supposition asking ourselves[:] What could be the intention of wise honest and well informed men in this particular case?" Ibid. As this quotation suggests, in an age in which reliable legislative history was a rare exception rather than the rule, classical equity hermeneutics inevitably relied heavily upon presumptions of various kinds. One of the most important of these was that legislators "may be presumed not to have intended, because they ought not to have intended, any thing which is unjust or unreasonable." Rutherforth, *Institutes of Natural Law*, II, p. 427. By treating this and other similar presumptions as conclusive rather than defeasible, one could easily arrive at the view (as Hamilton apparently did) that the key interpretive question is not "What did the lawmaker actually intend?" but rather "What could be the intention of wise, honest, and well-informed men in this particular case?" Hamilton's oft-cited later view that "[n]othing is more common than for laws to *express* and *effect*, more or less than was intended" (Hamilton, "Opinion on the Constitutionality of an Act to Establish a Bank," 1791, in *The Papers of Alexander Hamilton*, ed. by H. C. Syrett et al., 26 vols. (New York: Columbia University Press, 1961–79), VIII, p. 111) marks a decisive break with the traditional canon that "a thing which is within the intention of the makers of a statute is as much within the statute as if it were within the letter; and a thing which is within the letter of a statute is not within the statute unless it be within the intention of the makers." Riggs v. Palmer, 115 N.Y. 506, 507, 22 N.E. 188, 189 (1889).

18. Goebel and Smith, eds., *Law Practice of Alexander Hamilton*, I, p. 391.

19. James Wilson, "Lectures on the Law," in *The Works of James Wilson*, ed. by Robert McCloskey, 2 vols. (Cambridge, Mass.: Harvard University Press, 1967), I, p. 75.

20. Ibid., II, p. 478.

21. Letter from Jefferson to Justice William Johnson, June 12, 1823, in *The Writings of Thomas Jefferson,* ed. by Albert E. Bergh, 20 vols. (Washington, D.C.: Jefferson Memorial Association, 1907), XV, p. 449.

22. Letter from Madison to John Jackson, December 27, 1821, in *Letters and Other Writings of James Madison,* 4 vols. (Philadelphia: J. P. Lippincott, 1865), III, p. 245. See also "Essays of Brutus," reprinted in *The Anti-Federalist: Writings by the Opponents of the Constitution,* ed. by Herbert J. Storing (Chicago: University of Chicago Press, 1985), p. 164 (noting that, on commonly accepted principles, courts "are empowered, to explain the constitution according to the reasoning spirit of it, without being confined to the words or letter").

23. Wilson, *Works*, II, 502.

24. Alexander Hamilton, James Madison, and John Jay, *The Federalist,* ed. by Jacob E. Cooke (Middletown, Conn.: Wesleyan University Press, 1961), p. 523 (No. 78). Cf. Osborn v. Bank of United States, 22 U.S. (9 Wheat.) 738,

866 (1824) ("Courts are the mere instruments of the law, and can will nothing").

25. John Hart Ely, *Democracy and Distrust: A Theory of Judicial Review* (Cambridge, Mass.: Harvard University Press, 1980), p. 7.

26. The rule is "referred to as thoroughly established in 1811." James Bradley Thayer, "The Origin and Scope of the American Doctrine of Constitutional Law," *Harvard Law Review* 7 (1893), p. 140. For early affirmations of the rule, see Hylton v. United States, 3 U.S. (3 Dall.) 171, 175 (1796) (Chase, J.); Calder v. Bull, 3 U.S. (3 Dall.) 386, 398 (1798) (Iredell, J.); Cooper v. Telfair, 4 U.S. (4 Dall.) 14, 18 (1800) (Washington, J.); ibid., p. 19 (Paterson, J.); Dartmouth College v. Woodward, 17 U.S. (4 Wheat.) 518, 625 (1819) (Marshall, C.J.).

27. Thayer, "Origin and Scope," pp. 129–52. Thayer's views on judicial review influenced generations of Harvard-educated jurists, including Oliver Wendell Holmes, Jr., Learned Hand, Louis Brandeis, and Felix Frankfurter. See, generally, Wallace Mendelson, "The Influence of James B. Thayer upon the Work of Holmes, Brandeis, and Frankfurter," *Vanderbilt Law Review* 31 (1978), pp. 71–87.

28. Henry Campbell Black, *Handbook on the Construction and Interpretation of the Laws*, 2d ed. (St. Paul, Minn.: West, 1911), p. 110. See also Lochner v. New York, 198 U.S. 45, 68 (1905) (Harlan, J., dissenting) ("the rule is universal that a legislative enactment, Federal or state, is never to be disregarded or held invalid unless it be, beyond question, plainly and palpably in excess of legislative power").

29. Francis Lieber, *Legal and Political Hermeneutics* (Boston: Little, Brown, 1839), p. 23.

30. See, e.g., Aristotle, *De Interpretatione,* in *The Basic Works of Aristotle*, p. 40 (16a3).

31. See, e.g., St. Thomas Aquinas, *Commentary on the Metaphysics of Aristotle,* trans. by John P. Rowan (Chicago: Henry Regnery, 1961), p. 480 ("words are the signs of concepts"). For an illuminating discussion of Aquinas's views on signification, see Mark D. Jordan, *Ordering Wisdom: The Hierarchy of Philosophical Discourses in Aquinas* (Notre Dame, Indiana: University of Notre Dame Press, 1986), pp. 13–15.

32. John Locke, *An Essay Concerning Human Understanding,* ed. by Peter H. Nidditch (Oxford: Clarendon Press, 1975), p. 405 (emphasis omitted). Norman Kretzmann ("The Main Thesis of Locke's Semantic Theory," *The Philosophical Review* 77 (1968), pp. 175–96) argues forcefully that Locke did not hold the naive view that words generally *name* ideas; whether rightly or wrongly, however, this view was widely attributed to Locke and became the orthodox semantic theory in eighteenth-century England and America. See Stephen K. Land, *From Signs to Propositions: The Concept of Form in Eighteenth-Century Semantic Theory* (London: Longmans, 1974), p. 13.

33. See, e.g., William K. Wimsatt, Jr., and Monroe Beardsley, "The Intentional Fallacy," in W. K. Wimsatt, Jr., *The Verbal Icon: Studies in the Meaning of Poetry* (New York: Noonday Press, 1954); Stanley Fish, *Is There a Text in This Class? The Authority of Interpretive Communities* (Cambridge, Mass.:

Harvard University Press, 1980); Terence Hawkes, *Structuralism and Semiotics* (London: Metheun, 1977); Jonathan Culler, *On Deconstruction: Theory and Criticism After Structuralism* (Ithaca, N.Y.: Cornell University Press, 1982). Terry Eagleton's *Literary Theory: An Introduction* (Minneapolis: University of Minnesota Press, 1983) provides an accessible introduction to this frequently difficult literature.

34. See, e.g., Hans-Georg Gadamer, *Truth and Method*, trans. by Garnett Barden and John Cumming (London: Sheed & Ward, 1975); Michel Foucault, "What Is an Author?" in *Perspectives in Post-Structuralist Criticism*, ed. by Josué V. Harari (Ithaca, N.Y.: Cornell University Press, 1979); Jacques Derrida, "Structure, Sign and Play in the Discourse of the Human Sciences," in *Writing and Difference*, trans. by Alan Bass (London: Routledge & Kegan Paul), pp. 278–300. For a lucid introduction to developments in twentieth-century analytic philosophy on the concept of "meaning" and related notions, see William Alston, "Meaning," in *The Encyclopedia of Philosophy*, ed. by Paul Edwards, 8 vols. (New York and London: Macmillan and The Free Press, 1967), V, pp. 233–41. For more recent work, see Michael Devitt and Kim Sterelny, *Language and Reality: An Introduction to the Philosophy of Language* (Cambridge, Mass.: The MIT Press, 1987), pp. 15–86.

35. See, e.g., Ferdinand de Saussure, *Course in General Linguistics*, trans. by Ware Baker (New York: McGraw-Hill, 1966; 1st ed. 1916). See also Ruth Kempson, *Semantic Theory* (Cambridge: Cambridge University Press, 1977), p. 2 (noting that in linguistics there is currently "no semantic theory which enjoys widespread acceptance, even in bare outlines").

36. See, e.g., United States v. American Trucking Association, 310 U.S. 534, 545 (1940) ("When aid to construction of the meaning of words, as used in a statute, is available, there can certainly be no 'rule of law' which forbids its use, however clear the words may appear on 'superficial examination') (footnotes omitted); Thornburgh v. American College of Obstetricians and Gynecologists, 476 U.S. 747, 789 (1986) (White, J., dissenting) ("As its prior cases clearly show, . . . this Court does not subscribe to the simplistic view that constitutional interpretation can possibly be limited to the 'plain meaning' of the Constitution's text").

37. Black, *Handbook on the Construction of Laws*, pp. 20–21.

38. See, e.g., Antonin Scalia, "Originalism: the Lesser Evil," *University of Cincinnati Law Review* 57 (1989), p. 861; Walter Berns, "Judicial Review and the Rights and Laws of Nature," *Supreme Court Review: 1982*, ed. by Philip B. Kurland (Chicago: Chicago University Press, 1982), p. 50; Henry Monaghan, "Our Perfect Constitution," *New York University Law Review* 56 (1981), p. 360; Bernard Siegan, *Economic Liberties and the Constitution*, p. 24; Raoul Berger, *Government by Judiciary*, p. 412; Letter from James Madison to Charles Jared Ingersoll, June 25, 1831, in *Letters and Other Writings of James Madison*, IV, pp. 183–87.

39. Black, *Handbook on the Construction of Laws*, p. 20 (italics added).

40. James Kent, *Commentaries on American Law*, 13th ed. 4 vols. (Boston: Little, Brown, 1884; 1st ed. 1826–30), I, p. 462.

41. By common consent, Story and James Kent rank as "the two most significant

figures in American legal literature in the first half of the 19th century." Lawrence M. Friedman, *A History of American Law* (New York: Simon & Schuster, 1973), p. 288.

42. Sedgwick's *Treatise on the Measure of Damages* (1847) has been described as "the most brilliant and boldly innovative antebellum legal treatise." Morton J. Horwitz, *The Transformation of American Law, 1780–1860* (Cambridge, Mass.: Harvard University Press, 1977), p. 83. For Sedgwick's objections to intentionalism, see his *Treatise on the Interpretation of Statutory and Constitutional Law*, 2d ed. (New York: Baker, Voorhis, and Co., 1874; 1st ed. 1857), p. 328.

43. Story, *Commentaries on the Constitution,* I, 289, n. 1.

44. See, generally, Black, *Handbook on the Construction of Laws*, pp. 311–16.

45. The *locus classicus* of the Mischief Rule is Heydon's Case, 3 Co. Rep. 7a, 76 Eng. Rep. 637 (1574), in which

> It was resolved by the Barons of the Exchequer that for the sure and true interpretation of all statutes in general . . . four things are to be discerned and considered: (1) What was the common law before the making of the act; (2) what was the mischief or defect for which the common law did not provide; (3) what remedy Parliament hath resolved and appointed to cure the disease of the commonwealth; (4) the true reason of the remedy. And then the office of all the judges is always to make such construction as shall suppress the mischief and advance the remedy, . . . according to the true intent of the makers of the act, *pro bono publico*.

Quoted in Black, *Handbook on the Construction of Laws*, p. 286.

The Literal Rule holds that "if the words of an Act are clear, [courts] must follow them, even if they lead to manifest absurdity." Regina v. City of London Court Judge, [1892] 1 Q.B. 273, 290. The Golden Rule permits departures from the plain import of a statute if, but only if, this is necessary to avoid manifest absurdity or inconsistency. Becke v. Smith, [1836] 2 M. & W. 191, 195; Grey v. Pearson, [1857] 6 H.L. Cas. 61, 106. By 1930, American courts had more or less decisively repudiated the literalist approach to statutory interpretation embodied in these latter two rules. See John W. Johnson, "Retreat from the Common Law? The Grudging Reception of Legislative History by American Appellate Courts in the Twentieth Century," *Detroit College Law Review*, 1978 (1978), p. 421, English courts, by contrast, have continued to insist as a rule that the literal, ordinary, or plain meaning of statutory language must be preferred to any alternative meaning indicated by legislative history or other extrinsic aids to construction. See F. A. R. Bennion, *Statutory Interpretation* (London: Butterworths, 1984), pp. 199–222.

46. Compare, e.g., United States v. Wiltberger, 18 U.S. (5 Wheat.) 76, 95 (1820) (Marshall, C.J.) ("The case must be a strong one indeed, which would justify a Court in departing from the plain meaning of words . . . in search of an intention which the words themselves do not suggest) with the following formulation of the rule by H. C. Black:

> For the courts the only rule is "ita lex scripta est." . . . Even if the court is fully persuaded that the legislature really meant and intended something entirely different from what it actually enacted, and that the failure to convey the real meaning was due to inadvertence or mistake in the use of language, yet, if the words chosen by the legislature are not obscure or ambiguous, but convey a precise and sensible meaning (excluding the case of obvious clerical errors or elliptical forms of expression), then the court must take the law as it finds it, and give it its literal interpretation, without being influenced by the probable legislative meaning lying back of the words.

Black, *Handbook on the Construction of Laws,* pp. 52–53.

47. Throughout the early years of our constitutional tradition, it was widely accepted that the written Constitution was not the sole source of binding fundamental law, and thus that governmental actions might be unconstitutional even though they violated no written constitutional provision. See, e.g., Calder v. Bull, 3 U.S. (3 Dall.) 386, 387–88 (1798) (Chase, J.); Fletcher v. Peck, 10 U.S. (6 Cranch) 87, 136 (1810) (Marshall, C.J.); Terrett v. Taylor, 13 U.S. (9 Cranch) 43, 50–52 (1815) (Story, J.); Gardner v. Newburgh, 2 Johns. Ch. 162, 166–67 (N.Y. 1816) (Kent, J.). For useful overviews see Suzanna Sherry, "The Founders' Unwritten Constitution," *University of Chicago Law Review*, 54 (1987), pp. 1127–77; Thomas C. Grey, "The Original Understanding and the Unwritten Constitution," in *Toward a More Perfect Union: Six Essays on the Constitution*, ed. by Neil L. York (Provo, Utah: Brigham Young University, 1988), pp. 145–73. By the beginning of this century, owing to the intervening triumph of legal positivism, invocations of unwritten principles of higher law had become rare. For a classic discussion of the relevant history, see Benjamin J. Wright, *American Interpretations of Natural Law* (Cambridge, Mass.: Harvard University Press, 1931), pp. 307–19.

48. Theodore Sedgwick, writing in 1857 and citing mostly English cases, announced that the traditional doctrine of equitable construction "is now looked on with distrust." Sedgwick, *Interpretation of Statutory and Constitutional Law*, p. 311. By 1891, the doctrine was pronounced "obsolete." J. G. Sutherland, *Statutes and Statutory Construction* (Chicago: Callaghan & Co., 1891), p. 529. But see U.S. v. Kirby 74 U.S. (7 Wall.) 482 (1868), and The Church of the Holy Trinity v. United States, 143 U.S. 457 (1892) (both relying on equitable restriction of the statutory language at issue).

49. Holmes, "The Path of the Law," reprinted in *The Mind and Faith of Justice Holmes,* ed. Max Lerner (New York: The Modern Library, 1943), p. 85.

50. For convenience, I use "legal realism" broadly to include the brands of legal pragmatism associated with Oliver Wendell Holmes, Jr., and Roscoe Pound, although, strictly, this is inaccurate. The literature on legal realism and its pragmatist forerunners is immense. Among the works I have found helpful are H. L. Pohlman, *Justice Oliver Wendell Holmes and Utilitarian Jurisprudence* (Cambridge, Mass.: Harvard University Press, 1984); William Twining, *Karl Llewellyn and the Realist Movement* (London: Willmer Bros., 1973); Wilfrid

E. Rumble, Jr., *American Legal Realism: Skepticism, Reform, and the Judicial Process* (Ithaca, N.Y.: Cornell University Press, 1968); Grant Gilmore, *The Ages of American Law* (New Haven, Conn.: Yale University Press, 1977); Thomas C. Grey, "Holmes and Legal Pragmatism," *Stanford Law Review* 41 (1989), pp. 787–870; and especially Robert S. Summers, *Instrumentalism and American Legal Theory* (Ithaca, N.Y.: Cornell University Press, 1982).

51. Oliver Wendell Holmes, Jr., *The Common Law*, reprinted in part in *The Mind and Faith of Justice Holmes*, pp. 51–52. For detailed discussions of legal formalism, see Thomas C. Grey, "Langdell's Orthodoxy," *University of Pittsburgh Law Review* 45 (1983), pp. 1–53; Steven M. Quevedo, "Formalist and Instrumentalist Legal Reasoning and Legal Theory," *California Law Review* 73 (1985), pp. 119–25.

52. See, e.g., Ernest Bruncken, "Interpretation of the Written Law," *Yale Law Journal* 25 (1915), p. 130; Max Radin, "Statutory Interpretation," *Harvard Law Review* 43 (1930), p. 870; Frederick J. de Sloovere, "Textual Interpretation of Statutes," *New York University Law Quarterly Review* 11 (1934), pp. 540–41; Frank E. Horack, "Cooperative Action for Improved Statutory Interpretation," *Vanderbilt Law Review* 3 (1950), p. 388.

53. To save words, I shall occasionally use "legislative intent" as shorthand for "legislative *or* framers' intent".

54. See, e.g., Jacobus ten Broeck, "Admissibility and Use by the United States Supreme Court of Extrinsic Aids in Constitutional Construction," *California Law Review* 27 (1939), p. 453. For a later expression of this view, see C. Herman Pritchett, *The American Constitution* (New York: McGraw–Hill, 1959), p. 45.

55. See, e.g., Bruncken, "Interpretation of the Written Law," pp. 129–30; Pritchett, *The American Constitution*, pp. 43–44; William Anderson, "The Intention of the Framers: A Note on Constitutional Interpretation," *American Political Science Review* 49 (1955), pp. 341–45.

56. See, e.g., Roscoe Pound, "Liberty of Contract," *Yale Law Journal* 18 (1909), p. 467; Edward S. Corwin, "Moratorium Over Minnesota," *University of Pennsylvania Law Review* 82 (1934), pp. 313–14. The quoted language is from McCulloch v. Maryland, 17 U.S. (4 Wheat.) 316, 415 (1819) (Marshall, C.J.).

57. See, e.g., Bruncken, "Interpretation of the Written Law," p. 136; Benjamin N. Cardozo, *The Nature of the Judicial Process* (New Haven, Conn: Yale University Press, 1921), pp. 14–18, 150–52; Corwin, "Moratorium Over Minnesota," p. 314; Morris R. Cohen, *Law and the Social Order: Essays in Legal Philosophy* (New York: Harcourt, Brace, 1933), pp. 131–33; Walton H. Hamilton and Douglass Adair, *The Power to Govern: The Constitution—Then and Now* (New York: W. W. Norton, 1937), p. 184.

58. This is, at any rate, one way of understanding realist arguments to the effect that legal meaning is, or is closely connected with, judicially assigned meaning. See, e.g., Morris R. Cohen, *The Faith of a Liberal* (New York.: Henry Holt, 1946), p. 176 ("It is not the man who writes a law or those who vote for it, but the one who has the last word in its interpretation who determines its

final meaning"); John Chipman Gray, *The Nature and Sources of the Law*, 2d ed. (New York: Macmillan, 1924), p. 170 ("[statutory] meaning is declared by the courts; and it is with the meaning declared by the courts, and with no other meaning, that they are imposed upon the country as law"); Edward S. Corwin, "Judicial Review in Action," *University of Pennsylvania Law Review* 74 (1926), p. 652 ("the judicial version of the Constitution *is* the Constitution"); Vincent M. Barnett, Jr., "Constitutional Interpretation and Judicial Self-Restraint." *Michigan Law Review* 39 (1940), p. 220 ("[statutory] words have meaning only when interpreted and applied by the courts"); Louis B. Boudin, *Government By Judiciary,* 2 vols. (New York: William Godwin, 1932), I, p. 463 ("practically, the meaning of the constitution is that which the majority of the Supreme Court for the time being chooses to give to it"); Walton H. Hamilton, "1937 to 1787, Dr.," in *The Constitution Reconsidered,* ed. by Conyers Read (New York: Columbia University Press, 1938), p. viii ("the Constitution is as it is expounded"). See also Charles Evans Hughes, *The Supreme Court of the United States* (New York: Columbia University Press, 1928), p. 230 ("a federal statute finally means what the Court says it means"). Hughes's more famous remark, "We are under a Constitution, but the Constitution is what the judges say it is," is quoted in Merlo J. Pusey, *Charles Evans Hughes,* 2 vols. (New York: Macmillan, 1951), I, 204.

59. Benjamin Hoadly, Sermon on "The Nature of the Kingdom or Church of Christ," March 31, 1717, in *The Works of Benjamin Hoadly,* 3 vols. (London, 1773), II, p. 404. Quoted in Thayer, "Origin and Scope of Constitutional Law," p. 152.

60. ten Broeck, "Admissibility and Use of Extrinsic Aids," pp. 406, 407.

61. *The Writings of Thomas Jefferson*, VII, 459. For discussions of Jefferson's views on the sovereignty of the present generation, see Garry Wills, *Inventing America: Jefferson's Declaration of Independence* (Garden City, N.Y.: Doubleday, 1978), pp. 123–28; Daniel Boorstin, *The Lost World of Thomas Jefferson* (Boston: Beacon Press, 1960), pp. 204–13.

62. Arthur S. Miller and Ronald F. Howell, "The Myth of Neutrality in Constitutional Adjudication," *University of Chicago Law Review* 27 (1960), p. 683.

63. See, e.g., Radin, "Statutory Interpretation," p. 871; Corwin, "Constitution Versus Constitutional Theory," (1925), reprinted in *American Constitutional History: Essays by Edward S. Corwin*, ed. by Alpheus Mason and Gerald Garvey (New York: Harper & Row, 1964), pp. 106–08. See also Oliver Wendell Holmes, Jr., *Collected Legal Papers* (New York: Harcourt, Brace, 1921), p. 139 ("the present has a right to govern itself so far as it can").

64. For a representative sampling, see Ernst Freund, "Interpretation of Statutes," *University of Pennslvania Law Review* 65 (1917), p. 212; John Chipman Gray, *Nature and Sources of the Law,* p. 173n. 1 (quoting Holmes with approval); Frederick de Sloovere, "Preliminary Questions in Statutory Interpretation," *New York University Law Quarterly* 9 (1932), p. 414; Cohen, *Law and the Social Order,* p. 130; Karl Llewellyn, "The Constitution as an Instrument," *Columbia Law Review* 34 (1934), p. 13; Robert Farley, "Interpretation Re-interpreted,"

Tulane Law Review 11 (1937), p. 271; Charles P. Curtis, "A Better Theory of Legal Interpretation," *Vanderbilt Law Review* 3 (1950), pp. 409–10; John E. Thornton, "Intent of the Draftsman as a Device to Construe Written Instruments," *Alabama Law Review* 5 (1952), p. 56.

65. Some critics apparently held that all talk of legislative intent is irremediably senseless, since mental states cannot be attributed to collective bodies of persons. See, e.g., Albert Kocourek, *An Introduction to the Science of Law* (Boston: Little, Brown, 1930), p. 201; John Willis, "Statutory Interpretation in a Nutshell," *Canadian Bar Review* 16 (1938), p. 3; D. J. Payne, "The Intention of the Legislature in the Interpretation of Statutes," *Current Legal Problems* 9 (1956), pp. 97–98.

66. Karl Llewellyn, "Remarks on the Theory of Appellate Decision and the Rules or Canons About How Statutes are to be Construed," *Vanderbilt Law Review* 3 (1950), p. 400.

67. Ibid.

68. Radin, "Statutory Interpretation," p. 870.

69. Ibid. p. 872. Cf. Gray, *Nature and Sources of Law*, p. 170 ("psychic transference of the thought of an artificial body must stagger the most advanced of ghost hunters").

70. For examples of Black's originalist jurisprudence, see Everson v. Board of Education, 330 U.S. 1, 8–18 (1947); Adamson v. California, 332 U.S. 46, 92–123 (1947) (Black, J., dissenting); Engel v. Vitale, 370 U.S. 421, 425–36 (1962); Wesberry v. Sanders, 376 U.S. 1, 7–18 (1964); Bell v. Maryland, 378 U.S. 226, 335–43 (1964) (Black, J., dissenting). For less than flattering assessments of Black's skills as a historian, see Charles Fairman, "Does the Fourteenth Amendment Incorporate the Bill of Rights? The Original Understanding," *Stanford Law Review* 2 (1949), pp. 5–139; Paul Murphy, "Time to Reclaim: The Current Challenge of American Constitutional History," *American Historical Review* 69 (1963), pp. 64–65; Alfred E. Kelly, "Clio and the Court: An Illicit Love Affair," in *Supreme Court Review: 1965*, ed. by Philip B. Kurland (Chicago: University of Chicago Press, 1965), p. 135; Leonard W. Levy, "Introduction," in Charles Fairman and Stanley Morrison, *The Fourteenth Amendment and the Bill of Rights: The Incorporation Theory* (New York: De Capo Press, 1970), pp. xii–xiii.

71. See especially Crosskey, *Politics and the Constitution*. See also Felix Frankfurter, "Some Reflections on the Reading of Statutes," *Columbia Law Review* 47 (1947), pp. 422–23; *Sutherland's Statutes and Statutory Construction,* 4th ed., 4 vols., ed. by C. Dallas Sands (Chicago: Callaghan, 1974), IIa, pp. 22–24.

72. Gerald MacCallum, Jr., "Legislative Intent," *Yale Law Journal* 75 (1966), p. 780.

73. Michael S. Moore, "The Semantics of Judging," *Southern California Law Review* 54 (1981), p. 266.

74. See, e.g., James M. Landis, "A Note on Statutory Interpretation," *Harvard Law Review* 43 (1930), pp. 888–89; Harry Willmer Jones, "Statutory Doubts and Legislative Intention," *Columbia Law Review* 40 (1940), p. 969.

75. See, e.g., Frank E. Horack, Jr., "In the Name of Legislative Intention,"

West Virginia Law Quarterly 38 (1932), pp. 126–30; J. A. Corry, "Administrative Law and the Interpretation of Statutes," *University of Toronto Law Journal* 1 (1936), pp. 290–92; Jones, "Statutory Doubts," p. 973; Note, "A Re-evaluation of the Use of Legislative History in the Federal Courts," *Columbia Law Review* 52 (1952), p. 126; Henry M. Hart and Albert Sacks, "The Legal Process: Basic Problems in the Making and Application of Law" (unpublished mimeographed manuscript, 1958), pp. 166–67, 1201; Lon L. Fuller, *The Morality of Law* (New Haven, Conn.: Yale University Press, rev. ed. 1964), pp. 82–91. By 1966, as Gerald MacCallum reports, this response had become "conventional." MacCallum, "Legislative Intent," p. 779.

76. Distinctions along these lines are of considerable antiquity. Medieval jurists, for example, routinely distinguished between the *mens legis*, which resides in the proper signification of the law's words themselves, from both the *ratio legis* (the purpose or final cause of the law) and the *mens legislatoris* (the meaning that the legislator subjectively intended). See John Rogg Schmidt, *The Principles of Authentic Interpretation in Canon 17 of the Code of Canon Law: A Commentary* (Washington D.C.: The Catholic University of America Press, 1941), pp. 142–47. For related distinctions in early modern jurisprudence, see Grotius, *De Jure Belli ac Pacis*, II, pp. 412–13; Rutherforth, *Institutes of Natural Law*, II, pp. 414–15.

77. Home Building and Loan Association v. Blaisdell, 290 U.S. 398, 442–43 (1934). Fourteen years earlier, in Missouri v. Holland, 252 U.S. 416, 433 (1920), Justice Holmes had sounded a similar note:

> [W]hen we are dealing with words that also are a constituent act, like the Constitution of the United States, we must realize that they have called into life a being the development of which could not have been foreseen completely by the most gifted of its begetters. It was enough for them to realize or to hope that they had created an organism; it has taken a century and has cost their successors much sweat and blood to prove that they created a nation. The case before us must be considered in the light of our whole experience and not merely in that of what was said a hundred years ago.

78. United States v. Classic, 313 U.S. 299, 316 (1941).

79. Brown v. Board of Education, 347 U.S. 483, 489 (1954); Loving v. Virginia, 388 U.S. 1, 9 (1967).

80. Brown. v. Board of Education, 347 U.S. 483, 492 (1954).

81. Harper v. Virginia Board of Elections, 383 U.S. 663, 669 (1966).

82. The leading case here is of course *Brown*. For powerful arguments that the Fourteenth Amendment was not intended to prohibit states from segregating blacks in public schools, see Alexander M. Bickel, "The Original Understanding and the Segregation Decision," *Harvard Law Review* 69 (1955), pp. 1–43; Berger, *Government by Judiciary*, pp. 117–33.

83. Leading cases on apportionment include Baker v. Carr, 369 U.S. 186 (1962); Gray v. Sanders, 372 U.S. 368 (1963); Wesberry v. Sanders, 376 U.S. 1 (1964); Reynolds v. Sims, 377 U.S. 533 (1964). For evidence that the Four-

teenth Amendment was not originally intended to affect State control over suffrage, see Reynolds v. Sims, 377 U.S. 533, 589–625 (1964) (Harlan, J., dissenting); Oregon v. Mitchell, 400 U.S. 112, 152–219 (1970) (Harlan, J., concurring in part and dissenting in part); Michael Les Benedict, *A Compromise of Principle: Congressional Republicans and Reconstruction, 1863–1869* (New York: W. W. Norton, 1974), pp. 108–87; Berger, *Government by Judiciary*, pp. 52–98.

84. See, e.g., Nixon v. Herndon, 273 U.S. 536 (1927) (striking down all-white primary); Gomillion v. Lightfoot, 364 U.S. 339 (1960) (invalidating racially motivated redistricting plan); Harper v. Virginia Board of Elections 383 U.S. 663 (1966) (barring levying of poll taxes); Oregon v. Mitchell, 400 U.S. 112 (1970) (upholding congressional power to bar use of state literacy tests in state elections); Hunter v. Underwood, 471 U.S. 222 (1985) (striking down provision of Alabama Constitution that disenfranchised people convicted of crimes of moral turpitude, because the provision as enforced had a racially disparate impact). For countervailing historical evidence, see the studies cited in note 83 above.

85. Leading cases include Reed v. Reed, 404 U.S. 71 (1971); Frontiero v. Richardson, 411 U.S. 677 (1973); Craig v. Boren, 429 U.S. 190 (1976). For evidence that the framers of the Fourteenth Amendment generally expected that the amendment would not affect traditional sex-based state classifications, see Judith A. Baer, *Equality Under the Constitution: Reclaiming the Fourteenth Amendment* (Ithaca, N.Y.: Cornell University Press, 1983), pp. 89–91. See also Bradwell v. Illinois, 83 U.S. (16 Wall.) 130, 141 (1872) (Bradley, J., concurring) ("Man is, or should be, women's protector and defender. The natural and proper timidity and delicacy which belongs to the female sex evidently unfits it for many of the occupations of civil life . . . The paramount destiny and mission of woman are to fulfill the noble and benign offices of wife and mother. This is the law of the Creator.").

86. See especially McLaughlin v. Florida, 379 U.S. 184 (1964) (striking down a statute that punished interracial cohabitation more severely than cohabitation by persons of the same race); Loving v. Virginia, 388 U.S. 1 (1967) (invalidating Virginia's antimiscegenation law). See Bickel, "The Original Understanding and the Segregation Decision," and Berger, *Government by Judiciary,* pp. 161–2, 174, for historical evidence that cuts against these decisions.

87. National Mutual Insurance Co. v. Tidewater Transfer Co., 337 U.S. 582, 646 (1947) (Frankfurter, J., dissenting). See also Williams v. Florida, 399 U.S. 78, 124–25 (1970) (Harlan, J., concurring in part and dissenting in part) ("history should not imprison the broad guarantees of the Constitution whose proper scope is to be determined in a given instance by a blend of historical understanding and the adaptation of purpose to contemporary circumstances"); Oregon v. Mitchell, 400 U.S. 112, 274–75 (1970) (Brennan, Marshall, and White, JJ., dissenting in part) (The Fourteenth Amendment "was framed by men who . . . papered over their differences with the broad, elastic language of [section] 1 and left to future interpreters of their Amendment the task of resolving in accordance with future vision and future needs the issues that they left unresolved").

88. See, generally, John E. Nowack, Ronald D. Rotunda, and J. Nelson Young,

Constitutional Law, 3d ed. (St. Paul, Minn.: West, 1986), pp. 350–419, 451–520.

89. See, e.g., United States v. Darby, 312 U.S. 100 (1941); Wickard v. Filburn, 317 U.S. 111 (1942); Heart of Atlanta Motel v. United States, 379 U.S. 241 (1964); Katzenbach v. McClung, 379 U.S. 294 (1964). As long ago as 1926, Edward Corwin noted that constitutional words "defining the subject-matter of power or of right like 'commerce' . . . have been deliberately molded to the views of contemporary society." Corwin, "Judicial Review in Action," p. 659.

90. Compare, e.g., New York Times Co. v. Sullivan, 376 U.S. 254, 276 (1964) (the attack upon the validity of Sedition Act of 1798 "has carried the day in the court of history") with Leonard W. Levy, *Freedom of Speech and Press in Early American History: Legacy of Suppression* (New York: Harper Torchbooks, 1963) (demonstrating that "freedom of speech and press," as originally understood, did not bar prosecution for the common-law crime of seditious libel).

91. See, e.g., Thompson v. Oklahoma, 487 U.S. 815, 821 (1988) ("The authors of the Eighth Amendment drafted a categorical prohibition of cruel and unusual punishments, but they made no attempt to define the contours of that category. They delegated that task to future generations of judges who have been guided by the 'evolving standards of decency that mark the progress of a maturing society'") (quoting Trop v. Dulles, 356 U.S. 86, 101 (1958) (plurality opinion of Warren, C.J.)).

92. Board of Education v. Barnette, 319 U.S. 627, 639 (1943) (majority opinion of Jackson, J.).

93. The phrase is taken from Robert H. Jackson's classic account of the events leading up to the constitutional revolution of 1937, *The Struggle for Judicial Supremacy* (New York: Knopf, 1941).

94. *Ecclesiastes* 1:11.

95. *Nomination of Thurgood Marshall to be Associate Justice of the Supreme Court of the United States: Hearings Before the Committee on the Judiciary*, 90th Cong., 1st Sess. (1967), p. 49.

96. *Nomination of William H. Rehnquist to be Associate Justice of the Supreme Court of the United States: Hearings Before the Committee on the Judiciary*, 92th Cong., 1st Sess. (1971), p. 19.

97. Quoted in "A New Chief Justice: A New Court Era," *Congressional Quarterly Weekly Report* 27 (May 23, 1969), p. 798.

98. Quoted in Sue Davis, *Justice Rehnquist and the Constitution* (Princeton, N.J. : Princeton University Press, 1989), pp. 3–4.

99. *Indiana Law Journal* 47 (1971), pp. 1–35.

100. Ibid., p. 6.

101. As Michael Perry has noted (*Morality, Politics, and Law: A Bicentennial Essay* (New York. Oxford University Press, 1989), p. 54), versions of moral skepticism or moral conventionalism are now extremely common among academic lawyers. For apparent endorsements of one or another of these views by leading originalists, see William H. Rehnquist, "The Notion of a Living Constitution," *Texas Law Review* 54 (1976), p. 704; Raoul Berger, "The Constitution and the Rule of Law," reprinted in Berger, *Selected Writings on the Constitution*

(Cumberland, Va.: James River Press, 1987), p. 295; Richard S. Kay, "Adherence to the Original Intentions in Constitutional Adjudication: Three Objections and Responses," *Northwestern University Law Review* 82 (1988), p. 229. Cf. John Hart Ely, "Foreward: On Discovering Fundamental Values," *Harvard Law Review* 92 (1978), pp. 5–55.

102. Ibid., pp. 9, 10, 8.

103. Ibid., p. 12.

104. Ibid., p. 30.

105. Ibid., p. 3.

106. Ibid., p. 6.

107. Ibid., pp. 3–4.

108. Ibid., pp. 10–11.

109. On the originalist side, see especially John Hart Ely, "The Wages of Crying Wolf: A Comment on *Roe v. Wade*," *Yale Law Journal* 82 (1973), pp. 920–49; Rehnquist, "The Notion of a Living Constitution." On the nonoriginalist side, see, e.g., Arthur S. Miller, "An Inquiry into the Relevance of the Intentions of the Founding Fathers, With Special Emphasis Upon the Doctrine of Separation of Powers," *Arkansas Law Review* 27 (1973), pp. 583–602; Paul Brest, *Processes of Constitutional Decisionmaking: Cases and Materials* (Boston: Little, Brown, 1975), pp. 102–71; C. J. Antieau, "Constitutional Construction: A Guide to the Principles and Their Application," *Notre Dame Lawyer* 51 (1976), pp. 358–95.

110. Dworkin, "The Jurisprudence of Richard Nixon," *New York Review of Books* 18 (May 4, 1972), reprinted, with revisions, in Dworkin, *Taking Rights Seriously*, pp. 131–49.

111. Dworkin, *Taking Rights Seriously*, pp. 134–36. For a discussion of this distinction, see pp. 62–63.

112. Grey, "Do We Have an Unwritten Constitution?" *Stanford Law Review* 27 (1975), p. 713. Grey also suggested, without arguing the point in detail, that in the founding generation "there was an original understanding, both implicit and textually expressed, that unwritten higher law principles had constitutional status." The obvious implication was that true fidelity to the framers' intentions might at times require that judges not "stick close to the text and the history, and their fair implications," as Bork and other originalists had urged, but instead require that they give constitutional effect to values that the written Constitution has not expressly marked as special.

113. Berger's main arguments for originalism—that it is the only theory of constitutional interpretation consistent with our nation's commitment to democratic self-rule (*Government by Judiciary*, pp. 296, 410) and the rule of law (ibid., pp. 370–71)—were both standard originalist fare. His further claim, frequently repeated, that nonoriginalist adjudication "aborts [the Founders'] design" (ibid., p. 315), is manifestly circular, as many commentators have noted. See, e.g., Michael S. Moore, "Originalist Theories of Constitutional Interpretation," *Cornell Law Review* 73 (1988), p. 364; Perry, *Morality, Politics, and Law*, p. 128.

114. In relevant part, that section provides: "No state shall make or enforce

any law which shall abridge the privileges or immunities of citizens of the United States; nor shall any State deprive any person of life, liberty, or property, without due process of law; nor deny to any person within its jurisdiction the equal protection of the laws."

115. Civil Rights Act of 1866, quoted in Berger, *Government by Judiciary,* p. 24.

116. To cite just a few of the more influential discussions: see Ely, *Democracy and Distrust,* pp. 1–72; Paul Brest, "The Misconceived Quest for the Original Understanding," *Boston University Law Review* 60 (1980), pp. 204–38; Ronald Dworkin, "The Forum of Principle," *New York University Law Review* 56 (1981), reprinted in Dworkin, *A Matter of Principle*, pp. 33–71; Monaghan, "Our Perfect Constitution," *New York University Law Review* 56 (1981), pp. 353–96; Perry, *The Constitution, the Courts, and Human Rights*, pp. 9–36, 91–145; Mark Tushnet, "Following the Rules Laid Down: A Critique of Interpretivism and Neutral Principles," *Harvard Law Review* 96 (1983), pp. 781–827; Michael Perry, "The Authority of Text, Tradition, and Reason: A Theory of Constitutional 'Interpretation,'" *Southern California Law Review* 58 (1985), pp. 551–602; Michael S. Moore, "A Natural Law Theory of Interpretation," *Southern California Law Review* 58 (1985), pp. 277–398; H. Jefferson Powell, "The Original Understanding of Original Intent," *Harvard Law Review* 98 (1985), pp. 885–948; Raoul Berger, "New Theories of 'Interpretation': The Activist Flight from the Constitution," *Ohio State Law Journal* 47 (1986), pp. 1–45. For samplings of more recent literature, see note 118 below.

117. For Bork's own view of the confirmation battle, see Robert H. Bork, *The Tempting of America: The Political Seduction of the Law* (New York: Free Press, 1990), pp. 267–349. Two years earlier, in 1985, Attorney General Edwin Meese had also aroused considerable public attention when he announced, in a series of widely publicized addresses, that the Reagan Justice Department was committed to a "jurisprudence of original intent." See Edwin Meese III, "Construing the Constitution," *University of California, Davis Law Review* 19 (1985), pp. 22–30; *Original Meaning Jurisprudence: A Sourcebook* (Washington D.C.: Justice Department Office of Legal Policy, 1987). This announcement evoked a highly unusual public response by Supreme Court Justice William Brennan, who eloquently defended the Court's long standing commitment to a "living constitution." See William J. Brennan, "The Constitution of the United States: Contemporary Ratification," *South Texas Law Review* 27 (1986), pp. 433–45.

118. In addition to the recent works already cited, see, e.g., Michael J. Perry, "The Legitimacy of Particular Conceptions of Constitutional Interpretation," *Virginia Law Review* 77 (1991), pp. 669–719; James A. Gardner, "The Positivist Foundations of Originalism: An Account and Critique," *Boston University Law Review* 71 (1991), pp. 1–45; Richard A. Posner, "Bork and Beethoven," *Stanford Law Review* 42 (1990), pp. 1365–82; Ronald Dworkin, "Bork's Jurisprudence," *University of Chicago Law Review* 57 (1990), pp. 657–77; Daniel A. Farber, "The Originalist Debate: A Guide to the Perplexed," *Ohio State Law Journal,* 49 (1989), pp. 1085–1106; Henry Monaghan, "Stare Decisis and Constitutional Adjudication," *Columbia Law Review* 88 (1988), pp. 723–73; Leonard W. Levy,

Original Intent and the Framers' Constitution (New York: Macmillan, 1988); Erwin Chemerinsky, *Interpreting the Constitution* (New York: Praeger, 1987); Earl Maltz, "The Failure of Attacks on Originalism," *Constitutional Commentary* 4 (1987), pp. 43–56; Richard H. Fallon, Jr., "A Constructivist Coherence Theory of Constitutional Interpretation," *Harvard Law Review* 100 (1987), pp. 1189–1287.

CHAPTER 2

1. Francis Bacon, *The Proficience and Advancement of Learning, Divine and Moral,* in *The Works of Lord Bacon*, 2 vols. (London, 1871; 1st ed. 1605), I, p. 50.

2. Dworkin, *Law's Empire,* p. 357.

3. In 1975, Thomas Grey coined the expression "the pure interpretive model" (later simply "interpretivism") to name the view "that the only norms used in constitutional adjudication must be those inferable from the text—that the Constitution must not be seen as licensing courts to articulate and apply contemporary norms not demonstrably expressed or implied by the framers." Grey, "Do We Have an Unwritten Constitution?" p. 706, n. 9. The label caught on, and for some years "interpretivism" became the standard designation for originalist theories of constitutional interpretation. See, e.g., John Hart Ely, "Constitutional Interpretivism: Its Allure and Impossibility," *Indiana Law Journal* 53 (1978), pp. 399–448 (1978); Perry, *The Constitution, the Courts, and Human Rights*, p. 10. Beginning in the early 1980s, however, constitutional scholars on the left began to challenge the aptness of the term. As Grey himself came to admit, "the real arguments are not over whether judges should stick to interpreting, but over what they should interpret and what interpretive attitudes they should adopt." Grey, "The Constitution as Scripture," *Stanford Law Review* 37 (1984), p. 1. For similar criticisms, see Brest, "The Misconceived Quest for the Original Understanding," p. 204, n.1 (suggesting that "interpretivism" is misleading and proposing a neologism—"originalism"—as a substitute); Dworkin, *A Matter of Principle*, pp. 34–36. Since roughly the mid-1980s, "originalism" has been the generally accepted label for the class of theories examined in this study.

4. See, e.g., Powell, "The Original Understanding of Original Intent," p. 886; Pierre Schlag, "Framers' Intent: The Illegitimate Uses of History," *University of Puget Sound Law Review* 8 (1985), p. 287; Walter Benn Michaels, "Intentionalism, Again," *Cardozo Studies in Law and Literature* 1 (1989), p. 89.

5. Lief H. Carter, *Contemporary Constitutional Lawmaking* (Elmsford, N.Y.: Pergamon Press, 1985), p. 42.

6. Dworkin, *Law's Empire*, p. 360.

7. See, e.g., Charles A. Miller, *The Supreme Court and the Uses of History* (Cambridge, Mass.: Harvard University Press, 1969), p. 26 ("the intent theory"); Kent Greenawalt, "The Enduring Significance of Neutral Principles," *Columbia Law Review* 78 (1978), p. 1115 ("the framers' intent approach"); Munzer

and Nickel, "Does the Constitution Mean What It Always Meant?" p. 1030 ("the historical approach"); *Original Meaning Jurisprudence: A Sourcebook* (Washington D.C.: Justice Department Office of Legal Policy, 1987) ("original meaning jurisprudence"); Bork, *The Tempting of America,* p. 144 ("the philosophy of the original understanding").

8. William N. Eskridge, "Dynamic Statutory Interpretation," *University of Pennsylvania Law Review* 135 (1987), pp. 1479–80. Cf. Nicholas S. Zeppos, "Judicial Candor and Statutory Interpretation," *Georgetown Law Journal* 78 (1989), p. 357 (discussing "originalism as a method of statutory interpretation"); Steven D. Smith, "Law Without Mind," *Michigan Law Review* 88 (1989), p. 106 (asserting that the "essential contention [of originalion] is that in interpreting a statute or constitutional provision, a judge should try to determine what the law meant, or was intended to mean, at the time it was enacted").

9. Berger, "New Theories of Constitutional 'Interpretation,'" p. 2. Cf. Erwin Chemerinsky, "The Constitution Is Not 'Hard Law': The Bork Rejection and the Future of Constitutional Jurisprudence," *Constitutional Commentary* 6 (1989), p. 31 (originalism "claims that the Constitution's meaning is limited to that explicitly stated or clearly intended").

10. Note, "In Defense of the Framers' Intent: Civic Virtue, the Bill of Rights, and the Framers' Science of Politics," *Virginia Law Review* 75 (1989), p. 1312. Cf. Fallon, "A Constructivist Coherence Theory of Constitutional Interpretation," p. 1209 (interpretivists assert that "a court should hold government action unconstitutional only on the basis of one or both of two privileged factors: arguments from text and the intent of the framers").

11. Ely, *Democracy and Distrust,* p. 1. Cf. Maltz, "The Failure of Attacks on Originalism," p. 43 (originalism is "the theory that in constitutional adjudication judges should be bound by the intent of the framers"); J. Clifford Wallace, "Whose Constitution? An Inquiry into the Limits of Constitutional Interpretation," in *Still the Law of the Land? Essays on Changing Interpretations of the Constitution*, ed. by Joseph F. McNamara and Lissa Roche (Hillsdale, Mich.: Hillsdale College Press, 1987), p. 2 (interpretivism is the view "that judges, in resolving constitutional questions, should rely on the express provisions of the Constitution or upon the norms that are clearly explicit in the text").

12. John Valauri, "The Varieties of Constitutional Theory: A Comment on Perry and Hoy," *Northern Kentucky Law Review* 15 (1988), p. 500. Cf. Robert W. Bennett, "Objectivity in Constitutional Law," *University of Pennsylvania Law Review* 132 (1984), pp. 445–46 (constitutional interpretivists or originalists "argue that constitutional language, understood in light of the substantive intentions or values behind its enactment, is the sole proper source for constitutional interpretation"); Robert N. Clinton, "Original Understanding, Legal Realism, and the Interpretation of 'This Constitution,'" *Iowa Law Review* 72 (1987), p. 1180 (originalism is "the view that the Constitution or any amendment thereto should be interpreted as its spirit and language were understood when the relevant provision was drafted").

13. See notes 9–12 above and accompanying text.

14. See note 8 above and accompanying text.

15. Until recently, as we have seen, legal interpretation was widely conceived as a unity: *all* legal instruments, whether statutes, treaties, contracts, wills, or written constitutions, were held to have a fixed original intent which judges were charged with ascertaining and applying. This view, which we might call *classical originalism*, is now widely rejected. However, the opposite view—that originalist strategies are mistaken for *all* kinds of legal interpretation—also seems now to command little support. Most contemporary legal theorists, accordingly, seem to hold variants of what we might call *hybrid originalism.* Thus, it might be held, for example, that original intent is the proper interpretive standard for wills and contracts, but not for constitutions or for (some kinds of) statutes, or whatever the actual mix might be. In a broad sense, each of these combinations might count as a form of originalism. Used in this broad sense, "originalism" would be a kind of indeterminate or incomplete expression in much the same way that "relativism" now is. Thus, just as it conveys little information to describe someone as a "relativist" without making clear just which notions he claims to be relative to which framework, so it is similarly uninformative to characterize someone as an "originalist" without indicating at least roughly which form of the theory he or she holds.

16. It is noteworthy that most older discussions of originalist jurisprudence clearly assume that in essentials the theory applies to both federal *and state* constitutional interpretation. See, e.g., Thomas M. Cooley, *A Treatise on the Constitutional Limitations Which Rest Upon the Legislative Power of the States of the American Union,* 5th ed. (Boston: Little, Brown, 1883), pp. 49–102; and Black, *Handbook on the Construction of Laws,* pp. 17–44. However, there are important differences between federal and state constitutional politics that bear on the issue of originalism. Most significantly, state judges are often electorally accountable and state constitutions are generally far easier to amend than is the U.S. Constitution. See *The Book of the States* (Lexington, Ky.: Council of State Governments, 1988), XXVII, pp. 163–65, 16–20. These differences seem significant enough to justify separate treatment of federal and state constitutional interpretation.

17. See, e.g., Kay, "Adherence to the Original Intentions," pp. 230–36.

18. See pp. 28–34.

19. See, e.g., Berger, *Government by Judiciary,* pp. 300–311; William Bradford Reynolds, "Originalism and the Separation of Powers," *Tulane Law Review* 68 (1989), p. 1550; Bork, *The Tempting of America*, p. 154.

20. For additional examples of such extratextual intentions, see the discussion of interpretive purposes on p. 25.

21. See, e.g., Earl Maltz, "Some New Thoughts on an Old Problem: The Role of the Intent of the Framers in Constitutional Theory," *Boston University Law Review* 63 (1983), p. 816, n. 14 ("The heart of interpretivist theory is the notion that courts should strike down only those actions that the Framers themselves would have struck down"); Siegan, *Economic Liberties,* p. 14.

22. See, e.g., Raoul Berger, "Originalist Theories of Constitutional Interpretation," *Cornell Law Review* 73 (1988), p. 353.

23. Although it sounds jarring to nonlegal ears, legal writers do often speak

of the "intent" of documents or particular provisions. See, e.g., Powell, "The Original Understanding of Original Intent," p. 896; and Wolfe, *The Rise of Modern Judicial Review* p. 57. I shall follow this usage here.

24. Cf. Hirsch, *Validity in Interpretation,* pp. 122–23.

25. John Rawls, *A Theory of Justice* (Cambridge, Mass.: Harvard University Press, 1971), p. 8.

26. See, e.g., Hutto v. Davis, 454 U.S. 370, 375 (1982) (per curiam) ("[U]nless we wish anarchy to prevail within the federal judicial system a precedent of this Court must be followed by lower federal courts, no matter how misguided the judges of those courts may think it to be"); *Original Meaning Jurisprudence,* p. 54 ("Lower courts are, of course, bound to continue to follow Supreme Court precedent until that precedent is changed"); Bork, *The Tempting of America*, pp. 156–57; Richard A. Posner, *The Federal Courts: Crisis and Reform* (Cambridge, Mass: Harvard University Press, 1985), pp. 251–52. See also Martin v. Hunter's Lessee, 14 U.S. (1 Wheat.) 304 (1816) (state courts must conform to the decisions of the Supreme Court so that federal laws will have a uniform construction throughout the nation); Abelman v. Booth, 62 U.S. (21 How.) 506, 517–22 (1859). For contrary views, see Jaffree v. Board of School Commissioners of Mobile County, 554 F. Supp. 1104, 1126–28 (SD Ala. 1983); James McClellan, "Introduction," *Benchmark* 3 (1987), p. 123.

27. Cf. Rawls, *A Theory of Justice*, p. 8.

28. In addition to the writers cited on p. 147, n. 10, see, e.g., Mark Tushnet, *Red, White, and Blue: A Critical Analysis of Constitutional Law* (Cambridge, Mass.: Harvard University Press, 1988), p. 22; Kay, "Adherence to the Original Intentions," p. 230.

29. A statement, in other words, of necessary and sufficient conditions for the concept's correct application.

30. That is, the theories exhibit overlapping similarities but no common "essence." See Ludwig Wittgenstein, *Philosophical Investigations*, 3d ed. (New York: Macmillan, 1953), sections 66 and 67.

31. In the language of lawyers, a "practical construction" of the Constitution refers to an interpretation that is impliedly put upon constitutional language by legislative or executive action. For examples of this usage, see Black, *Handbook on the Construction of Laws*, p. 40; Ray v. Blair, 343 U.S. 219, 229–30 (1952). For brevity, I shall generally omit this rider when characterizing originalist positions.

32. Here, and throughout this essay, I employ "original intent" abstractly, without meaning to endorse any particular theory of this notion. In terms of Dworkin's useful distinction, I employ the notion as a "concept" rather as a "conception." For more on this distinction, see p. 28.

33. See, e.g., Dallin H. Oaks, "When Judges Legislate," in *Views From the Bench: The Judiciary and Constitutional Politics,* ed. by Mark Cannon and David O'Brien (Chatham, N.J. : Chatham House, 1985), p. 150 (interpretivism is the view that "a statute or other act of government cannot be unconstitutional unless it is inconsistent with the *express or clearly implied* words and phrases in the Constitution") (emphasis added); Meese, "Construing the Con-

stitution, p. 29 (A jurisprudence of original intent "is not a jurisprudence of political results . . . The power to declare acts of Congress and the laws of the states null and void is truly awesome. This power must be used when the Constitution clearly speaks. It should not be used when it does not."). See also Tushnet, *Red, White, and Blue,* p. 22 (originalism asserts that "judges should confine themselves to enforcing norms that are *stated or clearly implied* in the written Constitution") (emphasis added). Contrast these formulations with statements of the theory that contain no suggestion that judges should refrain from enforcing probable but uncertain original intentions. See, e.g., Kay, "Adherence to the Original Intentions in Constitutional Adjudication," p. 230 (original intentions adjudication "calls for judges to apply the rules of the written Constitution in the sense in which those rules were understood by the people who enacted them") (emphasis omitted).

34. See pp. 4–5.

35. Thayer, "Origin and Scope of Constitutional Law," pp. 143–44. Strictly, Thayer limited his doctrine to judicial review of the acts of *coordinate* branches of government, that is, federal court review of federal action and state court review of state action. See ibid., pp. 153–55. As Michael Perry has observed (*The Constitution, the Courts, and Human Rights*, p. 176n. 61), this is a subtlety that most commentators who discuss Thayer fail to note.

36. See, e.g., Perry, *The Constitution, the Courts, and Human Rights,* p. 91; Grey, "Do We Have an Unwritten Constitution?" pp. 710–14; Terrance Sandalow, "Constitutional Interpretation," *Michigan Law Review* 79 (1981), pp. 1035–45.

37. Scalia, "Originalism: the Lesser Evil," p. 861. Scalia himself seems to be a strong originalist. See, e.g., South Carolina v. Gathers, 109 S. Ct. 2207, 2218–19 (1989) (Scalia, J., dissenting).

38. See pp. 14–15 and accompanying notes.

39. See Epstein, *Takings*, p. *x*.

40. See, e.g., *Nomination of William H. Rehnquist to Be An Associate Justice*, p. 19 (in constitutional adjudication precedent is entitled to "great weight"); Payton v. New York, 445 U.S. 573, 621 (1978) (Rehnquist, J., dissenting) (arguing that, although the Court has in recent decades seriously misinterpreted the original intent of the Fourth Amendment, some of these rulings must now be accepted as settled law).

41. During the course of his Senate confirmation hearings, Bork repeatedly affirmed that "a judge must have great respect for precedence." "Bork Faces Tough Questions on Privacy and Equal Rights," *Congressional Quarterly*, Sept. 19, 1987, p. 2258. But see Bork, "Neutral Principles and Some First Amendment Problems," pp. 11–35 (urging a radical revision of existing constitutional doctrine). In fact, as late as 1985, Bork had stated that "in the field of constitutional law, precedent is [not] all that important." Quoted in "Bork Wraps Up His Testimony, Followed by Critics, Admirers," *Congressional Quarterly*, Sept. 26, 1987, p. 2331. This naturally gave rise to concerns of a mere "confirmation conversion." See *Nomination of Robert H. Bork to Be An Associate Justice of the United States Supreme Court: Report of the Committee on the Judiciary,* 100th Cong., 1st Sess. (Oct. 13, 1987), p. 93. For Bork's most recent discus-

sion of the role of precedent in constitutional adjudication, see Bork, *The Tempting of America*, pp. 155–59. There he argues that clearly incorrect precedents should presumptively be overruled unless they "have become so embedded in the life of the nation, so accepted by the society, so fundamental to the private and public expectations of individuals and institutions, that the result should not be changed now." Ibid., p. 158.

42. Brest, "The Misconceived Quest for the Original Understanding," p. 204.

43. Ibid., p. 222.

44. Ibid., p. 223. As standardly used in legal theory, a term is said to be "open textured" if it has a "core" of settled meaning and a "penumbra" or "periphery" where its meaning is indeterminate or controverted. For a classic exposition, see H. L. A. Hart, "Positivism and the Separation of Law and Morals," *Harvard Law Review* 71 (1958), pp. 607–608.

45. Brest, "The Misconceived Quest for the Original Understanding," p. 223.

46. Cf. Board of Education v. Barnette, 319 U.S. 624, 666 (Frankfurter, J., dissenting) ("Equally inadmissible is the claim to strike down legislation because to us as individuals it seems opposed to the 'plan and purpose' of the Constitution. That is too tempting a basis for finding in one's personal views the purposes of the Founders"). Cf. Sandalow, "Constitutional Interpretation," p. 1045 ("all the decisions shaping constitutional law to contemporary values can . . . be understood as coming within the general intentions of the framers . . . [by stating] those intentions at a sufficiently high level of abstraction").

47. Jacobson v. Massachusetts, 197 U.S. 11 (1905). Cf. Hepburn v. Griswold, 75 U.S. (8 Wall.) 603, 628 (1870) (Miller, J., dissenting) (strongly criticizing Chief Justice Chase's appeal to the preamble in the latter's majority opinion).

48. See, e.g., South Carolina v. United States, 199 U.S. 437 (1905).

49. James M. Beck, *The Constitution of the United States Today, Yesterday—and Tomorrow?* (New York: George H. Doran, 1924), p. 221.

50. Ward Elliott, *The Rise of Guardian Democracy: The Supreme Court's Role in the Voting Rights Disputes, 1845–1969* (Cambridge, Mass.: Harvard University Press, 1974), p. viii ("The Constitution is not a blank check to posterity"). Cf. Harper v. Virginia Board of Elections, 383 U.S. 663, 676 (1966) (Black, J. dissenting).

51. See Schmidt, *Principles of Authentic Interpretation*, p. 143 (commenting on the medieval maxim *ratio juris non facit jus)*.

52. Rutherforth, *Institutes of Natural Law,* II, p. 415.

53. Ibid., II, p. 414.

54. Ibid., II, p. 415.

55. The one great exception to this intentionalist principle, recognized in at least some strands of traditional equity hermeneutics, were "laws" that were seriously unjust, either intrinsically or as applied to particular cases. Thus, to return to an earlier example: Imagine that a lawmaker enacts a law requiring all deposits to be restored upon their owner's request. Suppose, too, that the lawmaker clearly intends the law to apply literally, with no exceptions. Must a judge apply this law in its intended meaning to a defendant who refuses to return

a sword to its temporarily deranged and homicidal owner? For many in this tradition, the answer would apparently be no. See Riley, *History, Nature, and Use of Epikeia*, pp. 165–66. See also Rutherforth, *Institutes of Natural Law*, II, p. 414 ("All civil laws . . . are to be so construed, where the words are of doubtful meaning, as to produce no other effect, but what is consistent with reason, or with the law of nature").

56. Blackstone, *Commentaries*, I, p. 35 (emphasis in original).

57. Not all would agree that available legislative histories are even now reasonably reliable indicia of legislative intent. See, e.g., Reed Dickerson, *The Interpretation and Application of Statutes* (Boston: Little, Brown, 1975), pp. 155–56; Blanchard v. Bergeron, 109 S. Ct. 939, 946–47 (1989) (Scalia, J., dissenting).

58. Prigg v. Pennsylvania, 41 U.S. 539, 610–11 (1842) (upholding the constitutionality of the Fugitive Slave Law of 1793).

59. Story, *Commentaries on the Constitution*, I, p. 283.

60. See Brest, "The Misconceived Quest for the Original Understanding," p. 212; Dworkin, *A Matter of Principle*, pp. 52–55.

61. Ibid., p. 216.

62. Questions, that is, that courts refuse to hear or decide because they implicate inherently nonjusticiable issues of public policy. For example, whether a state has a "republican" form of government under the Constitution's guaranty clause (Art. IV, Sec. 4) has been declared a question that courts are incompetent to answer. For a careful discussion of the current state of the political-questions doctrine, see Tribe, *American Constitutional Law*, pp. 96–107.

63. See, e.g., Raoul Berger, "'Original Intention' in Historical Perspective," *The George Washington Law Review* 54 (1986), pp. 101–42 (arguing that the founders accepted original intentionalism); and Charles A. Lofgren, "The Original Understanding of Original Intent?" *Constitutional Commentary* 5 (1988), pp. 77–115 (arguing that the framers intended that only the ratifiers' intent be binding on future interpreters).

64. As we shall see, however, originalists court disaster if they insist that both the framers' substantive and interpretive intentions be enforced. For the framers themselves may have intended that their own substantive intentions *not* be treated as binding law. In that case, the originalists' theory will be contingently self-defeating. For a fuller discussion of this point, see pp. 67–71.

65. I here speak of voting paradoxes in a less rigorous sense than is standard in social choice or voting theory. See pp. 88–89 for a fuller discussion of preference intransitivities in majoritarian voting.

66. Hugo Black came perhaps as close as anybody. See, e.g., Baldwin v. New York, 399 U.S. 66, 74–75 (1970) (Black, J., concurring) (urging that the Sixth Amendment's guarantee of a jury trial in "all criminal prosecutions" applies even to petty offenses); Mishkin v. New York, 383 U.S. 502, 518 (1966) (Black, J., dissenting) (claiming that the Free Speech and Press Clauses of the First Amendment should be read literally). But see Schmerber v. California, 384 U.S. 757, 776–77 (1966) (Black, J., dissenting) (arguing against a literal reading of the Fifth Amendment Self-Incrimination Clause); Cox v. Louisiana, 379 U.S.

559, 578 (1965) (Black, J., concurring in part and dissenting in part) (urging that picketing, even on public streets, is not protected by the Free Speech Clause).

67. For related but somewhat different uses of "textualism," see Philip Bobbitt, *Constitutional Fate: Theory of the Constitution* (New York: Oxford University Press, 1982), pp. 25–38; Tushnet, *Red, White, and Blue* p. 60.For a very different use of the term, see Thomas C. Grey, "The Uses of an Unwritten Constitution," *Chicago-Kent Law Review* 64 (1988), p. 211.

68. Art. III, sec. 2.

69. For a brief historical discussion, see United States v. Barnett, 376 U.S. 681, 740–53 (1964) (Goldberg, J., dissenting). In this case the Court reaffirmed its decision in Green v. United States, 356 U.S. 165 (1958), upholding the power of courts to find a person guilty of criminal contempt without trial by jury.

70. Cf. McKeiver v. Pennsylvania, 403 U.S. 528 (1971).

71. Cf. Ex Parte Milligan, 71 U.S. (4 Wall.) 2, 123 (1866).

72. Cf. Patton v. United States, 281 U.S. 276 (1930).

73. Art. I, sec. 8.

74. Moderate textualism in this sense should not be confused with the "plain meaning rule," discussed on pp. 5–6. The latter basically says that where constitutional language has a clear and definite *prima facie* meaning, it must be applied in that sense (with a few possible exceptions). It says nothing about what judges are to do in the many cases in which there is no "plain" meaning, as, for example, where the Constitution speaks of an "establishment of religion" or of an "ex post facto Law." Strict and moderate textualism, by contrast, aspire to be more comprehensive theories of constitutional adjudication. As we shall see shortly, textualist theories basically direct judges to construe constitutional provisions as a typical informed literalist would have construed them in their original social and linguistic contexts. In principle, given standard theories of counterfactual implication, these counterfactual questions will always have answers. See, generally, David Lewis, *Counterfactuals* (Cambridge, Mass.: Harvard University Press, 1973). Whether judges can reliably know these answers is of course another question.

75. Cf. Reynolds v. U.S., 98 U.S. (8 Otto) 145 (1879) (upholding application of a federal law prohibiting polygamy to a Mormon whose religious convictions required that he engage in that practice.)

76. Cf. Jehovah's Witnesses v. King County Hospital, 390 U.S. 598 (1968) (per curiam) (upholding statute that permitted children to be declared wards of the court in cases where their parents opposed blood transfusions for them).

77. My analysis of moderate textualism is here indebted to Douglas Laycock, "Text, Intent, and the Religion Clauses," *Notre Dame Journal of Law, Ethics, and Public Policy* 4 (1990), pp. 687–88.

78. Kay, "Adherence to the Original Intentions," p. 232. Kay's discussion of this approach, however, alternates dizzyingly between the "pure text" approach as I describe it and the quite different view, discussed below, that a constitutional provision should be construed as a then-contemporaneous typical reader would have construed it.

79. For accessible discussions of sentence meaning in this sense, see Rob-

ert M. Martin, *The Meaning of Language* (Cambridge, Mass.: The MIT Press, 1987), p. 92; Stephen C. Levinson, *Pragmatics* (Cambridge: Cambridge University Press, 1983), p. 17. An alternative, but related, way of understanding sentence meaning is to view it as what a speaker can be presumed to mean in the absence of any reason to the contrary. See Kent Bach, *Thought and Reference* (Oxford: Clarendon Press, 1987), p. 70.

80. Art. I, sec. 9.

81. The expression's "illocutionary force," in other words, is indeterminate. For persuasive arguments against distinguishing sharply between the "meaning" and "force" of expressions, see G. P. Baker and P. M. S. Hacker, *Language, Sense, and Nonsense: A Critical Investigation of Modern Theories of Language* (Oxford: Basil Blackwell, 1984); Francois Recanati, *Meaning and Force: The Pragmatics of Performative Utterances* (Cambridge: Cambridge University Press, 1987).

82. E.g., "Suits" (Amend. 7), "article" (Amend. 13), "magazines" (Art. I, sec. 8), "Party" (Art. III, sec. 2).

83. E.g., "Indians" (Art. I, sec. 2), "free Persons" (Art. I, sec. 2), "Duty" (Art. I, sec. 10), "Seat" (Art. II, sec. 1). The rule of thumb semanticists use in distinguishing cases of homonymy from those of multivocality (or "polysemy") is this: in cases of multivocality the different senses in question are related either historically or psychologically, or both. For a clear nontechnical discussion, see Geoffrey Leach, *Semantics* (Harmondsworth, Eng.: Penguin Books, 1974), pp. 228–30.

84. E.g., "they" (Amend. 12), "he" (Art. 2, sec. 2), "it" (Amend. 10).

85. In addition to these semantic ambiguities or indeterminacies, the Constitution also contains ambiguities of syntax. For instance, in the phrase "high Crimes and Misdemeanors" (Art. II, sec. 4), should "high" be taken as modifying only "Crimes" or both "Crimes" *and* "Misdemeanors"?

86. See Ely, *Democracy and Distrust*, p. 13.

87. See, e.g., Brest, "The Misconceived Quest for the Original Understanding," p. 206; Kay, "Adherence to the Original Intentions," p. 231. Because so much of constitutional language is drawn from the common law, some originalists add a qualifier that the reader be "informed" or "careful." See, e.g., Kuhn v. Curran, 294 N.Y. 207, 217, 61 N.E. 2d 513, 517–18 (1945); Arthur W. Machen, Jr., "The Elasticity of the Constitution," *Harvard Law Review* 14 (1900), p. 282 ("the test to be applied [by courts reviewing the constitutionality of challenged statutes] is whether the framers of the Constitution, that is, the intelligent, reasonable men of their day, would regard the statutes in question" as unconstitutional).

88. See, e.g., Cooley, *Treatise on Constitutional Limitations*, p. 68; Black, *Handbook on the Construction of Laws*, p. 20; Monaghan, "Stare Decisis and Constitutional Adjudication," p. 725; *Original Meaning Jurisprudence* p. 19 (judges should seek to determine "the original meaning of a provision as understood by the entire society that adopted it"); Bork, *The Tempting of America*, p. 144. In state constitutional adjudication, this form of intentionalism has long been dominant. See, e.g., Scribner v. Oklahoma, 9 Okl. Cr. 465, 467, 132 P. 933, 935 (1915)

("In construing constitutional provisions the question is not so much what the convention meant which framed the Constitution, but the supreme and controlling question is what the people whose votes adopted and placed the Constitution in force intended"); New Jersey v. Lanza, 27 N.J. 516, 527, 143 A2d. 571, 577 (1958) ("The Constitution derives its force, not from the Convention which framed it, but from the people who ratified it; and the intent to be arrived at is that of the people").

89. Some historians have suggested that the Joint Congressional Committee that drafted the Fourteenth Amendment in 1866 deliberately used the word "person" (rather than "citizen") in both the Due Process and Equal Protection Clauses so that courts would someday extend these protections to corporations. For a representative statement of this "conspiracy theory" of the Fourteenth Amendment, see Charles A. Beard and Mary R. Beard, *The Rise of American Civilization*, 2 vols. (New York: Macmillan, 1927), II, pp. 111–14. For an extended critical examination of the theory, see Howard J. Graham, *Everyman's Constitution: Historical Essays on the Fourteenth Amendment, the "Conspiracy Theory," and American Constitutionalism* (Madison: State Historical Society of Wisconsin, 1968), pp. 23–97. That corporations *are* "persons" within the meaning of the Equal Protection and Due Process Clauses was first officially accepted by the Court in Santa Clara County v. Southern Pacific Railroad Co.,118 U.S. 394 (1886). For a sharp textualist attack on this reading of the amendment, see Connecticut General Insurance Co. v. Johnson, 303 U.S. 77, 85–90 (1938) (Black, J., dissenting)

90. See Roe v. Wade, 410 U.S. 113, 157–58 (1973) (concluding, after a lengthy review of nineteenth-century state abortion laws, that fetuses were not originally considered "persons" under either the equal protection or due process guarantees of the Fourteenth Amendment).

91. The major problem, of course, is that for many constitutional clauses there is no real evidence of public understanding aside from the actual language adopted and the recorded discussions of those who framed and ratified that language. We know, for instance, that the Philadelphia Framers were divided on the question whether the Ex Post Facto Clause applied to civil as well as to criminal retroactive laws, with a majority, perhaps, favoring the broader construction. See Levy, *Original Intent and the Framers' Constitution*, pp. 65–74. But as to the *public's* understanding of the clause, any historical judgment would be the merest conjecture.

92. See, e.g., Black, *Handbook on the Construction of Laws*, pp. 445–46 ("A 'strict' construction of a [law] is a construction of it according to its letter, which recognizes nothing that is not expressed, takes the language used in its exact and technical meaning, and admits of no equitable considerations or implications").

93. To read a constitutional clause *narrowly* is to read it restrictively. In this sense, intentionalists often construe constitutional language far more narrowly than do textualists. Intentionalists, for example, have often read the term "persons" in the Equal Protection Clause quite narrowly—the extreme case being Chief Justice Miller's view in the *Slaughter-House* Cases, 83 U.S. (16 Wall.)

36, 82 (1873), that the term applies only to *blacks*. Textualists, on the other hand, would tend to read the clause far more expansively.

94. Inevitably, there will be cases that fall on the borderline between original textualism and original intentionalism. Joseph Story, for example, maintained that constitutional words should never "be stretched beyond their fair [conventional] sense; but within that range, the rule of interpretation must be taken, which best follows out the apparent intention." Story, *Commentaries on the Constitution*, III, p. 293. I have chosen to classify Story as a textualist (see pp. 7–8), but it is clear that his interpretive differences with the intentionalist members of the Marshall Court, including Marshall himself, were matters more of emphasis than of kind. See Powell, "The Original Understanding of Original Intent," pp. 942–44.

95. See p. 149, n. 32.

96. Dworkin, *Law's Empire*, p. 70. Cf. Rawls, *A Theory of Justice*, pp. 5, 10.

97. This is also Dworkin's view. See Dworkin, *A Matter of Principle*, p. 39.

98. See pp. 23–26.

99. Dworkin suggests that intentionalists are stuck with an unattractive choice. They can view original "intentions" as either the framers' *expectations* or their *hopes* about how constitutional language will be interpreted. Neither view, as Dworkin persuasively argues (*Law's Empire*, pp. 321–24), is satisfactory. My notion of the framers' "scope beliefs" largely avoids difficulties of the sort Dworkin raises. Furthermore, it is closer, I believe, to the way (strict) intentionalists typically think about the notion of original intent.

100. Cf. McCulloch v. Maryland, 17 U.S. (4 Wheat.) 316 (1819) (upholding the power of Congress to establish a national bank). For a forceful argument that this landmark decision was indefensible on originalist grounds, see Siegan, *The Supreme Court's Constitution*, pp. 7–18.

101. I owe this expression to Moore, "A Natural Law Theory of Interpretation," pp. 339–41. Cf. Dworkin, "Bork's Jurisprudence," *University of Chicago Law Review* 57 (1990), pp. 661–63 (distinguishing the framers' "linguistic" intentions from their "legal" intentions).

102. Cf. Story, *Commentaries on the Constitution of the United States*, 4th ed., 3 vols. (Boston: Little, Brown, 1873), III, p. 606 ("The real object of the [First Amendment Establishment Clause] was not to countenance, much less to advance, Mahometanism, or Judaism, or infidelity, by prostrating Christianity; but to exclude all rivalry among Christian sects, and to prevent any national ecclesiastical establishment which should give to a hierarchy the exclusive patronage of government"). See also Mark Tushnet, "The Origins of the Establishment Clause," *Georgetown Law Review* 75 (1987), pp. 1515–16.

103. See p. 25.

104. For a classic discussion, see MacCallum, "Legislative Intent," pp. 756–63. See also Michael Hancher, "Three Kinds of Intention," *Modern Language Notes* 87 (1972), pp. 827–51; Paul N. Cox, "Ruminations on Statutory Interpretation in the Burger Court," *Valparaiso Law Review* 19 (1985), pp. 287–395.

105. Brest, "The Misconceived Quest for the Original Understanding," p. 222.

106. See, e.g., Raoul Berger, "Paul Brest's Brief for an Imperial Judiciary," *Maryland Law Review* 40 (1981), p. 26 (denying that his view requires judges to be "soothsayer[s]" regarding counterfactual intentions).

107. See p. 25.

108. Art. IV, sec. 4.

109. Should we say that the framers' specific intent extends only to those specific acts or practices that the framers' actually had in mind while drafting or debating constitutional language? As Richard Kay has noted ("Adherence to the Original Intentions," pp. 254–55), there is nothing linguistically odd in saying that the framers "intended" the ban on "cruel and unusual punishments" to prohibit the use of electric as well as manual thumbscrews, even though they could have consciously adverted only to the latter. Gerald MacCallum brilliantly evokes the absurdity of the view that only consciously contemplated objects can fall within an agent's intentions in this classic example:

> Suppose that, needing a large number of ashtrays for an impending meeting in a building unfamiliar to me, I ask my assistant to scout around and bring back all the ashtrays he can find in the building. He comes back emptyhanded, saying the following: "I found a good many ashtrays, but naturally wanted to bring back only those you intended me to bring back. So, as I picked up each one, I asked myself—did he intend me to bring this ashtray back? Upon doing this, I realized in each case that it would certainly be a strange use of language to say that you 'intended' me to bring back that ashtray, as it was virtually certain that the thought of that ashtray had never occurred to you—after all, you had never even been in this building before. In the end, therefore, I found it most sensible to return without any."

MacCallum, "Legislative Intent," p. 771. "Clearly," MacCallum notes (ibid.), "such behavior would be idiotic." The idiocy results from a failure to grasp the elementary point that "intentions often relate . . . to *categories* of action rather than to particular people or instances of conduct." Kay, "Adhererence to the Original Intentions," p. 254 (emphasis added).

110. The view that I call moderate intentionalism is close, I believe, to the view Michael Perry terms "sophisticated originalism." See Perry, *Morality, Politics, and Law,* pp. 125–28; Perry, "The Legitimacy of Particular Conceptions of Constitutional Interpretation," p. 705. It may also be close to the originalist theory Robert Bork has recently defended. See Bork, *The Tempting of America,* pp. 144–51, 162–63.

111. Dworkin, *Taking Rights Seriously*, p. 134.

112. See ibid., p. 136; Dworkin, *A Matter of Principle*, p. 55. Cf. Duncan v. Louisiana, 391 U.S. 145, 175 (1968) (Harlan, J., dissenting) ("the very breadth and generality of the [Fourteenth] Amendment's provisions suggest that its authors did not suppose that the Nation would always be limited to mid-19th century conceptions of 'liberty' and 'due process of law' but that the increasing expe-

rience and evolving conscience of the American people would add new 'intermediate premises'").

113. Dworkin, *Taking Rights Seriously,* p. 136.

114. In deciding, for example, whether the death penalty is cruel and unusual punishment within the Eighth Amendment, "[i]t would be a mistake for the court," Dworkin argues, "to be much influenced by the fact that when the clause was adopted capital punishment was standard and unquestioned. That would be decisive if the framers of the clause had meant to lay down a particular conception of cruelty ... But it is not decisive of the different question the court now faces, which is this: Can the court, responding to the framers' appeal to the concept of cruelty, now defend a conception that does not make death cruel?" Ibid., pp. 135–36.

115. Cf. Scalia, "Originalism: the Lesser Evil," p. 861. Four members of the Court now argue that this is essentially how the clause should be read. See, generally, Gregory Bassham, "Rethinking the Emerging Jurisprudence of Juvenile Death," *Notre Dame Journal of Law, Ethics, and Public Policy* 5 (1991), pp. 467–84.

116. Moore, "A Natural Law Theory of Interpretation," p. 341.

117. Ibid.

118. This example is adapted from a well-known example in Hilary Putnam, "The Meaning of 'Meaning,'" reprinted in Putnam, *Mind, Language and Reality* (Cambridge: Cambridge University Press, 1975), pp. 226–27. Cf. Brink, "Legal Theory," p. 117.

119. With very slight changes, I have borrowed this example from Brink, "Legal Theory," pp. 123–24.

120. This seems to be Raoul Berger's view. See Berger, "'Original Intention' in Historical Perspective," pp. 113–20.

121. See, e.g., Kay, "Adherence to the Original Intentions," pp. 259–60.

122. In actual litigation, of course, there will often be no need for courts to settle on any very precise interpretation of the framers' intended meaning. They can say, for instance: "It's hard to say exactly what the framers may have meant by an 'establishment of religion.' But whatever exactly they meant, *this* clearly does [or does not] constitute such an establishment." As Richard Kay reminds us ("Adherence to the Original Intentions," pp. 243–44), the Court's principal task is to decide litigated issues of federal law, not to answer abstract questions of constitutional or statutory meaning.

123. See p. 133, n. 17.

124. Riggs v. Palmer, 115 N.Y. 506–07, 22 N. E. 188–89 (1889).

125. Cf. James E. Bond, "The Original Understanding of the Fourteenth Amendment in Illinois, Ohio, and Pennsylvania," *Akron Law Review* 18 (1985), p. 443 (The single most common explanation of the first section of the Fourteenth Amendment was that "it constitutionalized the Civil Rights Bill"). The relevant section of this Bill is quoted in part on pp. 14–15.

126. For more on such procedures, see pp. 83–90.

127. See, e.g., Scalia, "Originalism: the Lesser Evil," pp. 856, 863; Bork, *The Tempting of America*, p. 163. Proponents of moderate intentionalism do

not, in general, claim that their preferred mode of originalist jurisprudence is easy or wholly value-neutral, only that it is better than any alternative approach.

128. This approach would probably limit the reach of both the Establishment and Free Exercise Clauses to *theistic* religions. See Arlin M. Adams and Charles J. Emmerich, "A Heritage of Religious Liberty," *University of Pennsylvania Law Review* 137 (1989), p. 1666. Indeed, through at least the nineteenth century, courts routinely defined "religion" even more narrowly than that. See, e.g., Late Corporation of the Church of Jesus Christ of Latter-Day Saints v. United States, 136 U.S. 1, 49–50 (1890) (holding that the Mormon Church was not a religious corporation since one of its supposed religious tenets, polygamy, was a "pretense" according to "the enlightened sentiments of mankind"). In recent decades the Court has adopted substantially broader definitions of "religion" in both constitutional and statutory contexts. See, e.g., United States v. Seeger, 380 U.S. 163, 166 (1965); Welsh v. United States, 398 U.S. 333, 344 (1970).

129. National Mutual Insurance Co. v. Tidewater Transfer Co., 337 U.S. 582, 646 (1949) (Frankfurter, J., dissenting).

130. The language is from Trop v. Dulles, 356 U.S. 86, 101 (1958) ("evolving standards of decency that mark the progress of a maturing society").

131. See, e.g., Scalia, "Originalism: the Lesser Evil," p. 862. Cf. Chemerinsky, *Interpreting the Constitution*, pp. 77–8 (arguing that there is no meaningful distinction between moderate originalism and nonoriginalism).

132. Brest, "The Misconceived Quest for the Original Understanding," p. 237.

133. See, e.g., Oregon v. Mitchell, 400 U.S. 112, 202 (1970) (Harlan, J., dissenting) (urging that, although courts can look to the "underlying purposes of the Framers in giving constitutional language an unforseen application," they may not disregard the express intent and understanding of the framers).

134. See, e.g., Berger, *Government by Judiciary*, pp. 412–13; (conceding that *Brown* should not be overruled, although the decision was clearly mistaken on originalist grounds); Bork, *The Tempting of America*, p. 158.

135. See p. 22.

136. Perry, *Morality, Politics, and Law*, pp. 133–36.

137. See, e.g., Bork, *The Tempting of America*, pp. 213–14 (criticizing Dworkin's claim that the Constitution's framers enacted broad concepts); Scalia, "Originalism: The Lesser Evil," pp. 861–62 (arguing against those who "make up (out of whole cloth) an original evolutionary intent" for the Due Process, Equal Protection, and Privileges or Immunities Clauses of the Fourteenth Amendment); Wolfe, *The Rise of Modern Judicial Review*, pp. 141–42 (arguing that even if the framers did in some cases intend to enact relatively broad concepts, they also intended courts to defer to legislative interpretations of those broad concepts, except in cases in which those interpretations are clearly mistaken).

138. References to the intent of the "drafters" or "draftsmen" are common in originalist discussions. See, e.g., Trimble v. Gordon, 430 U.S. 762, 785 (1977) (Rehnquist, J., dissenting); Marsh v. Chambers, 463 U.S. 783, 790–91 (1983). In many cases, however, the context suggests that these terms are being used in some wider sense than that which I adopt.

139. Note the capital "F." All intentionalists agree that the intent of the framers (with a lower-case "f") is controlling; only some, however, identify the framers with the Framers. These latter intentionalists, in other words, adopt a particular conception of the abstract concept of the framers.

140. See, e.g., Rhode Island v. Massachusetts, 37 U.S. (12 Pet.) 657, 721 (1838) (in construing the Constitution courts must rely on "the meaning and intention of the convention which framed and proposed it for adoption and ratification"); Earl Maltz, "Foreword: The Appeal of Originalism," *Utah Law Review* 1987 (1987), p. 803. That it is the Framers' intent which ultimately matters for purposes of originalist history is more often assumed than explicitly asserted. See, e.g., Michael J. Malbin, *Religion and Politics: The Intentions of the Authors of the First Amendment* (Washington D.C.: American Enterprise Institute for Public Policy Research, 1978) (assuming, without explanation, that it is the intentions of members of the First Congress that fix the original meaning of the religion clauses of the First Amendment).

141. See, e.g., Monaghan, "Our Perfect Constitution," p. 375, n. 130. This view was apparently endorsed by a number of the Founders, including James Madison. See Lofgren, "The Original Understanding of Original Intent?" pp. 77–113.

142. See, e.g., Cooley, *Treatise on Constitutional Limitations*, p. 80; *Original Meaning Jurisprudence*, p. 19; *Corpus Juris Secundum: A Complete Restatement of the Entire American Law*, ed. by Arnold O. Ginnon and Milorad Nikolic, 101 vols. (St. Paul, Minn.: West Publishing Co., 1984), XVI, pp. 101–2 ("Ultimately, it is the final product, the constitution actually submitted to the people for adoption, as they understood it, which is controlling").

143. See, e.g., Berger, *Federalism: The Founders' Design*, pp. 70–71 (both the framers' and the ratifiers' intent is binding, but ratifiers' intent takes precedence in cases of conflict); Kay, "Adherence to the Original Intentions," pp. 246–47 (for amendments, both the Framers' and the ratifiers' intent is authoritative, but for the original Constitution only the ratifiers' intent is binding). Cf. Brest, "The Misconceived Quest for the Original Understanding," p. 214 (claiming that intentionalists should treat both the Framers' and the ratifiers' intent as binding).

144. I borrow this useful expression from Brest, "The Misconceived Quest for the Original Understanding," p. 212.

145. Most intentionalists who have addressed the issue have concluded that the intentions of *opponents* of constitutional provisions should not be counted. See, e.g., Berger, *Government by Judiciary*, p. 160; Kay, "Adherence to the Original Intentions," p. 248. But cf. Kent Greenawalt, *Speech, Crime, and the Uses of Language* (New York: Oxford University Press, 1989), p. 183 n. 16. The rationale for such a claim is perhaps least clear for those intentionalists who take seriously the notion that judges should enforce constitutional rules in the sense in which a typical reader of the time would have understood them.

146. For more on such procedures, see pp. 83–90.

147. See, e.g., Michael Kent Curtis, *No State Shall Abridge: The Fourteenth Amendment and the Bill of Rights* (Durham, N.C.: Duke University Press, 1986),

pp. 57–91, 131–53; Adamson v. California, 332 U.S. 46, 92–125 (1947) (Black, J., dissenting).

148. See, e.g., Fairman, "Does the Fourteenth Amendment Incorporate the Bill of Rights?" pp. 81–126; Bond, "The Original Understanding of the Fourteenth Amendment," p. 450. But see C. J. Antieau, *The Original Understanding of the Fourteenth Amendment* (Tucson, Ariz.: Mid–America Press, 1981), p. 40 (concluding that evidence of what the American people believed on the incorporation issue is simple too meager to warrant any particular conclusion).

149. But see Maltz, "Foreword," pp. 802–4 (suggesting that for constitutional amendments only the Framers' intent counts, that only intentions shared by at least two-thirds of each house of Congress are constitutionalized, and that in cases of uncertainty judges should assume that the expressed views of the House and Senate floor managers represent the views of the required supermajorities).

150. Kay, "Adherence to the Original Intentions," p. 249.

151. But see Payton v. New York, 445 U.S. 553, 604–11 (1980) (White, J., dissenting) (concluding that the framers of the Fourth Amendment did not intend to derogate from the constable's broad inherent authority to arrest).

152. See pp. 17–18.

153. Ibid., pp. 18–21.

154. Ibid., p. 21.

155. Ibid., p. 20.

156. Ibid., pp. 21–22.

157. Ibid., p. 22.

158. Brest, "The Misconceived Quest for the Original Understanding."

159. See, e.g., Lyons, "Constitutional Interpretation and Original Meaning," pp. 77, 84–85; Charles A. Cole, "Constitutional Interpretation: A Bicentennial Reflection," *Cumberland Law Review* 18 (1987–88), pp. 9–13; Chemerinsky, *Interpreting the Constitution*, pp. 75–78.

160. See pp. 26–27.

161. Ibid., p. 28.

162. See ibid., p. 26.

163. Ibid., pp. 22–26.

164. Ibid., pp. 23–26.

165. Ibid., pp. 25.

166. Ibid., p. 30.

167. Ibid.

168. Ibid., pp. 34–36.

CHAPTER 3

1. Twining, "Talk About Realism," *New York University Law Review* 60 (1985), p. 337.

2. Perry, *Morality, Politics, and Law*, p. 125.

3. Steven Macedo, *The New Right v. the Constitution* (Washington D.C.: The Cato Institute, 1987), p. 101.

4. See, e.g., Mark Tushnet, "The U.S. Constitution and the Intent of the

Framers," *Buffalo Law Review* 36 (1987), p. 218 ("'original intention' just doesn't make any sense at all, and everyone who has thought about the question knows that"). In extreme cases, attempts to portray originalism as lunacy have themselves been almost farcical. See, e.g., Chemerinsky, *Interpreting the Constitution*, p. 53 (arguing that originalists must admit that the Constitution permits censorship of radio and TV, and does not permit regulation of interstate commerce by motor vehicles, since the framers could not have foreseen these inventions).

5. But see, generally, Kay, "Adherence to the Original Intentions."

6. Perry, *Morality, Politics, and Law*, p. 122.

7. Grey, "Do We Have an Unwritten Constitution?" p. 705.

8. Perry, *Morality, Politics, and Law*, pp. 123–36.

9. Wilson, *The Works of James Wilson,* II, p. 577.

10. See pp. 20–21.

11. Bickel, T*he Least Dangerous Branch: The Supreme Court at the Bar of Politics,* 2d ed. (New Haven, Conn.: Yale University Press, 1986; 1st ed. 1962), p. 35 (calling Thayer's Rule "the rule of the clear mistake").

12. See, e.g., Perry, *The Constitution, the Courts, and Human Rights,* pp. 9–10; Ely, *Democracy and Distrust,* p. 7. For a forceful criticism of these theorists' views on majoritarianism, see Chemerinsky, *Interpreting the Constitution,* pp. 1–21.

13. For representative statements of this criticism, see Bickel, *The Least Dangerous Branch,* p. 102; Sandalow, "Constitutional Interpretation," p. 1035; and Brennan, "The Constitution of the United States," p. 435.

14. Thayer, "Origin and Scope of Constitutional Law," pp. 140–43.

15. Though doubtless hyperbolical, there is a kernel of truth to Leonard Levy's characterization of Chief Justice John Marshall as the "most activist judge in our constitutional history." Levy, *Original Intent and the Framers' Constitution,* p. 54. Although Marshall professed "that in no doubtful case, would [this Court] pronounce a legislative act to be contrary to the constitution" (Dartmouth College v. Woodward, 17 U.S. (4 Wheat.) 517, 625 (1819); see also Fletcher v. Peck, 10 U.S. (6 Cranch) 87, 128 (1810), it is clear that a number of his landmark decisions must be judged indefensible by the standard of Thayer's Rule. See, e.g., Bickel, *The Least Dangerous Branch*, pp. 1–14 (powerfully criticizing Marshall's reasoning in Marbury v. Madison, 5 U.S. (1 Cranch) 137 (1803), the case that established the power of the Court to review the constitutionality of acts of Congress); David P. Currie, *The Constitution in the Supreme Court: The First Hundred Years, 1789–1888* (Chicago: University of Chicago Press, 1985), p. 135 (noting that the Contract Clause was probably not originally intended to apply to public contracts, contrary to Marshall's holding in *Fletcher*).

16. See, e.g., Berger, *Government by Judiciary,* pp. 249–82; Wolfe, *The Rise of Modern Judicial Review* pp. 144–60; Bork, *The Tempting of America,* pp. 36–49.

17. See, e.g., Gordon S. Wood, *The Creation of the American Republic,* 1776–1787 (New York: W. W. Norton, 1969), pp. 471–518; Richard Hofstadter, "The Founding Fathers: An Age of Realism," in Robert H. Horwitz, ed., *The*

Moral Foundations of the American Republic, 3d ed. (Charlottesville: University of Virginia Press, 1986), pp. 62–74; J. Allen Smith, *The Spirit of American Government,* 2d ed. (Cambridge, Mass.: Harvard University Press, 1965; 1st ed. 1907), pp. 27–39; Charles A. Beard, *An Economic Interpretation of the Constitution of the United States* (New York: Macmillan, 1913); Donald Elfenbein, "The Myth of Conservatism as a Constitutional Philosophy," *Iowa Law Review* 71 (1986), pp. 468–79. For a valuable collection of readings on the subject, see Robert A. Goldwin and William A. Schambra, eds., *How Democratic Is the Constitution?* (Washington D.C.: American Enterprise Institute for Public Policy Research, 1980).

18. *The Federalist,* No. 78, p. 527.

19. Ibid., p. 526.

20. West Virginia State Board of Education v. Barnette, 319 U.S. 624, 638 (1943).

21. Cf. The Slaughter-House Cases, 83 U.S. (16 Wall.) 36, 129 (1872) (Swayne, J., dissenting) (charging that the majority's narrow construction of the Fourteenth Amendment's Privileges or Immunities Clause "turns, as it were, what was meant for bread into a stone").

22. Commager, *Majority Rule and Minority Rights* (New York: Oxford University Press, 1943), p. 55. Commager does note one "dubious" exception: Wong Wing v. United States, 163 U.S. 228 (1896) (striking down, as violative of the Fifth and Sixth Amendments, a provision of the 1892 Chinese Exclusion Act that subjected Chinese aliens to imprisonment at hard labor for up to one year if adjudged to be in the United States illegally following a summary hearing). Ibid. The Court's record on *state* infringements of civil liberties was somewhat less dismal this period. See, e.g., Strauder v. West Virginia, 100 U.S. 303 (1879) (invalidating a state statute that excluded blacks from jury service); McCabe v. A., T. & S. F. Railway Co., 235 U.S. 151 (1914) (overturning an Oklahoma law that permitted carriers to provide sleeping, dining, and chair cars for whites but not for blacks); Moore v. Dempsey, 261 U.S. 86 (1932) (holding that black petitioners sentenced to death under mob pressure were deprived of due process of law); Fiske v. Kansas, 274 U.S. 380 (1927) (reversing a conviction under a state criminal syndicalism statute); Powell v. Alabama, 287 U.S. 45 (1932) (ruling that defendants in capital cases must be provided with counsel if they are incapable of adequately making their own defense). For assessments of the Court's performance similar to Commager's, see Charles Grove Haines, *The American Doctrine of Judicial Supremacy,* 2d rev. ed. (New York: Russell & Russell, 1959), pp. 512–13; Rehnquist, "The Notion of a Living Constitution," pp. 700–704; Maltz, "Some New Thoughts on an Old Problem," pp. 844–45.

23. The period from roughly 1897 to 1937 when a deeply conservative Court routinely overturned economic and social legislation it believed unreasonably infringed on the "liberty of contract" protected by the Due Process Clauses of the Fifth and Fourteenth Amendments. The era derives its name from the most notorious example of the Court's laissez-faire activism, Lochner v. New York, 198 U.S. 45 (1905), in which the Court struck down a statute limiting the hours of bakery employees to sixty hours a week and ten hours a day. See, generally,

Paul Kens, *Judicial Power and Reform Politics: The Anatomy of* Lochner v. New York (Lawrence: University of Kansas Press, 1990).

24. See Brest, *Processes of Constitutional Decisionmaking,* p. 738.

25. Berger, *Government by Judiciary*, p. 332 (quoting Miller and Howell, "The Myth of Neutrality," p. 689).

26. Cf. Lochner v. New York, 198 U.S. 45, 75 (1905) (Holmes, J., dissenting) ("The Fourteenth Amendment does not enact Mr. Herbert Spencer's Social Statics"). Spencer's *Social Statics* (New York: D. Appleton & Co., 1864; 1st ed. 1850) is a radical defense of laissez-faire capitalism and what later came to be known as social Darwinism. Believing that the sole function of the state is to protect the right of individuals to do as they please, so long as the equal rights of others are not infringed, Spencer opposed all state aid to the poor and virtually all other social-welfare legislation, including state-sponsored education and protection from medical quacks. "The whole effort of nature," he wrote, "is to get rid of [the unfit], to clear the world of them, and make room for better . . . If they are not sufficiently complete to live, they die, and it is best they should die." *Social Statics*, pp. 415–16 (quoted in Richard Hofstadter, *Social Darwinism in American Thought*, rev. ed. (Boston: Beacon Press, 1955), p. 41).

27. Perry, *The Constitution, the Courts, and Human Rights,* p. 116.

28. See, generally, Herbert McCloskey and Alida Brill, *Dimensions of Tolerance: What Americans Believe about Civil Liberties* (New York: Russell Sage Foundation, 1983). When asked, for example, whether they agreed or disagreed with the statement "Atheists may preach against God in a civic auditorium," only 18 percent of those surveyed agreed, as compared to 66 percent of the polled lawyers and judges. Ibid., p. 124. Similarly, when asked whether they agreed or disagreed with the statement, "Accused rapists and child molesters are entitled to as fair a trial as anyone else," 73% of the mass public agreed, compared to 99% of lawyers and judges. Ibid., p. 162.

29. Bickel, *The Least Dangerous Branch*, p. 26.

30. See, e.g., the segregationist practices struck down in Smith v. Allwright, 339 U.S. 629 (1950) (all-white primary); McLaurin v. Oklahoma State Regents, 339 U.S. 637 (1950) (segregated graduate education); Brown v. Board of Education, 347 U.S. 483 (1954) (segregated public schools); Loving v. Virginia, 388 U.S. 1 (1967) (antimiscegenation law).

31. See Skinner v. Oklahoma, 316 U.S. 535 (1942) (striking down a state habitual criminal sterilization law).

32. See, e.g., Baker v. Carr, 369 U.S. 186 (1962) (invalidating a 1901 Tennessee apportionment statute under which 40 percent of Tennessee's voters elected nearly two-thirds of the members of the state's two legislative assemblies); Reynolds v. Sims, 377 U.S. 533 (1964).

33. See Griswold v. Connecticut, 381 U.S. 479 (1965) (striking down a Connecticut statute, as applied to married couples, that criminalized use of contraceptives); Moore v. East Cleveland, 431 U.S. 494 (1977) (invalidating a city zoning ordinance that barred a grandmother from living with her two grandchildren because the latter were not siblings).

34. See, e.g., Reed v. Reed, 404 U.S. 71 (1971) (overturning an Idaho law

that gave preferential treatment to males under rules for selecting administrators of intestate estates); Graham v. Richardson, 403 U.S. 365 (1971) (invalidating state statutes denying welfare benefits to resident aliens); Levy v. Louisiana, 391 U.S. 68 (1968) (striking down a Louisiana wrongful death statute that discriminated against illegitimate children).

35. See Klopfer v. North Carolina, 386 U.S. 213 (1967).

36. See, e.g., Duncan v. Louisiana, 391 U.S. (1968) (overturning a provision of the Louisiana Constitution that granted jury trials only in cases in which sentences of death or imprisonment at hard labor might be imposed); Parker v. Gladden, 385 U.S. 363 (1967) (incorporating Sixth Amendment guarantee of an impartial jury); Peters v. Kiff, 407 U.S. 493 (1972) (reaffirming and extending holding of Norris v. Alabama, 294 U.S. 587 (1935), that exclusion of blacks from juries violates the due process rights of black defendants).

37. See Washington v. Texas, 388 U.S. 14 (1967).

38. See Pointer v. Texas, 380 U.S. 400 (1965).

39. See Malloy v. Hogan, 378 U.S. 1 (1964); Murphy v. Waterfront Commission of New York Harbor, 378 U.S. 52 (1964).

40. See Benton v. Maryland, 395 U.S. 784 (1969).

41. See Gideon v. Wainwright, 372 U.S. 355 (1963); Argersinger v. Hamlin, 407 U.S. 25 (1972).

42. See *In re* Winship, 397 U.S. 358 (1970); Mullaney v. Wilbur, 421 U.S. 684 (1975).

43. See H. L. A. Hart, *The Concept of Law* (Oxford: Clarendon Press, 1961), pp. 121–32. For an earlier presentation of the theory, see Glanville Williams's neglected classic, "Language and the Law," *The Law Quarterly Review* 61 (1945), pp. 181–95, 301–3.

44. See Hart, "Positivism and the Separation of Law and Morals," pp. 607–8. In *The Concept of Law* (pp. 125–26), Hart suggests a related reason why legal rules may be open-textured: the fact that their makers suffer from limited knowledge and limited determinacy of aim. Because lawmakers cannot possibly anticipate all interpretive issues that may arise under a rule, they inevitably leave some questions of application unsettled. See also H. L. A. Hart, "Jhering's Heaven of Concepts and Modern Analytical Jurisprudence," in *Essays in Jurisprudence and Philosophy* (Oxford: Clarendon Press, 1983), p. 270. For a striking anticipation of Hart's distinction between core and penumbral meanings, see Lieber, *Legal and Political Hermeneutics,* p. 27.

45. See McBoyle v. United States, 283 U.S. 25 (1931) (holding that a federal statute outlawing the knowing transportation of stolen "motor vehicles" across state lines does not apply to aircraft). Speaking for the Court in *McBoyle,* Justice Holmes argued that while the conduct in question might fall within either the general purpose or the literal words of the statute at issue, justice requires "that a fair warning should be given to the world in language that the common world will understand" before the coercive power of the state is employed. Ibid., p. 27. Cf. *Ex Parte* Lockett, 178 P. 134 (Calif. 1919) (striking down a California law criminalizing "*fellatio*" and "*cunnilingus,*" since the use of the unexplained Latin terms failed to give adequate notice of the conduct intended to be

prohibited). These cases accord with the traditional rule, now somewhat infirm, that penal laws are to be construed strictly against the state and favorably to the accused.

46. See Robert Bork, "Original Intent and the Constitution," *Humanities* 7 (1986), p. 22.

47. Cf. Frank Easterbrook, "Statutes' Domains," *University of Chicago Law Review* 50 (1983), pp. 548–49.

48. An argument similar to this is critically discussed in Lyons, "Constitutional Interpretation and Original Meaning," p. 97. For simplicity, I have formulated the argument in textualist terms; complications could be added to accommodate intentionalist theories.

49. Ollman v. Evans, 705 F. 2d 970, 995 (D.C. Cir. 1984) (Bork, J., concurring).

50. See, e.g., Corwin, "Moratorium Over Minnesota," pp. 313–14; Eugene V. Rostow, *The Sovereign Prerogative: The Supreme Court and the Quest for Law* (New Haven, Conn.: Yale University Press, 1962), pp. 93–94; Rehnquist, "The Notion of a Living Constitution," p. 694.

51. For influential arguments to this effect, see Dworkin, *Taking Rights Seriously*, pp. 14–45, 81–130; Dworkin, *A Matter of Principle*, pp. 119–45.

52. See, e.g., Brink, "Legal Theory," pp. 114–16; Lyons, "Constitutional Interpretation and Original Meaning," pp. 83–88; Moore, "A Natural Law Theory of Interpretation," pp. 322–38.

53. Youngstown Sheet and Tube Co. v. Sawyer, 343 U.S. 579, 610–11 (1952) (Frankfurter, J., concurring).

54. See pp. 21–22.

55. F. A. Hayek, *The Road to Serfdom* (Chicago: University of Chicago Press, 1944), p. 72.

56. For a fuller discussion of the virtues of precedential constraint, see Frederick Schauer, "Precedent," *Stanford Law Review* 39 (1987), pp. 595–602. See also Moore, "A Natural Law Theory of Interpretation," pp. 371–77; Monaghan, "Stare Decisis and Constitutional Adjudication," pp. 744–54; Richard Wasserstrom, *The Judicial Decision: Toward a Theory of Legal Justification* (Stanford: Stanford University Press, 1961), pp. 60–81; Cardozo, *The Nature of the Judicial Process,* pp. 149–50; Moragne v. States Marine Lines, Inc., 398 U.S. 375, 403 (1970).

57. See Marbury v. Madison, 5 U.S. (1 Cranch) 137 (1803) (establishing the power of the Court to strike down unconstitutional acts of Congress).

58. Federalist Justice Samuel Chase was impeached by a Republican-controlled House in 1804, fundamentally for political reasons. After a protracted Senate trial, Chase narrowly escaped conviction and removal. See George L. Haskins and Herbert A. Jones, *Foundations of Power: John Marshall,1801–1815* (New York: Macmillan, 1981), pp. 205–45. Since that time, no really serious attempt has been made to impeach a Supreme Court Justice. But see Raoul Berger, *Impeachment: The Constitutional Problems* (Cambridge, Mass: Harvard University Press, 1973), p. 94 (discussing the politically motivated attempt by 110 House conservatives and Dixiecrats in 1970 to impeach Justice William O. Douglas).

59. Article 3, section 2, of the Constitution authorizes Congress to make "exceptions" to the Supreme Court's appellate jurisdiction. Only rarely has this power been used. The most famous instance occurred in 1868, when Congress, fearful that the Court would invalidate recently enacted Reconstruction legislation, withdrew the Court's power of appellate review in certain habeas corpus proceedings. The following year, in Ex Parte McCardle, 74 U.S. (7 Wall.) 506 (1869), the Court sustained this legislation. It should be noted, however, that a number of congressional attempts to limit the Court's jurisdiction have narrowly fallen short of passage. For detailed accounts of some of the most serious of these efforts, see Walter F. Murphy, *Congress Versus the Court: A Case Study in the American Political Process* (Chicago: University of Chicago Press, 1962); C. Herman Pritchett, *Congress Versus the Supreme Court, 1957–1960* (Minneapolis: University of Minnesota Press, 1961). For a discussion of more recent Court-curbing proposals, see Gary L. McDowell, *Curbing the Courts: The Constitution and the Limits of Judicial Power* (Baton Rouge: Louisiana State University Press, 1988), pp. 155–67.

60. Congressional reaction to the Court's decision in United States v. Lovett, 328 U.S. 303 (1946), provides an instructive example. In that case, the Court struck down, as violative of the Bill of Attainder Clause, a federal statute which prohibited the payment of compensation to certain named government employees who had been charged with subversive activities. An effort by House conservatives to negate the Court's decision by refusing to appropriate the needed funds failed by a single vote. See Jesse H. Choper, *Judicial Review and the National Political Process: A Functional Reconsideration of the Role of the Supreme Court* (Chicago: University of Chicago Press, 1980), p. 146.

61. In April 1802, congressional Republicans, concerned that the Federalist-dominated Supreme Court might overturn legislation that repealed the Judiciary Act of 1801, pushed through legislation that cancelled the upcoming June Term of the Court. As a consequence, the Court did not meet for a period of fourteen months. See Haskins and Johnson, *Foundations of Power,* p. 167.

62. The most famous Court-packing plan, Franklin Roosevelt's, failed of course. See Melvin I. Urofsky, *A March of Liberty: A Constitutional History of United States* (New York: Alfred A. Knopf, 1988), pp. 683–87. But on five occasions politically motivated attempts to alter the size of the Supreme Court succeeded. During one six-year stretch, from 1863–1869, Congress played political football with the Court's membership; raising it from nine to ten in 1863; lowering it from ten to seven in 1866, and raising it again from seven to nine in 1869. See James Q. Wilson, *American Government: Institutions and Policies,* 2d ed. (Lexington, Mass.: D. C. Heath and Co., 1983), p. 404.

63. The best-known examples are President Jackson's refusal to enforce the Court's decision in Worcester v. Georgia, 31 U.S. (6 Pet.) 515 (1832), and Lincoln's defiance of Chief Justice Taney's decision in Ex Parte Merryman, 17 Fed. Cas. 144 (No. 9487) (C.C.D. Md., 1861). See Murphy, *Congress Versus the Court,* pp. 26, 32–33. For more recent examples, see Choper, *Judicial Review* pp. 142–43.

64. For a brief survey of state resistance to Supreme Court rulings, see Choper, *Judicial Review*, pp. 140–42 and accompanying citations.

65. See ibid., pp. 146–50.

66. Ibid., pp. 129–70. For a contrasting view, see William Lasser, *The Limits of Judicial Power: The Supreme Court in American Politics* (Chaper Hill: University of North Carolina Press, 1988).

67. *The Federalist,* p. 532 (No. 78) (Hamilton).

68. Wills, *Explaining America: The Federalist* (London: The Athlone Press, 1981), p. 128.

69. See, e.g., Brown v. Board of Education, 347 U.S. 483 (1954) (striking down segregation in public education); Bolling v. Sharpe, 347 U.S. 497 (1954) (holding that congressionally mandated segregation in District of Columbia public schools violates a guarantee of equal protection implicit in the Fifth Amendment Due Process Clause); Shelley v. Kramer, 334 U.S. 1 (1948) (striking down racially restrictive housing covenants); Smith v. Allwright, 321 U.S. 649 (1944) (striking down all-white primary elections); Harper v. Virginia State Board of Elections, 383 U.S. 663 (1966) (invalidating state poll taxes); Loving v. Virginia, 388 U.S. 1 (1967) (overturning state antimiscegenation laws).

70. See, e.g., Reed v. Reed, 404 U.S. 71 (1971); Frontiero v. Richardson, 411 U.S. 677 (1973).

71. See, generally, Henry J. Abraham, *Freedom and the Court: Civil Rights and Liberties in the United States,* 5th ed. (New York: Oxford University Press, 1988), pp. 28–117.

72. See, e.g., Gideon v. Wainwright, 372 U.S. 335 (1963) (requiring provision of free legal assistance to indigent criminal defendants in felony cases); Miranda v. Arizona, 384 U.S. 436 (1966) (requiring police to inform criminal suspects of basic procedural rights prior to interrogation); Duncan v. Louisiana, 391 U.S. 145 (1968) (incorporating Sixth Amendment guarantee of trial by jury).

73. Leading historical studies suggest that the Eighth Amendment prohibition of cruel and unusual punishments was originally intended to bar only barbarous or torturous punishments, not disproportionately severe punishment. See Anthony F. Granucci, "'Nor Cruel and Unusual Punishments Inflicted': The Original Meaning," *California Law Review* 57 (1969), p. 839; Berger, *Death Penalties: The Supreme Court's Obstacle Course* (Cambridge, Mass.: Harvard University Press, 1982), p. 174. The Court has long held that the amendment does bar grossly excessive punishment. See, e.g., Weems v. United States, 217 U.S. 349 (1910); Coker v. Georgia, 433 U.S. 485 (1977); Solem v. Helm, 463 U.S. 277 (1983).

74. Originalist historians have made a strong case that the federal government was originally intended to possess only such powers as were either expressly enumerated or clearly essential to carry out those enumerated powers. See, e.g., Berger, *Federalism,* p. 94; Siegan, *The Supreme Court's Constitution,* p. 27. This "strict constructionist" view of enumerated and implied powers was definitively rejected by the Marshall Court. See especially McCulloch v. Maryland, 17 U.S. (4 Wheat.) 316 (1819) (holding that Congress is empowered, under the necessary and proper clause, to charter a national bank); American

Insurance Co. v. Canter, 26 U.S. (1 Pet.) 511 (1828) (deducing a power to acquire and govern territory from the power to make war and to conclude treaties). For a brief overview of Court decisions on implied federal powers, see Tribe, *American Constitutional Law*, pp. 300–15.

75. See, e.g., United States v. Curtiss-Wright Export Corp., 299 U.S. 304 (1936). For evidence that the Senate, rather than the president, was intended to be the principal architect of foreign policy, see Levy, *Original Intent and the Framers' Constitution*, pp. 30–53.

76. For much of American constitutional history, it was a settled maxim "that the power conferred upon the legislature to make laws cannot be delegated by that department to any other body or authority." Cooley, *Treatise on Constitutional Limitations*, p. 139. Twentieth-century courts, bowing to the exigencies of the modern administrative state, have generally sustained extensive delegations of lawmaking power to independent regulatory agencies and executive officials. See, e.g., J. W. Hampton & Co. v. U.S., 276 U.S. 394 (1928); United States v. Curtiss-Wright Corp., 299 U.S. 304 (1936). For a historical overview, see Sotirios A. Barber, *The Constitution and the Delegation of Congressional Power* (Chicago: University of Chicago Press, 1975).

77. Historians now generally agree that the Court's decision in Knox v. Lee, 79 U.S. (12 Wall.) 457 (1871) (overruling Hepburn v. Griswold, 75 U.S. (8 Wall.) 603 (1870), and establishing the power of Congress to make paper currency legal tender) was inconsistent with the framers' intent. See Kenneth Dam, "The Legal Tender Cases," *1981 Supreme Court Review* (1981), p. 389; see also Siegan, *The Supreme Court's Constitution*, pp. 22–38; Monaghan, "Stare Decisis and Constitutional Adjudication," p. 744.

78. Under current constitutional doctrine, congressional power to regulate "commerce . . . among the several States" (Art. 1, sec. 8) is viewed as a virtually "unlimited power to regulate everything and anything it wishe[s]." Monaghan, "Stare Decisis and Constitutional Adjudication," p. 731. That such an expansive reading is inconsistent with original intent of the Commerce Clause is widely acknowledged by constitutional historians. See, e.g., Berger, *Federalism*, pp. 120–57; Epstein, "The Proper Scope of the Commerce Power," *Virginia Law Review* 73 (1987), pp. 1387–1455; Henry Monaghan, "*Marbury* and the Administrative State," *Columbia Law Review* 83 (1983), pp. 1–34.

79. See, generally, Ethan Bronner, *Battle for Justice: How the Bork Nomination Shook America* (New York: W. W. Norton and Co., 1989).

80. "Let justice be done, though the heavens fall." Cf. *Black's Law Dictionary*, rev. 4th ed. (St. Paul, Minn.: West Publishing Co., 1968), p. 751.

81. See, e.g., Bork, "Neutral Principles," p. 6; Rehnquist, "The Notion of a Living Constitution," pp. 704–6.

82. See, e.g., Charles M. Lamb, "Judicial Restraint on the Supreme Court," in Charles M. Lamb and Stephen C. Halpern, eds., *Supreme Court Activism and Restraint* (Lexington, Mass.: Lexington Books, 1982), p. 24; J. Clifford Wallace, "The Jurisprudence of Judicial Restraint: A Return to Moorings," *George Washington Law Review* 50 (1980), p. 14; J. Skelly Wright, "The Judicial Right and the Rhetoric of Restraint: A Defense of Judicial Activism in an Age of Conservative Judges," *Hastings Constitutional Law Quarterly* 14 (1987), p. 490.

83. See p. 22.

84. Burnet v. Coronado Oil and Gas Co., 285 U.S. 393, 407 (1932) (Brandeis, J., concurring). Cf. C. I. R. v. Fink, 107 S. Ct. 2729, 2738n. 6 (1987) (Stevens, J., dissenting) (citing cases in which the Court has affirmed that the doctrine of *stare decisis* has a more limited application in constitutional law than in other areas of law).

85. Giuseppi v. Walling, 144 F. 2d 608, 624 (2d Cir. 1944).

86. See p. 28.

87. For a valuable discussion of the recent revival of textualism in statutory interpretation, see William N. Eskridge, Jr., "The New Textualism," *UCLA Law Review* 37 (1990), pp. 621–91. It should be noted, however, that Eskridge uses "textualism" in a sense somewhat different from that employed in the present study.

88. Suspicion of overweening judicial power and discretion apparently lay at the root of Justice Hugo Black's preference for textualist over intentionalist interpretive strategies. See, e.g., Connecticut General Life Insurance Co. v. Johnson, 303 U.S. 77, 85–90 (1938) (Black, J., dissenting); Griswold v. Connecticut, 381 U.S. 479, 521 (1965) (Black, J., dissenting); *In re* Winship, p. 397 U.S. 358, 385–86 (Black, J., dissenting). See also Frank Easterbrook, "The Role of Original Intent in Statutory Construction," *Harvard Journal of Law and Public Policy,*11 (1988), pp. 62–63.

89. Cf. Beswick v. Beswick, (1968) AC 58 at 74 (per Lord Reid).

90. Cf. Philip Bobbitt, *Constitutional Fate: Theory of the Constitution* (New York: Oxford University Press, 1982), p. 14.

91. See, e.g., Story, *Commentaries on the Constitution,* III, pp. 287–90; Sedgwick, *Treatise on the Interpretation of Statutory and Constitutional Law,* p. 328; Monahan, "Stare Decisis and Constitutional Adjudication," p. 725. Cf. Frank Easterbrook, "Statutes' Domains," pp. 548–49; Bobbit, *Constitutional Fate,* p. 14.

92. See, e.g., John Finnis, *Natural Law and Natural Rights* (Oxford: Clarendon Press, 1980), p. 270; Joseph Raz, *The Authority of Law: Essays on Law and Morality* (Oxford: Clarendon Press, 1979), p. 214; Moore, "A Natural Law Theory of Interpretation," p. 371.

93. Cf. P. S. Atiyah and Robert S. Summers, *Form and Substance in Anglo-American Law: A Comparative Study of Legal Reasoning, Legal Theory, and Legal Institutions* (Oxford: Clarendon Press, 1987), p. 105; Moore, "Semantics of Judging," p. 258, Harry Willmer Jones, "The Plain Meaning Rule and Extrinsic Aids in the Interpretation of Statutes," *Washington University Law Quarterly,* 25 (1939), p. 21. Cf. also George Van Camp and Sons Co. v. American Can Co., 278 U.S. 245, 253 (1928); McBoyle v. United States, 283 U.S. 25, 27 (1931).

94. See, e.g., Laycock, "Text, Intent, and the Religion Clauses," p. 686; Ruti Teitel, "Original Intent, History, and Levy's Establishment Clause," *Law and Social Inquiry* 15 (1990), p. 595. See also Frederick Douglass, "The American Constitution and the American Slave: An Address Delivered in Glasgow, Scotland on 26 March 1860," in *The Frederick Douglass Papers,* ed. by John W. Blassingame, 3 vols. to date (New Haven, Conn.: Yale University Press, 1985),

III, p. 347; Lysander Spooner, *The Unconstitutionality of Slavery* (New York: Burt Franklin, n.d.; 1st ed. 1860), pp. 157–58; Story, *Commentaries on the Constitution,* I, 288. Cf. Cass Sunstein, "Interpreting Statutes in the Regulatory State," *Harvard Law Review* 103 (1989), pp. 430–32.

95. See pp. 3–4. See also Bacon, *A New Abridgment*, VII, p. 457 ("Such a construction ought to be put upon a statute, as may best answer the intention which the makers had in view; for, *qui haeret in litera, haeret in cortice"* (He who considers merely the letter of an instrument goes but skin deep into its meaning)).

96. See Jay A. Sigler, *Double Jeopardy: The Development of a Legal and Social Policy* (Ithaca, N.Y. : Cornell University Press, 1969), pp. 27–32; Levy, *Original Intent and the Framers' Constitution,* p. 338.

97. See, e.g., Benton v. Maryland, 395 U.S. 784 (1969).

98. Art. 1, sec. 7.

99. *The Constitution of the United States: Analysis and Interpretation* (Washington D.C.: U.S. Government Printing Office, 1964), p. 135.

100. Art. IV, sec. 2.

101. See, e.g., Corfield v. Coryell, 6 Fed. Cas. 546, 551–52 (No. 3230) (C.C.E.D. Pa. 1823); Slaughter-House Cases, 83 U.S. (16 Wall.) 36, 76 (1873); Baldwin v. Montana Fish and Game Commission, 436 U.S. 371, 387 (1978).

102. See p. 26.

103. Art. 1, sec. 1.

104. See, e.g., J. W. Hampton, Jr., and Co. v. United States, 276 U.S. 394 (1928) (upholding an act of Congress authorizing the president to adjust customs duties under the Tariff Act of 1922); National Broadcasting Co. v. United States, 369 U.S. 190 (1943) (upholding the authority of the Federal Communications Commission to license broadcasting stations).

105. See, e.g., Bork, *The Tempting of America*, p. 158.

106. See Rexford G. Tugwell, *The Compromising of the Constitution: Early Departures* (Notre Dame, Ind.: University of Notre Dame Press, 1976), p. 155; Monaghan, "Stare Decisis and Constitutional Adjudication," p. 731. For historical background on the maxim, see Patrick W. Duff and Horace E. Whiteside, "*Delegata Potestas Non Potest Delegari*: A Maxim of American Constitutional Law," *Cornell Law Quarterly* 14 (1929), pp. 168–96. For Locke's discussion of the nondelegability of legislative powers, see his *Two Treatises of Government,* ed. by Peter Laslett (New York: New American Library, 1965), Book II, sec. 141, pp. 408–9.

107. Art. 1, sec. 8.

108. But see Epstein, *Takings,* p. x.

109. See p. 46, n. 78.

110. See pp. 3–4.

111. For representative recent statements of this view, see Richard A. Posner, "Legal Formalism, Legal Realism, and the Interpretation of Statutes and the Constitution," *Case Western Reserve Law Review* 37 (1986–87), pp. 189–90; Daniel A. Farber and Philip P. Frickey, "Legislative Intent and Public Choice," *Virginia Law Review* 74 (1988), pp. 460–61.

112. See p. 5.

113. See Arthur W. Murphy, "Old Maxims Never Die: the 'Plain-Meaning Rule' and Statutory Interpretation in the 'Modern' Federal Courts," *Columbia Law Review* 75 (1975), p. 1299.

114. See, e.g., Grant Gilmore, *The Ages of American Law* (New Haven, Conn.: Yale University Press, 1977), pp. 62–64; Sir Rupert Cross, *Statutory Interpretation,* 2d ed. (London: Butterworths, 1987) p. 11; Frederick Pollock, *Essays in Jurisprudence and Ethics* (London: Macmillan, 1882), p. 85. As Gilmore notes (ibid., p. 62), the paradigmatic expression of this older view was the interpretive canon, now wholly obsolete, that statutes in derogation of the common law should be strictly construed. See, generally, Jefferson B. Fordham and J. Russell Leach, "Interpretation of Statutes in Derogation of the Common Law," *Vanderbilt Law Review* 3 (1950), pp. 438–55. For a classic attack on this canon and the conception of judicial responsibility underlying it, see Roscoe Pound, "Common Law and Legislation," *Harvard Law Review* 21 (1908), pp. 383–407.

115. Hart and Sacks, *The Legal Process,* p. 99.

116. See, e.g., Cross, *Statutory Interpretation,* p. 154; Allen, *Law in the Making,* pp. 488–516; Fothergill v. Monarch Airlines Ltd. [1981] AC 251, 279–80 (per Lord Diplock).

117. See, e.g., Dickerson, *Interpretation and Application of Statutes,* pp. 152–56; Schwegmann Bros. v. Calvert Distilleries Corp., 341 U.S. 384, 395–97 (1952) (Jackson, J., concurring); Wallace v. Christensen, 802 F. 2d 1539, 1559–60 (9th Cir. 1986) (Kozinski, J., concurring). Cf. Tennessee Valley Authority v. Hill, 437 U.S. 153, 185 (1978).

118. Of course, a sufficiently obnoxious Court decision might goad the *American people* into reversing it by constitutional amendment. But this is extraordinarily unlikely. Only four Court decisions have been reversed in this way: Chisholm v. Georgia, 2 U.S. (2 Dall.) 419 (1793), by the Eleventh Amendment (1793) (removing federal jurisdiction over suits against a state); Dred Scott v. Sanford, 60 U.S. (19 How.) 393 (1856), by the Thirteenth and Fourteenth Amendments (1865 and 1868, respectively) (outlawing slavery and extending citizenship to all persons born or naturalized in the United States, respectively); Pollock v. Farmers Loan and Trust Co., 157 U.S. 429 (1895), by the Sixteenth Amendment (1913) (empowering Congress to levy income taxes); and Oregon v. Mitchell, 400 U.S. 112 (1970), by the Twenty-Sixth Amendment (1971) (granting eighteen-year-olds the right to vote). As Thomas Jefferson feared, the American people have come to regard the Constitution with "sanctimonious reverence," deeming it "like the ark of the covenant, too sacred to be touched." Letter from Jefferson to Samuel Kercheval, July 12, 1816, in *The Writings of Thomas Jefferson,* ed. by Paul L. Ford, 10 vols. (New York: G. P. Putnam's Sons, 1892–99), X, p. 42.

119. West Virginia Board of Education v. Barnette, 319 U.S. 634, 638 (1943).

120. See Lieber, *Legal and Political Hermeneutics,* p. 44 ("It is one of the most efficient agents in the civil progress of a nation that, certain principles being established, they should be left to unfold themselves gradually, and to be expanded, modified, and limited, by the civil action of the nation itself, by the practical intercourse of society").

121. See p. 28.

122. Chemerinsky, *Interpreting the Constitution,* pp. 36–41.

123. See, e.g., Judith A. Baer, "The Fruitless Search for Original Intent," in Michael W. McCann and Gerald L. Houseman, eds., *Judging the Constitution: Critical Essays on Judicial Lawmaking* (Boston: Scott, Foresman & Co., 1989), pp. 49–71; Macedo, *The New Right v. the Constitution,* pp. 16–17; Chemerinsky, *Interpreting the Constitution,* p. 67.

124. See p. 30.

125. Ibid.

126. For pioneering discussions of these or related notions, see J. S. Mill, *A System of Logic* (New York: Harper and Brothers, 1893; 1st ed., 1843), pp. 29–44 (distinguishing "connotation" from "denotation"); Gottlob Frege, "On Sense and Reference," in *Translations from the Philosophical Writings of Gottlob Frege,* ed. by Peter Geach and Max Black (Oxford: Basil Blackwell, 1970), pp. 56–78 (distinguishing "sense" (*Sinn*) from "reference" (*Bedeutung*)). For a discussion of more recent work on these notions, see John Lyons, *Semantics,* 2 vols. (Cambridge: Cambridge University Press, 1977), I, pp. 174–229.

127. See Berger, "'Original Intention' in Historical Perspective," pp. 101–42; Berger, *Government by Judiciary*, pp. 365–67.

128. See, e.g., Powell, "The Original Understanding of Original Intent," pp. 885–948; Lofgren, "The Original Understanding of Original Intent?" pp. 77–113; Robert N. Clinton, "Original Understanding, Legal Realism, and the Interpretation of 'This Constitution,'" *Iowa Law Review* 72 (1987), pp. 1186–1220.

129. What little evidence there is can be summarized briefly. Supporting the strict intentionalist view is the fact that the framers clearly assumed that traditional common-law techniques of legal interpretation would be used in construing the Constitution; that these techniques tended to favor "equitable" over literal constructions; and that equitable interpretation, as traditionally understood, required interpreters to answer questions of specific application as they believed the makers of a law would themselves have answered them if these questions could have been put to them at the time the law was enacted. See pp. 2–4. Critics of Berger's reading of the framers' interpretive intent have argued in response: (1) that many common lawyers apparently viewed the "intent" of legal instruments not as some hidden meaning locked into them by their authors, but rather as publicly determinable products of traditional interpretive methods (see Powell, "The Original Understanding of Original Intent," pp. 894–902); (2) that the framers deliberately chose abstract language in phrasing many constitutional provisions, suggesting an intention to enact broad concepts rather than specific conceptions (see Dworkin, "The Forum of Principle," p. 53); (3) that the framers made no effort to ensure that reasonably accurate and complete records of their specific intent were made and preserved, indicating that they did not view their own actual or counterfactual scope beliefs as crucial to correct constitutional interpretation (see Levy, *Original Intent and the Framers' Constitution,* pp. 1–29); and (4) that language users typically have "spare" rather than "rich" semantic intentions, and the framers were presumably no exception to this usual linguistic practice (see Moore, "A Natural Law Theory of Interpretation," pp. 340–41).

130. As late as 1972, Dworkin noted that many lawyers continued to adhere to the "crude" semantic theory that what the framers "'said' or 'meant' is limited to the instances of official action that they had in mind as violations, or, at least, to those instances that they would have thought were violations if they had them in mind." Dworkin, *Taking Rights Seriously,* p. 134.

131. See Dworkin, *A Matter of Principle*, pp. 54–55.

132. See pp. 49–50.

133. Cf. Dworkin, "The Bork Nomination," *New York Review of Books* (August 13, 1987), p. 6.

134. See p. 142, n. 85. Following the adoption of the Nineteenth Amendment, giving women the right to vote, state courts were inundated with suits challenging the traditional exclusion of women from juries. The issue in these cases was not whether such exclusions were barred by the constitutional guarantee of equal protection: it was settled law that they were not. See Gibson v. Mississippi, 162 U.S. 565 (1896). The issue was rather whether state statutes expressly extending jury eligibility to "persons" qualified to vote now extended to recently enfranchised women. In one case, in a remarkable feat of strict intentionalist reasoning, the Massachusetts Supreme Court held that its state's jury eligibility statute did not apply to women, since only men were qualified to vote at the time the statute was passed, and thus the "intent" of the legislature must have been to limit jury eligibility to men. See Commonwealth v. Welosky, 276 Mass. 398, 177 N.E. 656 (1931), *cert. denied,* 284 U.S. 684 (1932).

135. See p. 32.

136. In relevant part, the Fourth Amendment states, "The right of the people to be secure in their persons, houses, papers, and effects, against unreasonable searches and seizures, shall not be violated."

137. See p. 141, n. 82.

138. See Berger, *Government by Judiciary,* pp. 161–63.

139. See p. 142, n. 85.

140. See pp. 35–36.

141. For a brief discussion, see Dworkin, *Law's Empire,* p. 320. For recent qualified endorsement of a representative intention approach to legislative intent, see Farber and Frickey, "Legislative Intent and Public Choice," pp. 436–37.

142. See, generally, Levy, *Original Intent and the Framers' Constitution.*

143. Woody Allen, "My Speech to the Graduates," in *Side Effects* (New York: Random House, 1980), p. 57.

144. See Berger, *Death Penalties*, pp. 1–76; Walter Berns, *For Capital Punishment: Crime and the Morality of the Death Penalty* (New York: Basic Books, 1979), p. 31.

145. Compare, e.g., Grannuci, "'Nor Cruel and Unusual Punishments Inflicted,'" p. 865 (arguing that the framers intended to prohibit barbarous punishments but not disproportionately severe punishments); O'Neil v. Vermont, 144 U.S. 323, 339–40 (1892) (Field, J., dissenting) (contending that the framers intended to prohibit grossly excessive as well as torturous punishments); David A. J. Richards, "Interpretation and Historiography," *Southern California Law Review*

58 (1985), pp. 506–15 (arguing that the framers intended to constitutionalize an abstract concept of cruel punishment).

146. Cf. Kay, "Adherence to the Original Intentions," pp. 289–91. Cf. also Dworkin, *Law's Empire,* p. 365.

147. See, e.g., Tushnet, *Red, White, and Blue,* pp. 32–45; Laurence H. Tribe, "On Reading the Constitution," *Utah Law Review,* 1988 (1988), pp. 755–56; Chemerinsky, *Interpreting the Constitution,* pp. 50–51.

148. For a classic discussion of this theme, see Cardozo, *The Nature of the Judicial Process.*

149. See, e.g., Brennan, "The Constitution of the United States," p. 438; Chemerinsky, *Interpreting the Constitution,* pp. 52–56.

150. See Sotirios A. Barber, "*The Federalist* and the Anomalies of New Right Constitutionalism," *Northern Kentucky Law Review* 15 (1988), p. 445.

151. See Moore, "A Natural Law Theory of Interpretation," pp. 393–96.

152. Cf. Sotirios A. Barber, *On What the Constitution Means* (Baltimore: The Johns Hopkins University Press, 1984), p. 10; Perry, *Morality, Politics, and Law,* pp. 133–51.

153. Brennan, "The Constitution of the United States," p. 433.

154. See, e.g., Bork, "Original Intent and Constitution," pp. 26–27; Wolfe, *The Rise of Modern Judicial Review* p. 57; William Bradford Reynolds, "*The Burger Years:* A Critical Look at the Critics' Intent," *Northwestern University Law Review* 82 (1988), p. 821; Stephen J. Markman, "Interpretation and Non-Interpretation," *Benchmark* 3 (1987), p. 219n. 1. See also *Original Meaning Jurisprudence,* p. 16.

155. 347 U.S. 483 (1954) (holding that segregated public education violates the constitutional guarantee of equal protection).

156. 404 U.S. 71 (1971) (the first major case in which gender discrimination was held to violate the Equal Protection Clause).

157. For attempts to justify *Brown* on moderate intentionalist grounds, see, e.g., Bork, *The Tempting of America,* pp. 81–82; Reynolds, "*The Burger Years,*" p. 821; *Original Meaning Jurisprudence,* p. 51. For an argument that *Reed* is consistent with original intent, see Bork, *The Tempting of America,* pp. 319–20.

158. See Lester B. Orfield, *The Amending of the Federal Constitution* (Ann Arbor: University of Michigan Press, 1942), pp. 153–54. Article V also provides for proposal of amendments by a national convention, convened at the request of two-thirds of the states. This method of proposing amendments has never been used. In addition, at Congress's discretion, proposed amendments may be submitted for ratification to special state constitutional conventions rather than to state legislatures. This mode of ratifying amendments has been used only for the Twenty-first Amendment (repealing the Eighteenth). For simplicity, I ignore these alternate procedures for proposal and ratification.

159. See, e.g., Kay, "Adherence to the Original Intentions," p. 246. Cf. Perry, *Morality, Politics, and Law,* p. 124.

160. An often overlooked implication of this argument is that the intent of the president is entitled to some weight in originalist statutory interpretation. Cf. Eskridge, "The New Textualism," p. 633.

161. See, e.g., Bork, *The Tempting of America,* p. 144; Monaghan, "Stare Decisis and Constitutional Adjudication," p. 725; *Original Meaning Jurisprudence,* p. 16.

162. See Monaghan, "Stare Decisis and Constitutional Adjudication," p. 725; Epstein, *Takings,* p. 26.

163. See Bork, *The Tempting of America,* p. 144.

164. Cf. Scalia, *Address by Justice Antonin J. Scalia,* pp. 4–6.

165. See p. 27.

166. In a detailed exposition, a public-understanding originalist would need to specify just who "the people" are for purposes of his theory. One theory identifies "the people" with qualified American *voters.* See Cooley, *Treatise on Constitutional Limitations*, p. 38; H. C. Black, *Handbook on American Constitutional Law*, 3d ed. (St. Paul, Minn.: West Publishing Co., 1910), p. 30. Another view identifies them with American *citizens,* whether enfranchised or not. See, e.g., Dred Scott v. Sanford, 60 U.S. (19 How.) 393, 404 (1856); Edward S. Corwin, *The Constitution and What It Means Today,* 13th rev. ed. (Princeton, N.J. : Princeton University Press, 1974), p. 1. A third theory, supported by nineteenth-century abolitionists, identifies the American people with all permanent inhabitants of the United States. See Jacobus ten Broeck, *The Antislavery Origins of the Fourteenth Amendment* (Berkeley: University of California Press, 1951), p. 87. In a few cases, it might make a difference which of these views a public-meaning originalist accepts. For example, non-Garrisonian abolitionists regularly argued that slavery was unconstitutional, in part because it violated the Article IV requirement that the United States "guarantee to every State in this Union a Republican Form of Government." See William M. Wiecek, *The Sources of Antislavery Constitutionalism in America, 1760–1848* (Ithaca, N.Y.: Cornell University Press, 1977), pp. 119–22. If eighteenth-century blacks, both free and slave, were indeed entitled to an intention vote, this reading of the original meaning of the clause may well have been correct.

As noted earlier (see p. 154, n. 87), many public-understanding originalists qualify their commitment to the original "public" understanding by limiting intention votes to those members of the public who are "informed" or "knowledgeable." See, e.g., Scalia, *Address by Justice Antonin J. Scalia,* p. 3. Something like this qualification is clearly needed, since the Constitution is full of technical and quasi-technical terms drawn from the common law. But how does one determine who is sufficiently "informed"? Article VI declares that all federal laws made "in Pursuance" to the Constitution shall be the supreme law of land. Highly informed Americans presumably knew that in the leading dictionary of the day, Samuel Johnson's, "pursuant to" meant "in consequence of." See Edward S. Corwin, *Court Over Constitution: A Study of Judicial Review as an Instrument of Popular Government* (Princeton, N.J.: Princeton University Press, 1938), p. 35; Crosskey, *Politics and the Constitution*, II, pp. 991–92. But most of the Founders apparently were not that well informed: they seem to have thought that "pursuant to" meant "consistent with." See Raoul Berger, *Congress Versus the Supreme Court* (Cambridge, Mass.: Harvard University Press, 1969), pp. 229–36. Which of these readings should public-meaning originalists treat as authoritative?

167. Even textualists, however, cannot completely avoid summing problems, since many constitutional terms have more than one literal meaning, and textualists must decide which of these multiple meanings a "typical" literalist of the day would have understood the terms to express.

168. Cf. C. J. Antieau, *Constitutional Construction* (New York: Oceana Publications, Inc., 1982), pp. 76–78.

169. Cf. p. 155, n. 89.

170. Article 1, section 9, provides that "[n]o bill of attainder . . . shall be passed [by Congress]"; the following section extends the same prohibition to the states.

171. A "bill of attainder," at common law, was "a legislative conviction for alleged crime, with judgment of death." Cooley, *Treatise on Constitutional Limitations*, p. 316. Legislative acts decreeing lesser penalties were known as "bills of pains and penalties." Ibid., p. 218. As early as 1810 (see Fletcher v. Peck, 10 U.S. (6 Cranch) 87, 132 (1810)), the Court declared (in dicta) that bills of attainder, for federal constitutional purposes, were not limited to legislative sentences of death. There is some evidence that this accorded with the framers' intent. See Dennis J. Mahoney, "Bill of Attainder," in Kurland and Lerner, *Encyclopedia of the American Constitution,* I, p. 112.

172. Currently, there are four leading interpretations of the intended meaning of the Privileges or Immunities Clause. One view holds that it was meant only to protect a limited range of civil rights—those enumerated in the Civil Rights Act of 1866—against state infringement. See Berger, *Government by Judiciary,* pp. 208–9. A second view is that it was designed to make applicable to the states all and only the provisions of the Bill of Rights. See Adamson v. California, 332 U.S. 46, 74 (1947) (Black, J., dissenting); Duncan v. Louisiana, 391 U.S. 145, 166 (1968) (Black, J., concurring). A third theory holds that it was intended to protect the "fundamental" or "natural" rights of citizens of the United States, thus incorporating some but not all of the provisions of the Bill of Rights. See ten Broeck, *The Antislavery Origins of the Fourteenth Amendment,* pp. 218–20; Antieau, *The Original Understanding of the Fourteenth Amendment*, p. 28. Finally, some historians argue that the clause was designed to incorporate all of the provisions of the Bill of Rights *plus* other, unspecified, "fundamental" rights. See Curtis, *No State Shall Abridge,* pp. 113–20. The one view almost nobody seriously defends is that adopted in the Slaughter-House Cases, 83 U.S. (16 Wall.) 36 (1872), and never subsequently overruled: that the clause protects only those few rights that belong to citizens of the United States *as such*, i.e., rights that bear peculiarly on a citizen's relationship to the national government, such as the right of access to federal buildings and courts, the right to travel to the seat of national government, and the right to share in the benefits of a national postal system.

173. For a list of the states that ratified the Fourteenth Amendment (some of which later sought to withdraw that consent), see Nowak, Rotunda, and Young, *Constitutional Law,* p. 1124.

174. See p. 10.

175. This is particularly true of the Bill of Rights. The House debates on

these amendments survive (albeit in garbled form), but the debates in the Senate and in the twelve ratifying states are wholly missing. See Levy, *Original Intent and the Framers' Constitution,* pp. 292–94. For most later amendments, including the Fourteenth, surviving records of the state ratifying legislatures are typically much scantier than the surviving records of congressional debates and reports. See Ely, *Democracy and Distrust,* p. 17; Antieau, "Constitutional Construction," p. 363.

176. See, generally, Levy, *Original Intent and the Framers' Constitution*, pp. 284–99.

177. For instance, no records survive of the Senate debates on the Bill of Rights because the Senate met in secret session from 1789 to 1794. See Levy, *Original Intent and the Framers' Constitution,* p. 292.

178. In 1796, Washington sent a message to the House, then embroiled in debate over Jay's Treaty, in which he argued that the Constitution vests the treaty-making power solely in the president and the Senate. He clinched his argument by citing a passage from the official *Journal* of the Convention, which showed that the delegates had considered and rejected a proposition "that no Treaty should be binding on the United States which was not ratified by a law." This *Journal*, however, had never been published; it remained in Washington's custody from 1787 to 1796, and was under seal at the State Department from 1796 until 1818, when Congress ordered its publication. See Levy, *Original Intent and the Framers' Constitution,* p. 12. Commenting on Washington's resort to the *Journal* in the 1796 debate, Justice Scalia writes (*Address by Justice Antonin Scalia*, p. 6):

> Although George Washington did write a wonderful letter to the Jewish Community of Newport, Rhode Island, it is not recorded that he was familiar with the word "chutzpah." The above quoted message, however, relying upon documentation that only he and his administration knew about, since it was under seal at the State Department, suggests that he had some grasp of the substance of the thing.

179. See, e.g., p. 133, n. 21.

180. See, e.g., Madison's letter to Nicholas P. Trist (Dec. 1831), reprinted in *The Writings of James Madison,* ed. by Gaillard Hunt, 9 vols. (New York: Putnams, 1900–1910), IX, p. 477, where he writes:

> Another error has been in ascribing to the *intention* of the *Convention* which formed the Constitution, an undue ascendancy in expounding it. Apart from the difficulty of verifying that intention[,] it is clear, that if the meaning of the Constitution is to be sought out of itself, it is not in the proceedings of the Body that proposed it, but in those of the State Conventions which gave it all the validity & authority it possesses.

This letter was written in 1831, four years after Jonathan Elliot began publishing his *Debates in the Several State Conventions on the Adoption of the Federal Constitution,* rev. ed., 5 vols. (Philadelphia: J. B. Lippincott Co., 1836–1845), which for the first time made readily available the records of the five state ratifying conventions in which more than skeletal records were preserved. See Levy, *Original Intent and the Framers' Constitution,* pp. 289–91. However, Madison had expressed a similar view well before Elliot's *Debates* appeared. See, e.g., Letter from Madison to Thomas Ritchie (Sept. 15, 1821), reprinted in *The Writings of James Madison,* IX, p. 72.

181. Cf. also Rhode Island v. Massachusetts, 37 U.S. (12 Pet.) 657, 721 (1838) (endorsing resort to the intent of the Philadelphia Framers as a touchstone of correct constitutional interpretation, despite the fact that the only reasonably accurate and full record of the Convention debates, James Madison's *Notes of Debates in the Federal Convention,* would not be published for another two years).

182. For expressions of this view during the founding era, see Wood, *The Creation of the American Republic,* pp. 527–36. For later expressions, see Orfield, *The Amendment of the Federal Constitution,* pp. 141–42.

183. "He who acts through another acts himself." *Black's Law Dictionary,* p. 1413.

184. *The Federalist* No. 10 (Madison), p. 62.

185. See Maltz, "Foreword," p. 803.

186. Cf. Alfred Avins, "Preface," in *The Reconstruction Amendments' Debates: The Legislative History and Contemporary Debates in Congress on the 13th, 14th, and 15th Amendments,* ed. by Alfred Avins (Richmond: Virginia Commission on Constitutional Government, 1967), n.p.

187. See p. 5.

188. See William N. Eskridge, Jr., and Philip P. Frickey, *Cases and Materials on Legislation: Statutes and the Creation of Public Policy* (St. Paul, Minn.: West Publishing Co., 1988), p. 29.

189. Cf. Kay, "Adherence to the Original Intentions," p. 246. I deliberately state the view in oversimplified form. Complications would need to be added to handle acts of lawmaking unauthorized by prior existing law, such as when a new political system is established by force or by other extraconstitutional means.

190. See, e.g., Remarks of Rep. Roger Sherman (Aug. 13, 1789), quoted in Joseph Gales and W. W. Seaton, comps., *The Debates and Proceedings of the Congress of the United States (Annals of Congress)*, 42 vols. (Washington D.C.: Gales & Seaton, 1834–56), I, p. 708 ("The Constitution is the act of the people. . . . But the amendments will be the act of the State Governments").

191. See, e.g., *The Federalist* No. 39 (Madison), p. 254.

192. See, e.g., Story, *Commentaries on the Constitution* (5th ed.), I, p. 264.

193. Indeed, I have been unable to locate a single explicit discussion of the issue during the founding period. What little indirect evidence there is points in both directions. Compare, e.g., Remarks of Rep. Roger Sherman, quoted on p. 62 (n. 190), with James Madison, "Report on the Virginia Resolutions," (1800), reprinted in Kurland and Lerner, *The Founders' Constitution,* V, pp. 142–43 (arguing that the "most satisfactory and authentic proof" that the Free Press Clause is "a denial to Congress of all power over the press" is a statement by *Congress* that the clause, like the rest of the Bill of Rights, was intended to be "restrictive" or merely "declaratory" of existing Federal powers).

194. See pp. 69–71.

195. See, generally, Richard S. Kay, "The Illegality of the Constitution," *Constitutional Commentary* 4 (1987), pp. 57–80.

196. Marbury v. Madison, 5 U.S. (1 Cranch) 137, 176 (1803).

197. Rhode Island, rightly suspecting that the Convention would be hostile to debtor-relief legislation, declined to attend. See Samuel Eliot Morison, *The Oxford History of the American People* (New York: Oxford University Press, 1965), p. 305.

198. See Thomas A. Bailey and David M. Kennedy, *The American Pageant: A History of the Republic*, 7th ed. (Lexington, Mass.: D. C. Heath and Co., 1983), p. 130.

199. In February 1787, Congress issued a call for a federal convention for "*the sole and express purpose of revising* the Articles of Confederation." Max Farrand, ed., *The Records of the Federal Convention*, 4 vols. (New Haven, Conn.: Yale University Press, 1911), III, p. 13 (emphasis added). Some of the delegates, it should be noted, were under explicit instructions to agree only to *revisions* of the Articles. See Jackson Main Turner, *The Antifederalists: Critics of the Constitution, 1781–1788* (New York: W. W. Norton and Co., 1974), p. 126, n. 26.

200. *Annals of Congress*, V, p. 776. See also *The Federalist* No. 40, p. 264 (Madison); Farrand, *Records of the Federal Convention,* I, p. 295 (remarks of A. Hamilton); ibid., p. 253 (remarks of J. Wilson).

201. See, generally, Farber, "The Originalism Debate," pp. 1087–89.

202. See, generally, Antieau, "Constitutional Construction," pp. 360–63.

203. Cf. Berger, "'Original Intention' in Historical Perspective," p. 132.

204. See, generally, Beard, *An Economic Interpretation of the Constitution,* pp. 73–151.

205. To be precise, eight Senators and seven House members had been among the signers. Compare Saul K. Padover, ed., *The Living U.S. Constitution*, rev. ed. (New York: The New American Library, 1968), p. 43 (listing the thirty-nine signers) with Merrill Jensen, Robert A. Berker, and Gordon DenBoer, eds., *The Documentary History of the First Federal Elections, 1788–1790*, 3 vols. to date (Madison: University of Wisconsin Press, 1976–), I, pp. xxv–xxvi (listing the members of the First Congress).

206. See pp. 69–71.

207. For more on the notion of a contingently self-defeating set of propositions, see p. 182, n. 8.

CHAPTER 4

1. Powell, "The Original Understanding of Original Intent," *Harvard Law Review* 98 (1985), pp. 885–948.

2. Dworkin, "The Bork Nomination," p. 3, n. 1 (arguing that "the origi-

nal intention theory appears to be self-defeating, because there is persuasive historical evidence that the framers intended that their own interpretations of the abstract language they wrote should not be regarded as decisive in court").

3. Tushnet, "The U.S. Constitution and the Intent of the Framers," p. 219 (contending that originalists appear to be "caught in a contradiction," because they want "courts to do what the framers intended, but the framers intended that courts should ignore their intentions").

4. See, e.g., Macedo, *The New Right v. the Constitution*, pp. 16–17; Chemerinsky, *Interpreting the Constitution*, p. 63; John Arthur, *The Unfinished Constitution: Philosophy and Constitutional Practice* (Belmont, Calif.: Wadsworth Publishing Co., 1989), p. 6.

5. See, e.g., Berger, "'Original Intention' in Historical Perspective," pp. 101–42; Lofgren, "The Original Understanding of Original Intent?" pp. 77–115; Clinton, "Original Understanding, Legal Realism, and the Interpretation of 'This Constitution,'" pp. 1186–1220; Kay, "Adherence to the Original Intentions," pp. 273–81.

6. See, generally, pp. 2–4. Powell does not deny that the framers expected courts to employ traditional common-law techniques of legal interpretation in construing the Constitution. Nor does he deny that the cardinal rule of common-law hermeneutics was that legal instruments were to be construed in accordance with their original intent. He argues, however, that when common lawyers spoke of the original "intent" of a legal text, they referred not to any subjective meaning its framers wished to communicate, but rather to the meaning that interpreters were warranted in *deriving* from the text employing the "artificial reason and judgment of law," i.e., traditional techniques of legal interpretation. Powell, "The Original Understanding of Original Intent," p. 896 (quoting Prohibitions del Roy, 12 Co. Rep. 63, 65, 77 Eng. Rep. 1342, 1344 (1608)). Powell claims that the Constitution's framers accepted this view of original "intent," and thus held that the canonical meaning of constitutional provisions was not "something locked into the text by its author[s]" (ibid., p. 899), but was instead a product of a correctly conducted interpretive process. Ibid., pp. 902–24. However, as Berger and others have shown, Powell reaches this conclusion largely by relying on two time-honored techniques of "law-office history": selective quotation and selective presentation of relevant evidence. Powell's incredible assertion, for example, that "[p]olitical and legal scholars in both Britain and the American colonies viewed strict judicial adherence to the legislature's language as a constitutional necessity" (ibid., p. 898) is supportable only if one completely ignores (as Powell does) the entire tradition of equitable interpretation.

7. In 1839, Francis Lieber (*Legal and Political Hermeneutics*, pp. 139–40) wrote that if "the subject to which the text relates [is] of that elementary, vital and absorbing importance to society, that every other interest, or consideration, must yield; . . . we are obliged to regulate our decision rather by the meaning which the words would now have considering things and circumstances as they now exist, than by the known meaning which the utterer attached to

them." This is the earliest clear rejection of originalism by an American legal theorist or jurist I have found.

8. To describe a proposition, or set of propositions, as "self-defeating" or "self-refuting" is scarcely self-explanatory. In a well-known article ["Self-Refutation—A Formal Analysis," *The Philosophical Quarterly* 14 (1964), pp. 193–203], J. L. Mackie helpfully distinguishes three senses in which a proposition may be self-refuting. *Absolutely self-refuting* propositions (e.g., "It can be proved that nothing can be proved") refute themselves by being either directly self-contradictory or logically entailing their contradictories. *Pragmatically self-refuting* propositions are refuted by certain facts that are given in and by the assertion of the proposition. "I am not speaking loudly," spoken loudly, is an example of this second type of self-refutation. Finally, a proposition is *operationally self-refuting* if it is falsified by any attempt to assert it. Examples of this third type of self-refutation include: "I do not exist" and "No sentences are intelligible." Unfortunately, none of these senses of "self-refuting" seems to capture the sense in which critics claim that intentionalism is self-refuting. Very loosely, their claim seems to be this: that intentionalists are *committed* to formally contradictory statements owing to certain unanticipated *contingent* features of reference. Claims that suffer from this infirmity I shall term *contingently self-defeating*. There are myriad ways in which a claim, or set of claims, can be contingently self-defeating. If I assert, for example, speaking attributively, both "The murderer of Smith is a dunce" and "The assailant of Jones is a genius," I am committed to contingently self-defeating claims if, unknown to me, the murderer of Smith and the assailant of Jones are the same man. Cf. Keith Donnellan, "Reference and Definite Descriptions," *Philosophical Review* 75 (1966), pp. 281–304. Likewise, if I assert "Whatever *S* says is true," my assertion is contingently self-defeating if, as it turns out, one of the things *S* says is "Sometimes I lie." Finally, if I believe that I should do whatever *S* wants, my belief is contingently self-defeating if I later learn that one of the things *S* wants is that I *not* always do as *S* wants. The argument that intentionalism is self-refuting most closely resembles this last example.

9. G. E. M. Anscombe, *Intention*, 2d ed. (Ithaca, N.Y.: Cornell University Press, 1963), p. 18. There is an extensive philosophical literature on the various uses or senses of the term "intention" and its cognates. For a recent critical discussion, see J. David Velleman, *Practical Reflection* (Princeton, N.J.: Princeton University Press, 1989), pp. 109–42. Much of this literature bears at most tangentially on the debates over original "intent." As we have seen, when originalists speak of original "intent" or of the "intentions" of the framers, this is often shorthand for notions such as the intended, understood, or textual meaning or scope of constitutional provisions. For this reason, work by philosophers of language and literary theorists is often of more relevance to the originalism debate than is philosophical work in the theory of agency.

10. See p. 23.

11. See Edward S. Corwin, *The President: Office and Powers, 1787–1957*, 4th rev. ed (New York: New York University Press, 1957), p. 34.

12. Thomas Hart Benton, quoted in Neal R. Peirce and Lawrence N. Longley, *The People's President: The Electoral College and the Direct Vote Alternative*, rev. ed. (New Haven, Conn.: Yale University Press, 1981), p. 96.

13. Ray v. Blair, 343 U.S. 214, 232 (1952) (Jackson, J., dissenting) (upholding party loyalty pledges for candidates for presidential elector).

14. Moore, "Semantics of Judging," p. 262. Traditionally, courts have been reluctant to inquire into the "motives" which may have influenced a lawmaking body to enact a law. See, generally, Tribe, *American Constitutional Law*, pp. 302–3 and accompanying citations; Ely *Democracy and Distrust,* pp. 136–38. However, courts have also traditionally held that it is often proper to inquire into the "purposes" that underlie legislative enactments. See Antieau, *Constitutional Construction,* pp. 23–24. Distinctions along these lines are of considerable antiquity. See Schmidt, *Principles of Authentic Interpretation*, p. 143 (noting that the distinguished fourteen–century jurist Baldus de Ubaldis held that "the *causa finalis* serves for the purposes of interpreting a law while a mere motivating cause [*causa impulsiva*] cannot be used to this end"). Very crudely, as Anscombe explains [*Intention,* p. 18], the difference seems to amount to this: an agent's purpose "is what he aims at or chooses; his motive is what determines the aim or choice." Thus, if a state legislature, thoroughly corrupted by bribery, enacts a law authorizing the sale of huge tracts of state-owned land, it might be said that while the (primary) *purpose* of the law was simply to sell the land, the (primary) *motive* was personal greed. Cf. Fletcher v. Peck, 10 U.S. (6 Cranch) 87 (1810). However, both in ordinary usage and in law, the distinction between motives and purposes is often obscure. For example, if a city council passes an ordinance banning motor vehicles from a local park, a search of the legislative history might reveal that the primary "intent" of the ordinance was to reduce noise in the park. Should we classify this "intent" as a legislative purpose or as a legislative motive? Would it matter if we added that the park was primarily used by affluent whites and that most of the vehicular noise was believed to be caused by clunkers driven by blacks coming from a nearby ghetto?

15. See, classically, Beard, *An Economic Interpretation of the Constitution*. For influential criticisms of Beard's view, see Robert E. Brown, *Charles Beard and the Constitution: A Critical Analysis of "An Economic Interpretation of the Constitution"* (Princeton, N.J.: Princeton University Press, 1956); Forrest McDonald, *We the People: The Economic Origins of the Constitution* (Chicago: Chicago University Press, 1956).

16. See, e.g., Berger, "New Theories of 'Interpretation,'" p. 43; Berger, "Constitution Law and the Constitution," *Suffolk University Law Review* 19 (1985), p. 11.

17. See, e.g., Bork, *The Tempting of America*, pp. 154, 177.

18. See Kay, "Adherence to the Original Intentions," p. 259.

19. See Maltz, "Foreword," p. 800.

20. See, generally, p. 24.

21. See p. 137, n. 47. Many liberal constitutional scholars argue that the Ninth Amendment, which provides that "[t]he enumeration in the Constitution

of certain rights shall not be construed to deny or disparage others retained by the people," is a *textual* affirmation of the principle that there are judicially enforceable fundamental rights that are neither expressly nor impliedly embodied in the written Constitution. See, e.g., Grey, "Do We Have an Unwritten Constitution?" p. 716; Ely, *Democracy and Distrust,* pp. 34–41; Levy, *Original Intent and the Framers' Constitution,* pp. 278–79; Randy E. Barnett, "Reconceiving the Ninth Amendment," *Cornell Law Review* 74 (1988), pp. 1–42. See, generally, Randy Barnett, ed., *The Rights Retained by the People: The History and Meaning of the Ninth Amendment* (Fairfax, Va.: George Mason University Press, 1989). For a powerful critique of this liberal reading, see Thomas B. McAffee, "The Original Meaning of the Ninth Amendment, " *Columbia Law Review* 90 (1990), pp. 1215–320. If these liberal scholars are correct, originalists are probably committed to enforcing the amendment in the sense and spirit intended. (I say "probably" because it is not *obviously* true that judges have any business attempting to enforce the amendment if, as many originalists believe, either there are no natural rights or judges have no reliable way of knowing what those rights are. Cf. Ely, *Democracy and Distrust,* p. 39; Barnett, "The Ninth Amendment Reconceived," pp. 27–29.) It is worth noting, however, that even if this liberal reading of the amendment is correct, originalists can sharply limit its scope by noting that it was originally understood to apply only to the federal government; that the framers of the Fourteenth Amendment probably did not intend to make the Ninth Amendment applicable to the states; and that no Supreme Court decision has ever held that the Ninth is "incorporated" by the Fourteenth.

22. See p. 63.

23. See p. 134, n. 26. See also Sanford B. Gabin, *Judicial Review and the Reasonable Doubt Test* (Port Washington, N.Y.: Kennikat Press, 1980), p. 4; and Levy, *Original Intent and the Framers' Constitution,* p. 375.

24. The traditional view has been that "[r]ules of interpretation are not imperative like the mandatory provisions of law," unless expressly provided by legislative or constitutional enactment. Thomas M. Cooley, quoted in Black, *Handbook on the Construction of Laws,* p. 9.

25. See, generally, Raoul Berger, *Impeachment: The Constitutional Problems* (Cambridge, Mass.: Harvard University Press, 1973), pp. 122–80.

26. It might be argued that originalism is self-defeating in a more obvious way, namely, that certain of the framers' *substantive* intentions are mutually inconsistent. See, e.g., Tribe, "On Reading the Constitution," pp. 765–76 (arguing that the Constitution embodies no unitary or fully coherent normative vision); Dworkin, *A Matter of Principle,* pp. 48–55 (suggesting that the framers typically had *both* abstract and concrete intentions and that these often pull in different directions). This is an important objection, which highlights the need for originalists to develop what I term "supplementary rules": rules designed to provide guidance to judges in cases in which the framers' intent is undiscoverable, inapplicable, inconsistent, or trumped by other considerations (e.g., by deeply rooted precedent). See pp. 89–90 for more on such rules. Since nothing in my subsequent argument turns on the choice of supplementary rules to handle cases of conflicting intentions, I shall not pursue the issue here.

27. See Dworkin, *Taking Rights Seriously*, pp. 134–36.

28. See Brink, "Legal Theory," pp. 111–24.

29. See, e.g., Moore, "The Semantics of Judging," pp. 202–70; "A Natural Law Theory of Interpretation," pp. 285–358; "The Constitution as Hard Law," *Constitutional Commentary* 6 (1989), pp. 62–66.

30. The distinction between concepts and conceptions was not invented by Dworkin, but was borrowed from the work of contemporary philosophers. See, especially, W. B. Gallie, "Essentially Contested Concepts," *Proceedings of the Aristotelian Society* 56 (1955–56), pp. 167–98; Rawls, *A Theory of Justice*, pp. 5, 10. A related set of distinctions, between abstract "standards" and "principles" on the one hand, and concrete "concepts" and "rules" on the other, had long been familiar to lawyers through the work of Roscoe Pound. See, e.g., Pound, "Hierarchy of Sources and Forms in Different Systems of Law," *Tulane Law Review* 7 (1933), pp. 482–86. Cf. Bruncken, "Interpretation of the Written Law," p. 137; Corwin, "Judicial Review in Action," pp. 664–68; John Dickinson, *Administrative Justice and the Supremacy of Law in the United States* (Cambridge, Mass.: Harvard University Press, 1927), pp. 128–50; G. W. Paton, *A Textbook of Jurisprudence* (Oxford: Clarendon Press, 1946), pp. 176–81; Hart and Sacks, *The Legal Process*, pp. 155–58; Hart, *The Concept of Law*, pp. 127–30.

31. See, e.g., Lyons, "Constitutional Interpretation and Original Meaning," pp. 85–87; Macedo, *The New Right v. the Constitution*, p. 14; Barber, *On What the Constitution Means*, p. 117; Richards, "Interpretation and Historiography," pp. 506–9; Tribe, "On Reading the Constitution," p. 753.

32. National Mutual Insurance Co. v. Tidewater Transfer Co., 337 U.S. 582, 646 (1949) (Frankfurter, J., dissenting). Cf. Cardozo, *The Nature of the Judicial Process*, p. 17 ("The great generalities of the Constitution have a content and a significance that vary from age to age"); Wallace Mendelson, *Justices Black and Frankfurter: Conflict in the Court* (Chicago: University of Chicago Press, 1961), p. vii, (suggesting that certain constitutional terms, such as "due process of law," "doubtless were designed to have the chameleon capacity to change their color with changing moods and circumstances").

33. See, e.g., Corwin, "Moratorium Over Minnesota," pp. 313–14; Willard Hurst, "Discussion," in Edmond Cahn, ed., *Supreme Court and Supreme Law* (New York: Greenwood Press, 1968; first published 1954), p. 60; Miller, *The Supreme Court and the Uses of History*, pp. 151–69; William J. Brennan, Jr., "Landmarks of Legal History," in Bernard Schwartz, ed., *The Fourteenth Amendment: Centennial Volume* (New York: New York University Press, 1970), p. 9.

34. See, e.g., Rochin v. California, 342 U.S. 165, 175–77 (1952) (Black, J., concurring); Hugo Black, *A Constitutional Faith* (New York: Knopf, 1969), pp. 11–14.

35. See, e.g., Griswold v. Connecticut, 381 U.S. 479, 514–16 (1965) (Black, J., dissenting); Rehnquist, "The Notion of a Living Constitution," pp. 702–4; Bork, The *Tempting of America*, p. 225.

36. See, e.g., Dworkin, *Taking Rights Seriously*, p. 136.

37. See, e.g., Dworkin, *Law's Empire*, p. 398.

38. I owe this term to Chemerinsky, *Interpreting the Constitution*, p. 75. Notice that conceptualism, in the sense specified, is a purely descriptive claim. It should not be confused with moderate originalism, which is a normative theory of adjudication.

39. Compare, e.g., Tushnet, *Red, White, and Blue*, p. 30 (treating conceptualism as consistent with originalism), and Kay, "Adherence to the Original Intentions," p. 259 (treating conceptualism as an objection to originalism).

40. See, e.g., Dworkin, *Law's Empire*, pp. 348–50, 388.

41. See, e.g., Dworkin, *A Matter of Principle*, p. 53; Richards, "Interpretation and Historiography," pp. 506–7.

42. See, e.g., Richards, "Interpretation and Historiography," pp. 507–8. Cf. Bickel, "The Original Understanding and the Segregation Decision," p. 61. The quoted language is from McCulloch v. Maryland, 17 U.S. (4 Wheat.) 316, 415 (1819) (Marshall, C.J.) (italics in original).

43. The leading early case is Adair v. United States, 208 U.S. 161 (1908) (striking down a federal law prohibiting interstate railroads from discharging an employee for union membership). Eleven years earlier, in Allgeyer v. Louisiana, 165 U.S. 578 (1897), the court had applied a substantive due process analysis to the Fourteenth Amendment's Due Process Clause.

44. Nebbia v. New York, 291 U.S. 502, 525 (1934).

45. Palko v. Connecticut, 302 U.S. 319, 325–26 (1937) (Cardozo, J.). Cf. Bowers v. Hardwick, 478 U.S. 186, 191 (1986).

46. Snyder v. Massachusetts, 291 U.S. 97, 105 (1934) (Cardozo, J.). Cf. Moore v. East Cleveland, 431 U.S. 494, 503 (1977) (Powell, J.); Michael H. v. Gerald D., 109 S. Ct. 2333, 2341 (1989) (plurality opinion).

47. See, e.g., Hamilton, *The Papers of Alexander Hamilton*, IV, 35 ("The words 'due process' have a precise technical import, and are only applicable to the process and proceedings of the courts of justice; they can never be referred to an act of the legislature"); Story, *Commentaries on the Constitution*, 4th ed, II, p. 547 (The Due Process Clause "in effect affirms the right of trial according to the process and proceedings of the common law"); Edward Corwin, "The Doctrine of Due Process of Law Before the Civil War," *Harvard Law Review* 24 (1911), pp. 372–73; W. W. Willoughby, *The Constitutional Law of the United States*, 2d ed., 3 vols. (New York: Baker, Voorhis and Co., 1929), III, pp. 1688–89; Crosskey, *Politics and the Constitution*, II, pp. 1102–10; Ely, *Democracy and Distrust*, 14–21; Levy, *Original Intent and the Framers' Constitution*, p. 273. Cf. Berger, *Government by Judiciary*, p. 197 (arguing that the framers understood "due process" to require only that "the appropriate *writ* be used to summon the accused before the court to answer the complaint against him," quoting Keith Jurow, "Untimely Thoughts: A Reconsideration of the Origins of Due Process of Law," *American Journal of Legal History* 19 (1975), at 267 (emphasis added)). For dissenting views, see Cooley, *Treatise on Constitutional Limitations*, pp. 433–34; Rodney L. Mott, *Due Process of Law* (Indianapolis: Bobbs-Merrill, 1926), pp. 141–42.

48. Charles P. Curtis, "Review and Majority Rule," in *Supreme Court and Supreme Law*, p. 177.

49. The clause provides: "Congress shall make no law ... abridging the freedom of speech, or of the press."

50. Schenck v. United States, 249 U.S. 47, 52 (1919) (Holmes, J.).

51. Chaplinsky v. New Hampshire, 315 U.S. 568, 568 (1942). As Tribe notes (*American Constitutional Law*, pp. 791–92), the Court has evolved a different and less "absolutist" test for governmental regulations that are not aimed at suppressing speech or expressive conduct, but do have an incidental suppressive impact. According to this "test," "the 'balance' between the values of freedom of expression and the government's regulatory interests is struck on a case-by-case basis, guided by whatever unifying principles may be articulated." Tribe, *American Constitutional Law*, p. 792. For examples of such "balancing," see United States v. O'Brien, 391 U.S. 367 (1968) (upholding a congressional ban on draft card burning); Heffron v. International Society for Krishna Consciousness, 452 U.S. 640 (1981) (upholding a state regulation limiting distribution of printed materials at a state fair to certain fixed locations).

52. James Madison, "Report on the Virginia Resolutions" (1799), reprinted in Kurland and Lerner, *The Founders' Constitution,* V, p. 143.

53. The best-known modern-day defender of this "absolutist" reading is of course Justice Hugo Black. See, e.g., Black, *A Constitutional Faith*, pp. 43–63. Leonard Levy, the foremost contemporary historian of the First Amendment, basically agrees with Black that the "framers meant Congress to be totally without power to enact legislation" respecting speech and press. Levy, *Emergence of a Free Press* (New York: Oxford University Press, 1985), p. 270. However, Levy traces this absolute prohibition not to the Free Speech Clause (which the framers understood narrowly, he argues), but rather to the framers' background assumption, later given explicit constitutional expression in the Tenth Amendment, that Congress could exercise only enumerated powers. Ibid., pp. 269–73.

54. See John Marshall, "Report of the Minority on the Virginia Resolution" (1799), reprinted in Kurland and Lerner, *The Founders' Constitution*, V, p. 138 ("In fact, the liberty of the press is a term which has a definite and appropriate signification, completely understood. It signifies a liberty to publish, free from previous restraints, anything and everything at the discretion of the printer only, but not the liberty of spreading with impunity false and scandalous slanders which may destroy the person and mangle the reputation of an individual or of a community"). See also Story, *Commentaries on the Constitution* (5th ed.), II, p. 635.

55. James Wilson, Remarks at the Pennsylvania Ratifying Convention (1787), quoted in Levy, *Emergence of a Free Press*, p. 204.

56. Ely, *Democracy and Distrust,* p. 58.

57. Perry, *The Constitution, the Courts, and Human Rights,* p. 70.

58. Tushnet, *Red, White, and Blue*, p. 31. For an elaboration of this claim, see pp. 79–82.

59. See, e.g., Wood, *The Creation of the American Republic,* pp. 298–305; Berger, *Government by Juciciary*, pp. 300–311; Morton J. Horwitz, *The Transformation of American Law, 1780–1860* (Cambridge, Mass.: Harvard University Press, 1977), pp. 4–5, 12–15.

60. Stephen P. Schwartz, "Introduction," in Schwartz, ed., *Naming, Necessity, and Natural Kinds* (Ithaca, N.Y.: Cornell University Press, 1977), pp. 15–16.

61. For representative statements of description theories, see Locke, *An Essay Concerning Human Understanding*, bk. 3, chaps. 2–10; Frege, "On Sense and Reference," pp. 57–58; Bertrand Russell, *The Problems of Philosophy* (New York: Oxford University Press, 1959; 1st publ., 1912), pp. 54–59; C. I. Lewis, *An Analysis of Knowledge and Evaluation* (Lasalle, Ill.: Open Court, 1946), pp. 39–48; Rudolph Carnap, *Meaning and Necessity: A Study in Semantics and Modal Logic*, 2d ed. (Chicago: University of Chicago Press, 1956), pp. 233–43; Alonzo Church, *Introduction to Mathematical Logic I* (Princeton, N.J. : Princeton University Press, 1956), pp. 3–9; Leonard Linsky, *Names and Descriptions* (Chicago: University of Chicago Press, 1977), pp. 66–111; Michael Dummett, *Frege: Philosophy of Language* (Cambridge, Mass.: Harvard University Press, 1981), pp. 110–51; Irving Copi, *Introduction to Logic*, 6th ed. (New York: Macmillan, 1982), pp. 154–58.

62. Standard, or classical, description theories typically view the meaning of a word as a *conjunction* of properties or descriptions, each of which is necessarily instantiated or satisfied by its referents. See Hilary Putnam, "Is Semantics Possible?" reprinted in Putnam, *Philosophical Papers II: Mind, Language, and Reality* (Cambridge: Cambridge University Press, 1975), p. 140. By contrast, "cluster" description theories hold that the meaning of a word is typically a cluster of descriptions and that a word refers to whatever object or objects, if any, most of these descriptions (or the most important of them) pick out. For influential statements of cluster theories, see John Searle, "Proper Names," *Mind* 68 (1958), pp. 161–73; P. F. Strawson, *Individuals* (London: Metheun, 1959), pp. 180–83, 190–94. Cf. Wittgenstein, *Philosophical Investigations*, pp. 36–38. For a justly famous critique of cluster theories, see Saul Kripke, *Naming and Necessity* (Cambridge, Mass.: Harvard University Press, 1980), pp. 60–95.

63. I borrow this example from Devitt and Sterelny, *Language and Reality*, p. 68. Cf. Kripke, *Naming and Necessity*, p. 119.

64. See, especially, Kripke, *Naming and Necessity*; Kripke, "Speaker's Reference and Semantic Reference," in P. French, T. Uehling, and H. Wettstein, eds., *Contemporary Perspectives in the Philosophy of Language* (Minneapolis: University of Minnesota Press, 1979), pp. 6–27.

65. See, e.g., Donnellan, "Proper Names and Identifying Descriptions," in D. Davidson and G. Harman, eds., *Semantics of Natural Language* (Dordrecht: D. Reidel, 1972), pp. 356–79.

66. See, especially, Putnam, *Philosophical Papers II*, pp. 196–290.

67. See, e.g., Kaplan, "Demonstratives: An Essay on the Semantics, Logic, Metaphysics, and Epistemology of Demonstratives and Other Indexicals," in J. Almog, J. Perry, and H. Wettstein, eds., *Themes From Kaplan* (New York: Oxford University Press, 1989), pp. 481–563.

68. For lucid discussions of the major arguments, see Nathan Salmon, *Reference and Essence* (Princeton, N.J. : Princeton University Press, 1981), pp. 23–32; and Devitt and Sterelny, *Language and Reality*, pp. 41–53, 67–70.

69. See, e.g., Kripke, *Naming and Necessity*, p. 30; Salmon, *Reference and Essence*, pp. 24–25; Devitt and Sterelny, *Language and Reality*, p. 42.

70. See, e.g., Kripke, *Naming and Necessity*, pp. 74–75; Salmon, *Reference and Essence*, pp. 24–27; Schwartz, "Introduction," p. 23.

71. See, e.g., Putnam, *Philosophical Papers II*, pp. 197–202; and Brink, "Legal Theory," pp. 114–15. Cf. Devitt and Sterelny, *Language and Reality*, p. 41. For an extended argument against the traditional view of theoretical disagreement, see Dworkin, *Law's Empire*, pp. 45–86.

72. I am indebted to Brink, "Legal Theory," pp. 114–15, for this example.

73. Locke, *An Essay Concerning Human Understanding*, bk. 3, chap. 9, sec. 10.

74. Many commentators have noted that the causal theory, to date, is more of a program or a picture than a developed theory. See, e.g., Howard Wettstein, "Has Semantics Rested on a Mistake?" *Journal of Philosophy* 83 (1986), p. 192; Robert M. Martin, *The Meaning of Language* (Cambridge, Mass.: The MIT Press, 1987), pp. 173–74.

75. See Gregory McCulloch, *The Game of the Name: Introducing Logic, Language, and Mind* (Oxford: Clarendon Press, 1989), p. 101.

76. Kripke, for example, extends the theory to natural kind terms and to certain natural phenomena nouns and adjectives such as "heat" and "hot." See Kripke, *Naming and Necessity*, p. 134. Putnam extends the theory to natural kind nouns, physical magnitude terms such as "temperature," certain natural kind verbs, certain adjectives such as "red," certain artifact terms such as "pencil" and "pediatrician," and to "the great majority of all nouns." See Putnam, *Philosophical Papers II*, pp. 199–204, 242–45. For an extended argument that the theory applies to indexical terms (e.g., "this," "now," "I"), see Kaplan, "Demonstratives," pp. 498–500 and *passim*.

77. Cf. Kripke, *Naming and Necessity*, pp. 119–20; Putnam, *Philosophical Papers II*, p. 140.

78. See Kripke, *Naming and Necessity*, p. 120.

79. See, e.g., Devitt and Sterelny, *Language and Reality*, p. 69; Martin, *The Meaning of Language*, p. 198.

80. See Locke, *An Essay Concerning Human Understanding*, bk. 3, chap. 3, sections ll, 18.

81. See, e.g., Bork, *The Tempting of America*, p. 177; Sparf v. United States 156 U.S. 51, 169 (1895) (Gray, J., dissenting) (arguing that all questions of constitutional interpretation are, at bottom, historical questions). Cf. *The Federalist* No. 78 (Hamilton), p. 532 (arguing that under our constitutional scheme judges properly exercise "neither Force nor Will, but merely judgment").

82. Cf. Brink, "Legal Theory," p. 113 (distinguishing "conventionalistic" from "individualistic" versions of descriptivist semantics).

83. See pp. 47–50

84. See, e.g., Henry Monaghan, "The Constitution Goes to Harvard," *Harvard Civil Rights—Civil Liberties Law Review* 13 (1978), pp. 127–28; Robert Bork, "The Impossibility of Finding Welfare Rights in the Constitution," *Washington University Law Quarterly*, 1979 (1979), p. 697; Kay, "Adherence to the Original Intentions," pp. 263–73.

85. Consider, for example, how a realist judge might handle the issue of whether the unborn are "persons" within the meaning of the Equal Protection and Due Process Clauses. By framing this as a question of how the framers would have resolved the issue, Justice Blackmun, in his majority opinion in *Roe v. Wade* (410 U.S. 113, 157–58 (1973)), found the answer easy: the clauses do not extend to the unborn. But for a realist this is bound to be a much harder question. Since the framers did not intend the clause to embody any particular conception of "persons," but meant it, instead, to protect those entities that really are persons, judges should seek to determine the true scope of the clause by examining the best contemporary theories of the nature of persons. Cf. Moore, "A Natural Law Theory of Interpretation," p. 358. Unfortunately, however, there is now deep disagreement over the best theory of personhood. Cf., e.g., Michael Tooley, *Abortion and Infanticide* (Oxford: Clarendon Press, 1983), pp. 309–425 (arguing that neither fetuses nor newborn infants are persons) and Judith Jarvis Thomson, "A Defense of Abortion," *Philosophy and Public Affairs* 1 (1971), p. 47 (conceding that at least more developed fetuses are persons). To invite judges to apply a realistic analysis to constitutional and statutory provisions featuring the word "person" is thus likely to result both in considerable uncertainty (since it is difficult to predict how individual judges will resolve disputes hinging on the "real" referents of the term) and in considerable judicial activism (since "pro-life" judges will presumably strike down laws that, as currently construed, deny basic rights or equal protection to the unborn).

86. For a vigorous recent critique of causal semantics, see Bach, *Thought and Reference,* pp. 149–74.

87. See Munzer, "Realistic Limits on Realist Interpretation," *Southern California Law Review* 58 (1985), pp. 463–66.

88. One important difference is that normative language is often applied to objects that have little or nothing of significance in common. "[F]or one man calleth *wisdom,*" Hobbes said, "what another calleth *fear;* and one *cruelty*, what another *justice.*" Thomas Hobbes, *Leviathan* (New York: Macmillan, 1962; 1st ed., 1651), p. 40. A realist theory of moral kind terms, accordingly, must reject the standard explanation of reference grounding offered by causal theorists, which keys the reference of a term *N* to those things that "[the present speaker] and other speakers in my linguistic community have on other occasions *called*" *N.* Putnam, *Philosophical Papers II,* p. 225 (emphasis added). If a natural kind term is conventionally applied to two distinct kinds (as the term "jade" is commonly applied to both jadeite and nephrite), causal theorists can say, among other things, that "jade" "partially refers" to both kinds. See Michael Devitt, *Designation* (New York: Columbia University Press, 1981), pp. 194–95. But a moral realist obviously does not wish to say that *both* race-conscious and race-blind employment policies are just, even though the term "just" is widely applied to both. He thus needs to develop an account of moral reference grounding and borrowing that permits reference to real moral properties independently of actual applications of moral language. But, in principle, I see no reason why this should not be possible.

89. McCulloch v. Maryland, 17 U.S. (4 Wheat.) 316, 415 (1819) (Marshall, C.J.).

90. Moore, "A Natural Law Theory of Interpretation," p. 322 (emphasis omitted).

91. See p. 186, n. 47.

92. See p. 187, n. 54.

93. Cf. Land, *From Signs to Propositions*, p. 13.

94. See Wills, *Inventing America*, p. 171.

95. Locke's notorious claim that "morality is capable of demonstration, as well as mathematics" (*Essay*, 4.12.8) is premised on the view that because moral notions are *constructed* by us, their content is, in principle, completely knowable (*Essay*, 4.4.7). For a comprehensive discussion of Locke's moral views, see John Colman, *John Locke's Moral Philosophy* (Edinburgh: Edinburgh University Press, 1983).

96. Locke, *An Essay Concerning Human Understanding*, bk. 3, chap. 3, sec. 12.

97. Ibid., bk. 3, chap. 3, sec. 15. See also bk. 3, chap. 10, sec. 19.

98. Ibid., bk. 3, chap. 3, sec. 13.

99. Ibid., bk. 3, chap. 2, sec. 2.

100. Ibid., bk. 3, chap. 3, sec. 15.

101. Moore, "A Natural Law Theory of Interpretation," p. 324.

102. Thus, Kripke (*Naming and Necessity*, p. 118):

> Could we discover that gold was not in fact yellow? Suppose an optical illusion was prevalent, due to the peculiar properties of the atmosphere in South Africa and Russia and certain other areas where gold mines are common. Suppose there were an optical illusion which made the substance appear to be yellow; but, in fact, once the peculiar properties of the atmosphere were removed, we would see that it is actually blue. Maybe a demon even corrupted the vision of all those entering the gold mines (obviously their *souls* were already corrupt), and thus made them believe that this substance is yellow, though it is not. Would there on this basis be an announcement in the newspapers: "It has turned out that there is no gold . . . ?" . . . It seems to me that there would be no such announcement. On the contrary, what would be announced would be that though it appeared that gold was yellow, in fact gold has turned out not to be yellow, but blue. The reason is, I think, that we use "gold" as a term for a certain *kind* of thing. . . . The kind of thing is *thought* to have certain identifying marks. Some of these marks may not really be true of gold.

103. See, generally, Nelson Goodman, *Fact, Fiction and Forecast*, 4th ed. (Cambridge, Mass.: Harvard University Press, 1983), pp. 1–27. See also Chemerinsky, *Interpreting the Constitution*, pp. 77–78; Eskridge and Frickey, "Statutory Interpretation as Practical Reasoning," pp. 329–30.

104. At common law, individual "liberty" was often defined narrowly, as "the power of loco-motion, of changing situation, or removing one's person to

whatsoever place one's own inclination may direct; without imprisonment or restraint, unless by due course of law." Blackstone, *Commentaries,* p. 133. For classic arguments that state and federal due process clauses were originally understood to enact this narrow common-law conception of liberty, see Charles E. Shattuck, "The True Meaning of the Term 'Liberty' in Those Clauses in the Federal and State Constitutions Which Protect 'Life, Liberty, and Property,'" *Harvard Law Review* 4 (1891), pp. 365–92; Charles Warren, "The New 'Liberty' Under the Fourteenth Amendment," *Harvard Law Review* 39 (1926), pp. 431–65.

105. See p. 58. The term "establishment of religion" is an example of how the meaning of a common–law term might be modified in response to uniquely American conditions and experiences. The American experience of religious tolerance and pluralism made it unthinkable, by 1791, for any state to "establish" any religious denomination in the robust sense in which the Anglican church was the established religion in England. Each of the six states that then retained religious "establishments" had so-called multiple establishments, in which not one but several or all (Christian) denominations received state aid on a nonpreferential basis. Leonard Levy concludes from this and other evidence that the term "establishment of religion" had, by 1791, "come to mean government support, primarily financial, for religion generally, without legal preference for any church." Levy, *Original Intent and the Framers' Constitution*, p. 185. For a contrasting view, see Cord, *Separation of Church and State*, pp. 11–15 and *passim.*

106. See, e.g., Stephen P. Schwartz, "Natural Kinds and Nominal Kinds," *Mind* 89 (1980), p. 184; Devitt and Sterelny, *Language and Reality,* p. 78. Significantly, Moore contends that the causal theory *does* extend to technical or specially defined legal terms (e.g., "malice," "death," "contract"). See Moore, "A Natural Law Theory of Interpretation," pp. 328–38. In at least many cases, however, as Stephen Munzer points out (Munzer, "Realistic Limits on Realist Interpretation," p. 461), this claim is clearly unsustainable. Consider the Treason Clause of the Federal Constitution: "Treason against the United States shall consist only in levying war against them, or in adhering to their enemies, giving them aid and comfort. No person shall be convicted of treason unless on the testimony of two witnesses to the same overt act, or on confession in open court." Art. III, sec. 3. History leaves little doubt that the framers would have been aghast at the suggestion that judges could properly treat this definition as a "conventional gloss," which is "provisional and hostage to a deeper theory about the nature of the thing to which the words refer." Moore, "A Natural Law Theory of Interpretation," p. 337. For historical background on the Treason Clause, see Bradley Chapin, *The American Law of Treason: Revolutionary and Early National Origins* (Seattle: University of Washington Press, 1964).

107. See pp. 48–49.

108. The clause reads, "No Person held to Service or Labour in one State, under the Laws thereof, escaping into another, shall, in Consequence of any Law or Regulation therein, be discharged from such Service or Labour, but shall be delivered up on Claim of the Party to whom such Service or Labour may be due." Art. IV, sec. 2. In opposition to abolitionist arguments that the clause, as part of a presumptively antislavery Constitution, should be read as applying

only to apprentices and other persons bound to service for a limited period, Justice Story wrote: "Historically, it is well known that the object of this clause was to secure to the citizens of the slaveholding States the complete right and title of ownership in their slaves, as property, in every State in the Union into which they might escape from the State where they were held in servitude." Prigg v. Pennsylvania, 41 U.S. (16 Pet.) 539, 609 (1842).

109. The best evidence of this is the shockingly inadequate procedural guarantees accorded putative runaway slaves in the Fugitive Slave Act of 1793. See, generally, Thomas D. Morris, *Free Men All: The Personal Liberty Laws of the North, 1780–1861* (Baltimore: The Johns Hopkins University Press, 1974), pp. 19–22. Relevant, too, is the fact that, by congressional acquiescence, slaves in Washington D.C. in the 1790s were governed by the law of slavery then in effect in Maryland, which provided few criminal or civil procedural protections for slaves. See, generally, Daniel J. Flanigan, "Criminal Procedure in Slave Trials in the Antebellum South," *Journal of Southern History* 40 (1974), pp. 537–64. Moreover, state courts regularly construed generally phrased state constitutional protections as being inapplicable to slaves. See, e.g., Hudgins v. Wright, 11 Va. (1 Hen. & M.) 133, 141 (Va. 1806) (opinion of Tucker, J.) (holding that the Free and Equal Clause in the Virginia Constitution, which declared that "all men are by nature equally free," "was meant to embrace the case of free citizens, or aliens only; and not by a side wind to overturn" the right of chattel slavery.) Cf. Thomas R. R. Cobb, *An Inquiry into the Law of Slavery in the United States* (New York: Negro Universities Press, 1968; 1st publ., 1858), p. 91 (noting that, as construed in most slave states, "[s]tatutory enactments never extend to or include the slave . . . unless specifically named, or included by necessary implication").

110. Scott v. Sandford, 60 U.S. (19 How.) 393, 572–76 (1856) (Curtis, J., dissenting).

111. Art. III, sec. 2.

112. *Dred Scott,* pp. 416–18.

113. The clause reads, "The Citizens of each State shall be entitled to all Privileges and Immunities of Citizens in the several States." Art. IV, sec. 2.

114. Standardly, courts have understood the Privileges and Immunities Clause as having the limited purpose of "relieving state citizens of the disabilities of alienage in other States and of inhibiting discriminatory legislation against them by other States." Paul v. Virginia, 75 U.S. (8 Wall.) 168, 180 (1869). Since free blacks were barred from even *setting foot* in many Southern states in the early national period, a strong case can be made that Taney's reading of the clause was correct. For discussions of the legal disabilities of free blacks in antebellum America, see Leon Litwack, *North of Slavery: The Free Negro in the Free States, 1790–1860* (Chicago: University of Chicago Press, 1961); Ira Berlin, *Slaves Without Masters: The Free Negro in the Antebellum South* (New York: Panther Books, 1974).

115. Moore, "A Natural Law Theory of Interpretation," p. 341.

116. See pp. 48–49.

117. See pp. 3–5.

118. See pp. 5–7.

119. In 1862, by overwhelming majorities, Congress passed legislation abolishing slavery in the federal territories. See Don E. Fehrenbacher, *The Dred Scott Case: Its Significance in American Law and Politics* (New York: Oxford University Press, 1978), p. 575. Remarkably, in the congressional debates over the bill, not a single representative or senator even mentioned that just six years before, in Scott v. Sandford, 60 U.S. (19 How.) 393 (1856), the Supreme Court had expressly declared that Congress had no such power. Ibid.

120. Cf. Moore, "A Natural Law Theory of Interpretation," p. 322. Moore's example involves an apparent drowning victim whose organs doctors wish to transplant but whom relatives allege to be revivable through new medical procedures.

121. Const. amend. XXV, sec. 4.

122. See Karen Grandstrand Gervais, *Redefining Death* (New Haven, Conn.: Yale University Press, 1986), p. 1. Cf. *Black's Law Dictionary,* p. 488 (defining "death" as "[t]he cessation of life; the ceasing to exist; defined by physicians as a total stoppage of the circulation of the blood, and cessation of the animal and vital functions consequent thereon, such as respiration, pulsation, etc.").

123. Moore, "A Natural Law Theory of Interpretation," p. 323.

124. President's Commission for the Study of Medicine and Biomedical and Behavioral Research, *Defining Death: A Report on the Medical, Legal and Ethical Issues in the Determination of Death* (1981), p. 73, quoted in Gervais, *Redefining Death,* p. 198.

125. *A Discourse Upon the Exposition and Understanding of Statutes,* ed. by S. E. Thorne (San Marino, Calif.: Huntington Library, 1942), p. 151.

126. See p. 140, n. 65.

127. Moore, "Semantics of Judging," p. 265.

128. Ibid., p. 266.

129. Ibid.

130. See, e.g., ibid, pp. 266–68; Tushnet, "The U.S. Constitution and the Intent of the Framers," p. 221; Chemerinsky, *Interpreting the Constitution,* p. 51. Cf. Sunstein, "Interpreting Statutes in the Regulatory State," pp. 427, 433.

131. Actually, as we shall see, three, since mixed theories are possible.

132. Dickerson, *The Interpretation and Application of Statutes,* p. 37.

133. See p. 35.

134. See p. 53.

135. See p. 10.

136. For discussions, see Comment, "The Privileges or Immunities Clause," pp. 147–48; Dworkin, *Law's Empire,* p. 320; Brest, "The Misconceived Quest for the Original Understanding," p. 214; MacCallum, "Legislative Intent," pp. 777–80.

137. Farber, "The Originalism Debate," p. 1093.

138. See p. 53.

139. See, generally, Eskridge and Frickey, *Cases and Materials on Legisla-*

tion, p. 31; Lief Carter, *Reason in Law,* 3d ed. (Glenview, Ill.: Scott, Foresman, and Co., 1988), pp. 80–81; MacCallum, "Legislative Intent," p. 783.

140. See, e.g., Federal Energy Administration v. Algonquin SNG, Inc., 426 U.S. 548, 564 (1976); National Association of Greeting Card Publishers v. U.S. Postal Service, 462 U.S. 810, 832n. 28 (1983). Cf. Dworkin, *Law's Empire,* p. 342.

Notice, however, that agency theories do not really solve the problem of summing intentions but merely push it back a step. This is because there is usually more than one legislator whose intentions are viewed as authoritative, and there is no guarantee that these legislators' intentions will coincide.

141. For example, in the debate over whether the Fourteenth Amendment was intended to incorporate the Bill of Rights, the fact that an incorporationist reading was clearly endorsed by both Representative John Bingham, the principal author of the amendment, and Senator Jacob Howard, the floor manager in the Senate, has generally not been regarded as decisive. See, generally, Berger, *Government by Judiciary,* pp. 134–156; Fairman, "Does the Fourteenth Amendment Incorporate the Bill of Rights?" pp. 5–139.

142. See Carl Van Doren, *The Great Rehearsal: The Story of the Making and Ratifying of the Constitution of the United States* (New York: Viking Press, 1948), pp. 27, 159.

143. See p. 175, n. 158.

144. A few states do require approval by supermajorities in one or both legislative bodies. Such schemes were upheld in Dyer v. Blair, 390 F. Supp. 1291 (N.D. Ill. E.D. 1975).

145. Brest, "The Misconceived Quest for the Original Understanding," p. 214.

146. See p. 53.

147. Article VII reads, "The Ratification of the Conventions of nine States, shall be sufficient for the Establishment of this Constitution between the States so ratifying the Same."

148. See, generally, *The Federalist,* pp. 296–98 (No. 43) (Madison). Cf. Akhil Reed Amar, "Philadelphia Revisited: Amending the Constitution Outside Article V," *University of Chicago Law Review* 55 (1988), pp. 1043–1104 (arguing that the framers believed that popular majorities have an inalienable right to alter or abolish existing governmental arrangements, even in ways not expressly provided for by law).

149. Ibid., p. 296.

150. See Blaise Pascal, *Pensees* (London: J. M. Dent & Sons, 1932), No. 233, p. 67 (arguing that it is rational to "wager" that God exists, despite the fact that there is no conclusive evidence that He does, because "[i]f you gain, you gain all; if you lose, you lose nothing").

151. Bork, *The Tempting of America,* p. 163. See also Comment, "The Privileges or Immunities Clause," p. 148 (noting that "[t]he majority model can in practice be applied only in a rather 'impressionistic' form").

152. See p. 152, n. 58 and accompanying text.

153. See, e.g., Perry, *Morality Politics, and Law*, p. 131 (suggesting that, "[g]iven originalism's democratic premises, presumably an originalist judge should resolve whatever doubt remains, after her historical inquiry is finished, in favor of the governmental action whose constitutionality is at issue").

154. See, e.g., Bork, *The Tempting of America*. p. 166 ("A provision whose meaning cannot be ascertained is precisely like a provision that is written in Sanskrit or is obliterated past deciphering by an ink blot. No judge is entitled to interpret an ink blot on the ground that there must be something under it").

155. It should be noted, however, that my account does not permit judges to enforce just *any* proposition as the originally intended reading of a provision; only readings receiving votes on at least some "intention ballots" are eligible. If we wished, of course, this eligibility requirement could be tightened even further by, say, permitting only the top two or three vote-getters to compete at the "run-off" stage of our voting procedure.

156. Space does not permit a discussion of numerous matters of detail that would need to be addressed in a full-scale theory of constitutional intention voting. For example: Should we count the intention votes of states that ratified a provision after the provision was adopted? (If we do, we may find that the meaning of the Constitution *changes* as late returns come in. Some of these returns may be *very* late: Massachusetts, Connecticut, and Georgia did not ratify the Bill of Rights until 1939. Levy, *Original Intent and the Framers' Constitution,* p. 171.) Again, should we count the intention-votes of states *coerced* into ratifying a provision—as the Southern states were coerced into ratifying the Fourteenth Amendment by the threat of continued military occupation? See, generally, Ferdinand F. Fernandez, "The Constitutionality of the Fourteenth Amendment," *Southern California Law Review* 39 (1966), pp. 378–407. Should the views of *opponents* of adopted provisions be given at least some weight? Should added weight be given to the intention votes of the *Framers* to prevent their votes from being swamped by the much greater voting strength of the ratifiers? Finally, and most importantly, what role, if any, should traditional interpretive "presumptions" (presumptions against absurdity, inconsistency, injustice, departure from the "popular" meanings of words, etc.) play in a theory of intention voting? For more on such presumptions, see Black, *Handbook on the Construction of Laws,* pp. 17–44.

157. 337 U.S. 582 (1949).

158. This was because three Justices concluded that Article III, but not Article I, confers this power; while two found that Article I, but not Article III, provides the needed warrant. The four remaining Justices took the view that no such power exists.

159. This is "Arrow's theorem," the most striking discovery of public choice theory. For discussions, see Willian H. Riker, *Liberalism Against Populism: A Confrontation Between the Theory of Democracy and the Theory of Social Choice* (Prospect Heights, Ill.: Waveland Press, 1982), pp. 115–36; Frank Easterbrook, "Ways of Criticizing the Court," *Harvard Law Review* 95 (1982), pp. 814–31; Farber and Frickey, "Legislative Intent and Public Choice," pp. 423–69.

160. Brest, "The Misconceived Quest for the Original Understanding," p.

221. Cf. Hand, *The Bill of Rights,* p. 34 ("[I]t would be fatuous to attempt imaginatively to concoct how the founding Fathers would have applied [the Bill of Rights] to the regulation of a modern society").

161. It might be found, for example, that the relevant general purposes and structural considerations *themselves* conflict. (Such conflicts are likely at the level of highly abstract purposes. See, generally, Dworkin, *Law's Empire*, pp. 176–275.) Even in this case, however, originalist judges should probably try to reconcile these conflicts by weighing these competing purposes in accordance with original values before throwing in the towel and turning to nonoriginal values.

162. Kay, "Adherence to the Original Intentions," p. 255. These "explicit rules," as Kay makes clear in a letter to the author, need not be *textually* explicit. Rather, any constitutional rule is "explicit" so long as the balance of historical evidence suggests that the framers intended to enact it. I am grateful to Professor Kay for this clarification of his argument.

163. Ibid., p. 256.

164. Ibid.

165. Ibid., p. 257.

166. For more on these and other perplexities connected with Article V conventions, see Laurence Tribe, "Issues Raised by Requesting Congress to Call a Constitutional Convention to Propose a Balanced Budget Amendment," *Pacific Law Journal* 10 (1979), pp. 627–40.

167. See, e.g., Charles Black, "The Proposed Amendment of Article V: A Threatened Disaster," *Yale Law Journal* 72 (1963), p. 964 (noting that "neither text nor history can give any real help" in answering such questions). For a determined effort to tease more positive conclusions out of the meager historical record, see Russell L. Caplan, *Constitutional Brinksmanship: Amending the Constitution by National Convention* (New York: Oxford University Press, 1988).

168. Kay's "back-up" rules may also result in certain strongly counterintuitive results. Imagine, for example, that the available evidence suggests that the framers never arrived at an agreed view about which agency of the national government has the power to remove subordinate officials from office. (The text of the Constitution, oddly enough, is completely silent on the question.) In that case, Kay's first back-up rule comes into play: the agencies of the national government may only do those things that the Constitution affirmatively empowers them to do. But this implies, absurdly, that neither Congress, nor the president, nor any other federal official has the power to remove subordinate officials from office. This suggests that even in those cases in which Kay's back-up rules do succeed in removing an apparent "gap," the price of closure may be higher than we should pay.

169. See, e.g., *The Federalist* No. 37 (Madison), p. 236 ("All new laws, though penned with the greatest technical skill, and passed on the fullest and most mature deliberation, are considered more or less obscure and equivocal, until their meaning be liquidated and ascertained by a series of particular discussions and adjudications").

170. See, e.g., Story, *Commentaries on the Constitution*, I, p. 289, n. 1.

171. See, e.g., Lieber, *Legal and Political Hermeneutics*, pp. 139–40. Anyone inclined to doubt that the original understanding must sometimes give way in the face of unforeseeable national emergencies should consult J. G. Randall's magisterial study, *Constitutional Problems Under Lincoln*, rev. ed (Urbana: The University of Illinois Press, 1951).

172. See p. 184, n. 26. The expression "supplementary rules" is borrowed from Tushnet, "Following the Rules Laid Down," p. 794; Cf. Maltz, "Foreword," pp. 803–4. It should be noted, however, that I conceive of these rules a bit differently than they do.

CHAPTER 5

1. F. W. Maitland, "A Survey of the Century," in *The Collected Papers of Frederic William Maitland*, 3 vols. (Cambridge: Cambridge University Press, 1911), III, p. 439.

2. Paul Freund, *On Law and Justice* (Cambridge, Mass.: Harvard University Press, 1968), p. 165.

3. Cf. Perry, "The Legitimacy of Particular Conceptions of Constitutional Interpretation," p. 681.

4. See, generally, p. 5. See also Berger, "New Theories of 'Interpretation,'" p. 24; Walter Benn Michaels, "Response to Perry and Simon," *Southern California Law Review* 58 (1985), p. 678.

5. Kay, "Adherence to the Original Intentions," p. 289.

6. See, e.g., Bork, *The Tempting of America*, p. 6; Bond, *The Art of Judging*, p. 21; Wolfe, *The Rise of Modern Judicial Review*, pp. 333–34; Rehnquist, "The Notion of a Living Constitution," pp. 699–706; Berger, *Government by Judiciary*, p. 296. Cf. Ely, *Democracy and Distrust*, pp. 4–8.

7. See, generally, Beard, *An Economic Interpretation of the Constitution*. Blacks, women, and Indians, of course, were almost totally excluded from the framing and ratification process. Owing to property qualifications, so too were 25–35 percent of adult white males. See Donald S. Lutz, "Political Participation in Eighteenth-Century America," *Albany Law Review* 53 (1989), p. 335. As a result of voting restrictions and widespread public apathy, only about five percent of the population participated in the ratification process. See Chemerinsky, *Interpreting the Constitution*, p. 19. Of these participants, it is doubtful that a majority actually favored ratification. See Beard, *An Economic Interpretation of the Constitution*, p. 251. As Gordon Wood notes, the Federalist victory "was actually more of an Antifederalist default." Wood, *The Creation of the American Republic*, p. 486. The Federalists out-financed, out-hustled, and out-maneuvered their poorly organized but possibly more numerous opponents.

8. See, e.g., Chemerinsky, *Interpreting the Constitution*, p. 7; Brennan, "The Constitution of the United States," pp. 436–37; Perry, "The Authority of Text, Tradition, and Reason," pp. 577–78.

9. See, generally, pp. 45–47.

10. One notable possible exception is John Hart Ely's "representation-re-

inforcing" theory of judicial review, which directs judges to interpret open-ended constitutional provisions in ways designed to enhance democratic processes and full representation. See, generally, Ely, *Democracy and Distrust,* pp. 73–179. For critical discussions of Ely's theory, see, generally, "Symposium: Constitutional Adjudication and Democratic Theory," *New York University Law Review* 56 (1981), pp. 259–582; "Symposium: Judicial Review Versus Democracy," *Ohio State Law Review* 42 (1981), pp. 1–434; Laurence Tribe, "The Puzzling Persistence of Process-Based Constitutional Theories," *Yale Law Journal*, 89 (1980), pp. 1063–80; Tushnet, *Red, White, and Blue,* pp. 70–107; Chemerinsky, *Interpreting the Constitution*, pp. 14–17; Bork, *The Tempting of America,* pp. 194–99.

11. See pp. 2–3.

12. See, generally, *Corpus Juris Secundum*, XVI, pp. 70–75.

13. Grey, "Do We Have an Unwritten Constitution?" p. 705.

14. George Washington, *Writings,* ed. by J. Fitzpatrick, 39 vols. (Washington D.C.: Government Printing Office, 1940), XXXV, pp. 228–29.

15. Letter from Thomas Jefferson to William Carey Nicholas, Sept. 7, 1803, in *The Writings of Thomas Jefferson,* ed. by P. L. Ford, 10 vols. (New York: Putnam, 1892–99), VIII, p. 247.

16. *The Federalist* No. 78 (Hamilton), p. 522.

17. See, e.g., Brest, *Processes of Constitutional Decisionmaking*, p. 285 (noting that "the policy views dominant on the Court are never for long out of line with the policy views dominant among the lawmaking majorities of the United States"); Moore, "A Natural Law Theory of Interpretation," p. 393.

18. See, e.g., Berger, *Government by Judiciary*, p. 410 ("Respect for the limits on power are [*sic*] the essence of a democratic society; without it the entire democratic structure is undermined and the way is paved from Weimar to Hitler").

19. Hand, *The Bill of Rights,* p. 73.

20. See p. 148, n. 16.

21. Monaghan, "Our Perfect Constitution," p. 376.

22. *The Federalist* No. 78 (Hamilton), pp. 527–28.

23. See pp. 3–7.

24. Holmes, *Collected Legal Papers,* p. 139.

25. T. Alexander Aleinikoff, "Updating Statutory Interpretation," *Michigan Law Review* 87 (1988), p. 58 (emphasis added).

26. Powell, "Rules for Originalists," *Virginia Law Review* 73 (1987), p. 680.

27. Macedo, *The New Right v. the Constitution,* p. 101.

28. Perry, *Morality, Politics, and Law,* p. 131.

29. See p. 45.

30. See pp. 97–100.

31. Grey, "Do We Have an Unwritten Constitution?" p. 713.

32. See, e.g., *Original Meaning Jurisprudence,* p. 54.

33. See, e.g., Pervear v. Commonwealth, 72 U.S. (5 Wall.) 455 (1867); Wilkerson v. Utah, 99 U.S. 130 (1878); *In re* Kemmler, 136 U.S. 436 (1890).

These punishments included, for capital offenses, burning at the stake, boiling in oil, burial alive, drowning, death by pressing, and disembowelment followed by beheading and quartering. For noncapital offenses, various forms of bodily mutilation were common. See James Fitzjames Stephen, *A History of the Criminal Law of England,* 3 vols. (London: Macmillan, 1883), I, pp. 476–78.

34. 144 U.S. 323 (1892).

35. Ibid., pp. 339–41 (Field, J., dissenting).

36. See Weems v. United States, 217 U.S. 349 (1910).

37. See, e.g., Trop v. Dulles, 356 U.S. 86 (1958); Robinson v. California, 370 U.S. 660 (1962); Furman v. Georgia, 408 U.S. 238, 266 (1972) (Brennan, J., concurring).

38. Grannuci, "'Nor Cruel and Unusual Punishments Inflicted': The Original Meaning," *California Law Review* 57 (1969), pp. 839–65.

39. See especially Berger, *Death Penalties*, p. 174. But see Comment, "The Eighth Amendment, Beccaria, and the Enlightenment: An Historical Justification for *Weems v. United States*' Excessive Punishment Doctrine," *Buffalo Law Review* 24 (1975), pp. 783–838.

40. See, e.g., The Slaughter-House Cases, 83 U.S. (16 Wall.) 36 (1873); Cruikshank v. United States, 92 U.S. 542 (1875). See, generally, Stanley Morrison, "Does the Fourteenth Amendment Incorporate the Bill of Rights? The Judicial Interpretation," *Stanford Law Review* 2 (1949), pp. 140–73. For early judicial proponents of incorporation, see United States v. Hall, 26 F. Cas. 79 (C.C.S.D. Ala. 1871) (No. 15, 282); Hurtado v. California, 110 U.S. 516, 546 (1884) (Harlan, J., dissenting); O'Neil v. Vermont, 144 U.S. 323, 361 (1892) (Field, J., dissenting).

41. See, e.g., William D. Guthrie, *Lectures on the Fourteenth Article of Amendment to the Constitution of the United States* (Boston: Little, Brown, 1898), pp. 58–65; Horace Flack, *The Adoption of the Fourteenth Amendment* (Baltimore: The Johns Hopkins University Press, 1908), p. 94; Edward S. Corwin, *The Constitution and What It Means Today,* 8th ed. (Princeton N.J.: Princeton University Press, 1948), p. 181. See also John N. Pomeroy, *An Introduction to the Constitutional Law of the United States* (New York: Hurd & Houghton, 1868), p. 151; John W. Burgess, *Political Science and Comparative Constitutional Law,* 2 vols. (Boston: Ginn & Co., 1890), I, p. 226.

42. 332 U.S. 46, 68–123 (1947).

43. Fairman, "Does the Fourteenth Amendment Incorporate the Bill of Rights? The Original Understanding," *Stanford Law Review* 2 (1949), pp. 5–139.

44. See, e.g., Bickel, *The Least Dangerous Branch,* p. 102; Grey, "Do We Have an Unwritten Constitution?" pp. 711–12; Berger, *Government by Judiciary,* pp. 134–56; Dean Alfange, Jr., "On Judicial Policymaking and Constitutional Change: Another Look at the 'Original Intent' Theory of Constitutional Interpretation," *Hastings Constitutional Law Quarterly* 5 (1978), p. 607; Philip Kurland, "The Irrelevance of the Constitution: The Religion Clauses of the First Amendment," *Villanova Law Review* 24 (1978–79), pp. 9–10; Brest, "The Misconceived Quest for the Original Understanding," p. 224; Perry, *The Constitution, the Courts, and Human Rights,* p. 63; Posner, *The Federal Courts,* p. 194; Lino Graglia,

"'Constitutional Theory': The Attempted Justification for the Supreme Court's Liberal Political Program," *Texas Law Review* 65 (1987), p. 797.

45. See, e.g., Jacobus ten Broeck, *The Antislavery Origins of the Fourteenth Amendment* (Berkeley: University of California Press, 1951), pp. 196–98 (selective incorporation); Howard Jay Graham, "Our 'Declaratory' Fourteenth Amendment," *Stanford Law Review* 7 (1954), pp. 3–39 (selective incorporation); William W. Crosskey, "Charles Fairman, 'Legislative History,' and the Constitutional Limitations on State Authority," *University of Chicago Law Review* 22 (1954), pp. 1–143; Joseph B. James, *The Framing of the Fourteenth Amendment* (Urbana: University of Illinois Press, 1956), p. 197; Alfred Avins, "Incorporation of the Bill of Rights: The Crosskey-Fairman Debates Revisited," *Harvard Journal on Legislation* 6 (1968), pp. 1–26; Alfred H. Kelly and Winfred A. Harbison, *The American Constitution: Its Origin and Developments*, 4th ed. (New York: W.W. Norton, 1970), p. 463; Robert Kaczorowski, "Searching for the Intent of the Framers of the Fourteenth Amendment," *Connecticut Law Review* 5 (1972), pp. 368–98; Corwin, *The Constitution and What It Means Today,* 13th rev. ed. (Princeton N.J.: Princeton University Press, 1974), p. 387; Harold M. Hyman and William M. Wiecek, *Equal Justice Under Law: Constitutional Development*, 1835–75 (New York: Harper & Row, 1982), pp. 386–438.

46. Curtis, *No State Shall Abridge: The Fourteenth Amendment and the Bill of Rights* (Durham, N.C.: Duke University Press, 1986).

47. See William E. Nelson, *The Fourteenth Amendment: From Political Principle to Judicial Doctrine* (Cambridge, Mass.: Harvard University Press, 1988), p. 4 (noting that the incorporation debate is currently at an impasse). Cf. Ely, *Democracy and Distrust,* p. 25 ("people are coming to realize that this is an argument no one can win"); Leonard W. Levy, *Judgments: Essays on American Constitutional History* (Chicago: Quadrangle Books, 1972), p. 64 (suggesting that the evidence is ultimately "inconclusive"); Antieau, *The Original Understanding of the Fourteenth Amendment,* p. 40 (same).

48. See, e.g., Story, *Commentaries on the Constitution*, 4th ed., 3 vols. (Boston: Little, Brown, 1873), III, p. 606; Cooley, *A Treatise on Constitutional Limitations,* pp. 582–83.

49. There is some evidence, however, that the framers intended to permit the national government, within limits, to favor Christianity over non-Christian religions and Protestantism over Catholicism. See Douglas Laycock, "'Nonpreferential' Aid to Religion: A False Claim About Original Intent," *William and Mary Law Review* 27 (1986), p. 918–19; Tushnet, "The Origins of the Establishment Clause," pp. 1515–16. Originalist critics of current establishment clause doctrine, not surprisingly, tend to ignore this disturbing reminder of less tolerant times.

50. 330 U.S. 1 (1947).

51. Ibid., p. 16. (quoting Letter from Thomas Jefferson to Danbury Connecticut Baptist Association, Jan. 1, 1802, in *The Writings of Thomas Jefferson,* Lipscomb and Bergh, eds., XVI, p. 282).

52. Ibid., p. 15.

53. See, e.g., Leo Pfeffer, *Church, State, and Freedom*, rev. ed. (Boston:

Beacon Press, 1967), p. 149; C. Herman Pritchett, *The American Constitution,* 2d ed. (New York: McGraw-Hill, 1968), pp. 567–68; Bernard Schwartz, *A Commentary on the Constitution of the United States,* 5 vols. (New York: Macmillan, 1963–68), V, pp. 650–53. See also Zorach v. Clauson, 343 U.S. 306, 312 (1952); Abington School District v. Schempp, 374 U.S. 203, 222 (1963); Lemon v. Kurtzman, 403 U.S. 602, 612–13 (1971); Wallace v. Jaffree, 472 U.S. 38, 60 (1985). But see Edward Corwin, "The Supreme Court as a National School Board," *Law and Contemporary Problems* 14 (1949), pp. 3–22; James M. O'Neil, *Religion and Education Under the Constitution* (New York: Harper and Bros., 1949); Chester J. Antieau, James Downey, and Edward C. Roberts, *Freedom from Federal Establishment: Formation and Early History of the First Amendment's Religion Clause* (Milwaukee: Bruce Publishing Co., 1964); Mark DeWolfe Howe, *The Garden and the Wilderness: Religion and Government in American Constitutional History* (Chicago: University of Chicago Press, 1967), p. 26.

54. See, e.g., Walter Berns, *The First Amendment and the Future of American Democracy* (New York: Basic Books, 1976), p. 31; Michael J. Malbin, *Religion and Politics: The Intentions of the Authors of the First Amendment*; Cord, *Separation of Church and State*; Jaffree v. Board of School Commissioners of Mobile County, 554 F. Supp. 1104, 1113–18 (S. D. Ala. 1983); Wallace v. Jaffree, 472 U.S. 38, 113 (1985) (Rehnquist, J., dissenting); Meese, "Toward a Jurisprudence of Original Intent," p. 5; Martin Nussbaum, "A Garment for the Naked Public Square: Nurturing American Public Theology," *Cumberland Law Review* 16 (1985), p. 62; Michael McConnell, "Accommodation of Religion," *1985 Supreme Court Review* (1985), pp. 13–21; Rodney K. Smith, *Public Prayer and the Constitution: A Case Study in Constitutional Interpretation* (Wilmington, Del.: Scholarly Resources Inc., 1987), p. 116; Gerard V. Bradley, *Church-State Relationships in America* (Westport, Conn.: Greenwood Press, 1987).

55. See Thomas J. Curry, *The First Freedoms: Church and State in America to the Passage of the First Amendment* (New York: Oxford University Press, 1986); Leonard W. Levy, *The Establishment Clause: Religion and the First Amendment* (New York: Macmillan, 1986); Laycock, "'Nonpreferential' Aid to Religion," pp. 875–923; Leo Pfeffer, "The Establishment Clause: An Absolutist's Defense," *Notre Dame Journal of Law, Ethics, and Public Policy* 4 (1990), pp. 699–729.

56. See, generally, Levy, *Original Intent and the Framers' Constitution,* pp. 300–21; Miller, *The Supreme Court and the Uses of History;* Murphy, "Time to Reclaim," pp. 64–79; Kelly, "Clio and the Court," pp. 119–58; Wofford, "The Blinding Light," pp. 502–33; Powell, "Rules for Originalists," pp. 655–99; Richard Neely, *How Courts Govern America* (New Haven, Conn.: Yale University Press, 1981), p. 18 (remarking that people who take seriously the Supreme Court's "historical scholarship as applied to the Constitution also probably believe in the Tooth Fairy and the Easter Bunny").

57. Bickel, *The Least Dangerous Branch,* p. 102.

58. See, generally, Monaghan, "Stare Decisis and Constitutional Adjudication," pp. 727–39.

59. See p. 22.

60. See, generally, Ethan Bronner, *Battle for Justice: How the Bork Nomination Shook America* (New York: W. W. Norton, 1989); Michael Pertschuk and Wendy Schaetzel, *The People Rising: The Campaign Against the Bork Nomination* (New York: Thunder's Mouth Press, 1989).

61. Quoted in Patrick B. McGuigan and Dawn M. Weyrich, *Ninth Justice: The Fight for Bork* (Washington D.C.: Free Congress Research and Education Foundation, 1990), p. 14.

62. See ibid.; Bork, *The Tempting of America,* p. 268.

63. See p. 150, n. 41.

64. See Thompson v. Oklahoma, 487 U.S. 815, 864 (1988) (Scalia, J., dissenting).

65. See Margaret Radin,"The Jurisprudence of Death: Evolving Standards for the Cruel and Unusual Punishments Clause," *University of Pennsylvania Law Review* 126 (1978), p. 1031.

66. Ruffin v. Commonwealth, 62 Va. (21 Gratt.) 790, 796 (1871). See, generally, Ben M. Crouch and James W. Marquart, *An Appeal to Justice: Litigated Reform of Texas Prisons* (Austin: University of Texas Press, 1989), pp. 4–5.

67. See Berger, *Government by Judiciary,* pp. 161–63.

68. See Bork, *The Tempting of America,* pp. 62–67 (criticizing Skinner v. Oklahoma, 316 U.S. 535 (1942), in which the Court struck down a state law providing for the sterilization of habitual offenders).

69. See Bork, *The Tempting of America,* pp. 95–100 (criticizing Griswold v. Connecticut, 381 U.S. 479 (1965), which invalidated a state anticontraceptive law).

70. See Tribe, *American Constitutional Law,* p. 1161n. 25.

71. See Cooley, *Treatise on Constitutional Limitations,* pp. 407–8; William M. Beaney, *The Right to Counsel in American Courts* (Ann Arbor: University of Michigan Press, 1955), pp. 25–29.

72. See Bowers v. Hardwick, 478 U.S. 186, 192–94 (1986); Carter v. State, 500 S.W. 2d. 368 (Ark. 1973) (upholding an eight-year prison sentence for consensual homosexual sodomy).

73. See, e.g., Bradwell v. Illinois, 38 U.S. (16 Wall.) 130 (1872). But Cf. Nelson, *The Fourteenth Amendment*, p. 163.

74. See Bork, *The Tempting of America,* p. 83; Ely, *Democracy and Distrust,* pp. 32–33; Grey, "Do We Have an Unwritten Constitution?" p. 711 (each noting that Bolling v. Sharpe, 347 U.S. 497 (1954), which held that the Fifth Amendment Due Process Clause embodies an equal protection component, is illegitimate on originalist premises).

75. See p. 169, n. 76. See also Bernard Schwartz, *The New Right and the Constitution: Turning Back the Legal Clock* (Boston: Northeastern University Press, 1990), pp. 10–14.

76. See p. 169, n. 76.

77. See p. 169, n. 75. See also Monaghan, "Stare Decisis and Constitutional Adjudication," pp. 736–39.

78. See p. 169, n. 78.

79. See pp. 46–47.

80. See p. 22.

81. Monaghan, "Stare Decisis and Constitutional Adjudication," p. 744.

82. Ibid., pp. 744–45.

83. William Wordsworth, "The Solitary Reaper," in *The Poetical Works of William Wordsworth*, ed. by E. de Selincourt and Helen Darbishire, 5 vols. (Oxford: Clarendon Press, 1940–49), III, p. 77.

84. See Bork, *The Tempting of America,* p. 158.

85. See, generally, Abraham, *Freedom and the Court,* pp. 28–117.

86. See, generally, pp. 73–74.

87. See, generally, Tribe, *American Constitutional Law*, pp. 1302–1435. Cf. Bork, *The Tempting of America,* pp. 95–100, 110–26 (criticizing privacy cases).

88. See p. 142, n. 85.

89. See, generally, pp. 95–96; Schwartz, *The New Right and the Constitution,* pp. 14–17.

90. See, generally, Mapp v. Ohio, 367 U.S. 643 (1961); Potter Stewart, "The Origins, Development, and Future of the Exclusionary Rule in Search-and Seizure Cases," *Columbia Law Review* 83 (1983), pp. 1365–1404.

91. See, generally, Miranda v. Arizona, 384 U.S. 436 (1966); Liva Baker, *Miranda: Crime, Law and Politics* (New York: Atheneum, 1983).

92. Cf., generally Bork, *The Tempting of America,* pp. 111–16, and Laurence Tribe, *Abortion: the Clash of Absolutes* (New York: W. W. Norton & Co., 1990).

93. See, generally, Tribe, *American Constitutional Law,* pp. 904–28.

94. Cf., generally, Cord, *Separation of Church and State,* and Levy, *Original Intent and the Framers' Constitution,* pp. 174–94.

95. Cf., generally, Stanford v. Kentucky, 109 S. Ct. 2969, 2979–80 (1989)(opinion of Scalia, J.), and ibid., pp. 2982–88 (Brennan, J., dissenting).

96. See, generally, Igor Primoratz, *Justifying Legal Punishment* (Atlantic Heights, N.J.: Humanities Press International, 1989), pp. 111–43.

97. See, e.g., Andrew Von Hirsch, *Past or Future Crimes: Deservedness and Dangerousness in the Sentencing of Criminals* (New Brunswick, N.J.: Rutgers University Press, 1985), pp. 38–46.

98. Weems v. United States, 217 U.S. 349, 373 (1910).

99. See pp. 93–94.

100. Quoted in Wood, *The Creation of the American Republic,* p. 379.

101. Simon, "The Authority of the Framers," p. 1499.

102. See William A. Edmondson, "Book Review," *1984 Duke Law Review,* p. 628, n. 18.

103. Stephen Carter, "Constitutional Adjudication and the Indeterminate Text: A Preliminary Defense of an Imperfect Muddle," *Yale Law Journal* 94 (1985), p. 842.

104. Corwin, "Constitution Versus Constitutional Theory," p. 107.

105. Ibid., p. 108.

106. Bickel, *The Least Dangerous Branch,* p. 26.

107. See, generally, Kent Greenawalt, *Conflicts of Law and Morality* (New York: Oxford University Press, 1987), pp. 67–93.

108. See, generally, Amar, "Philadelphia Revisited," pp. 147–60.

109. Cf. Bork, *The Tempting of America,* pp. 170–71.

110. McCulloch v. Maryland, 17 U.S. (4 Wheat.) 316, 415 (1819).

111. See, generally, *The Federalist* No. 85 (Hamilton), pp. 590–95; Wood, *The Creation of the American Republic*, pp. 613–14.

112. See, generally, Levinson, *Constitutional Faith,* pp. 9–17.

113. Joseph Long, "Tinkering with the Constitution," *Yale Law Journal* 24 (1915), p. 580.

114. For a valuable discussion of this theme, see Chemerinsky, *Interpreting the Constitution,* pp. 36–40.

115. Brennan, "The Constitution of the United States," p. 433.

116. The Propeller Genesee Chief v. Fitzhugh, 53 U.S. (12 How) 433 (1851). One recent constitutional historian has described Chief Justice Taney's majority opinion in the case as "one of the most satisfying of all early constitutional opinions." Currie, *The Constitution in the Supreme Court*, p. 259. Cf. Bernard L. Steiner, *The Life of Roger Brooke Taney, Chief Justice of the United States Supreme Court* (Baltimore: Williams & Wilkins Co., 1922), p. 292 (calling the decision "Taney's most important contribution to jurisprudence").

117. See Carl B. Swisher, *The Taney Period* (New York: Macmillan, 1974), p. 443.

118. See, e.g., The Steamboat Thomas Jefferson, 22 U.S. (10 Wheat.) 428, 429 (1825); Steamboat Orleans v. Phoebus, 36 U.S. (11 Pet.) 175, 183 (1837). See, generally, Milton Conover, "The Abandonment of the 'Tidewater' Concept of Admiralty Jurisdiction," *Oregon Law Review* 38 (1958), p. 39.

119. *Genesee Chief,* 53 U.S. at 451–52.

120. Ibid., p. 448.

121. In particular, Taney seized on some ambiguous language in the Judiciary Act of 1789 to argue that the First Congress—and hence presumably the framers—had not understood the constitutional grant of admiralty jurisdiction as necessarily limited to tidewaters. See ibid., pp. 457–58. In this, Taney was clearly mistaken. See, generally, Note, Development of Admiralty Jurisdiction in the United States, 1789–1857," *Western New England Law Review* 8 (1986), p. 188. Significantly, even Justice Story, whose broad views on the scope of admiralty jurisdiction prompted one wag to remark that "if a bucket of water were brought into court with a corn cob floating in it, he would immediately extend the admiralty jurisdiction of the United States over it" (quoted in Grant Gilmore and Charles Black, *The Law of Admiralty* (Mineola, N.Y.: The Foundation Press, 1957), p. 32), acknowledged that the tidewater rule was implicit in the original understanding of the Admiralty Clause. See The Steamboat Thomas Jefferson, 22 U.S. (10 Wheat.) 428, 429 (1825).

122. *Genesee Chief,* 53 U.S. at 464–65 (Daniel, J., dissenting).

123. Ibid., p. 465.

124. Ibid.

125. Ibid.

126. See Note, "From Judicial Grant to Legislative Power: The Admiralty

Clause in the Nineteenth Century," *Harvard Law Review* 67 (1954), pp. 1221–23; Swisher, *The Taney Period*, pp. 427–28.

127. Something the Court had last done almost half a century before, in Marbury v. Madison, 5 U.S. (1 Cranch) 137 (1803).

128. *Genesee Chief,* 53 U.S. at 454.

129. Ibid.

130. See ibid.

131. See, generally, Schmidt, *Principles of Authentic Interpretation,* p. 143.

132. See, generally, Francisco Suárez, *A Treatise on Laws and God the Lawgiver,* in *Selections from Three Works of Francisco Suárez, S.J.* (Oxford: Clarendon Press, 1944), pp. 419–37.

133. Moore, "A Natural Law Theory of Interpretation," p. 393.

134. Rostow, *The Sovereign Imperative,* p. xxxiv.

135. Chambers v. Florida, 309 U.S 227, 241 (1940).

136. Perry, *The Constitution, the Courts, and Human Rights,* p. 91.

137. 347 U.S. 483 (1954).

138. See Chemerinsky, *Interpreting the Constitution,* pp. 69–70.

139. Quoted in Richard Kluger, *Simple Justice: The History of Brown v. Board of Education and Black America's Struggle for Equality* (New York: Vintage Books, 1975), p. 690.

140. Ibid., p. 709. But see Ely, *Democracy and Distrust,* p. 66.

141. The title of Richard Kluger's definitive history of *Brown*, cited immediately above.

142. See p. 175, n. 157.

143. See, e.g., Bork, *The Tempting of America,* p. 82; *Original Meaning Jurisprudence,* p. 51; Meese, "Construing the Constitution," p. 27; Cf. Siegan, *The Supreme Court's Constitution*, p. 93 (arguing that the Equal Protection Clause was originally understood to bar discriminatory state action with respect to fundamental or natural rights).

144. *Brown*, 347 U.S. at 495.

145. See Kluger, *Simple Justice*, p. 635.

146. See Berger, *Government by Judiciary*, p. 118.

147. Bork, *The Tempting of America,* p. 149.

148. Ibid., p. 144.

CHAPTER 6

1. Benjamin Cardozo, *The Nature of the Judicial Process* (New Haven, Conn.: Yale University Press, 1921), p. 36.

2. Benjamin Cardozo, *The Paradoxes of Legal Science* (New York: Columbia University Press, 1928), p. 8.

3. See Richard A. Posner, *Cardozo: A Study in Reputation* (Chicago: University of Chicago Press, 1990), p. 20.

4. Benjamin Cardozo, *The Growth of the Law* (New Haven, Conn.: Yale University Press, 1924); and Cardozo, *The Paradoxes of Legal Science.*

5. Cardozo, *The Nature of the Judicial Process*, p. 18.

6. There are, of course, some significant differences between common-law and constitutional adjudication. Perhaps the two most important are (1) the existence of an authoritative text in constitutional law and (2) the fact that mistaken constitutional decisions are not ordinarily subject to legislative correction.

7. A "broadly" pragmatic theory, as I use the term, is not committed to any particular theory of truth or meaning. What makes a legal theory "pragmatic," in my broad use of the term, is the importance it places on avoiding the vices of "excessive abstraction, unwarranted generalization, formalistic rigidity, [and] insensitivity to context." Steven B. Smith, "The Pursuit of Pragmatism," *Yale Law Journal* 100 (1990), p. 446.

8. Ibid., p. 173.

9. A foundationalist, as I use the term, asserts either that there is a single legitimate method or principle by which judges should decide all legal questions (*privileged-factor foundationalism*), or that there is a small number of such methods or principles and that these methods or principles can be rank-ordered (*rank-order foundationalism*). I owe the expression "privileged-factor theory" to Fallon, "A Constructivist Coherence Theory," p. 1209 (though I use the term in a slightly different way). For different, though related, uses of the term "foundationalism," see Eskridge and Frickey, "Statutory Interpretation as Practical Reasoning," p. 321; Farber, "Legal Pragmatism," pp. 1331–32.

10. Lochner v. New York, 198 U.S. 45, 76 (1905) (Holmes, J., dissenting).

11. See Cardozo, *The Nature of the Judicial Process*, pp. 30–141.

12. Cardozo, *The Growth of the Law*, p. 108.

13. Cardozo never clearly explains what he means by "social welfare," but he does make clear that he does not employ the term in any narrow utilitarian sense. See Cardozo, *The Nature of the Judicial Process*, pp. 71–72. Cf. John C. P. Goldberg, "Community and the Common-Law Judge: Reconstructing Cardozo's Theoretical Writings," *New York University Law Review* 65 (1990), p. 1337.

14. Cardozo, *The Nature of the Judicial Process*, p. 66.

15. Ibid., p. 160.

16. Ibid., p. 58.

17. My argument here is indebted to Fallon, "A Constructivist Coherence Theory," pp. 1194–1209. For similar typologies see Bobbitt, pp. 3–8; Walter F. Murphy, James E. Fleming, and William F. Harris, *American Constitutional Interpretation*, pp. 291–301.

18. See pp. 45–47.

19. See, generally, Robert Nagel, *Constitutional Cultures: The Mentality and Consequences of Judicial Review* (Berkeley: University of California Press, 1989), pp. 12–17.

20. Joseph William Singer, "Legal Realism Now," *California Law Review* 76 (1988), p. 467.

21. Letter From Thomas Reed Powell to Benjamin Cardozo, quoted in Cardozo, *The Growth of the Law*, pp. 64–65.

22. See, generally, Andrew L. Kaufman, "Judges or Scholars: To Whom

Shall We Look for Our Constitutional Law?" *Journal of Legal Education* 37 (1987), pp. 184–202. Cf. Eskridge and Frickey, "Statutory Interpretation as Practical Reasoning," pp. 345–62.

23. Cardozo, *The Nature of the Judicial Process*, p. 162.

24. The best-known critic was Justice Hugo Black. See, e.g., Barenblatt v. United States, 360 U.S. 109, 141–44 (1959) (Black, J., dissenting); El Paso v. Simmons, 379 U.S. 497, 528–33 (1965) (Black, J., dissenting). For a recent critical appraisal, see Nancy Levitt, "Practically Unreasonable: A Critique of Practical Reason," *Northwestern University Law Review* 85 (1991), pp. 494–518.

25. Several leading legal pragmatists of Cardozo's generation endorsed what Cardozo rightly regarded as excessively result-oriented theories of judicial decision making. See, generally, Summers, *Instrumentalism and American Legal Theory*; Benjamin Cardozo, "Jurisprudence," in *Selected Writings of Benjamin Nathan Cardozo* (New York: Fallon Publications, 1947), pp. 7–46.

26. In recent years, as Richard Posner notes, legal pragmatism has been "dominated by persons of liberal or radical persuasion" who see the theory as a way to "justify extreme judicial activism on behalf of the oppressed." Posner, "What Has Pragmatism to Offer Law?," *Southern California Law Review* 63 (1990), p. 1658. See, generally, "Symposium: The Renaissance of Pragmatism in American Legal Thought," *Southern California Law Review* 63 (1990), pp. 1569–1853.

27. Cardozo, *The Growth of the Law*, p. 49.

28. See Cardozo, *The Nature of the Judicial Process*, p. 14.

29. See ibid., p. 129.

30. See ibid., p. 103. Cf. Southern Pacific Co. v. Jensen, 244 U.S. 205, 221 (1917) (Holmes, J., dissenting) ("I recognize without hesitation that judges do and must legislate, but they can do so only interstitially; they are confined from molar to molecular motions"), quoted in Cardozo, *The Nature of the Judicial Process*, p. 69.

31. See, e.g., Cardozo, *The Growth of the Common Law*, pp. 58–60; Cardozo, *The Nature of the Judicial Process,* pp. 164–65. On the frequency of easy cases in law, see Frederick Schauer, "Easy Cases," *Southern California Law Review* 58 (1985), pp. 399–440; Lawrence Solum, "On the Indeterminacy Crisis: Critiquing Critical Dogma," *University of Chicago Law Review* 54 (1987), pp. 471–76; Ken Kress, "Legal Indeterminacy," *California Law Review* 77 (1989), pp. 296–97.

32. Schauer, "Easy Cases," p. 409.

33. See, e.g., Otis v. Parker, 187 U.S. 606, 609 (1903) (per Justice Holmes).

34. Cardozo, *The Nature of the Judicial Process*, p. 91.

35. Ibid., p. 94.

36. See p. 22.

37. See pp. 41–43.

38. Cf. United States v. Carolene Products Co., 304 U.S. 144, 152–53 n. 4 (1938); Ely, *Democracy and Distrust,* chaps. 4–6; Choper, *Judicial Review and the National Political Process,* chaps. 4–5. Similarly, considerations of institu-

tional competence or other "prudential" concerns may justify the Court in refusing jurisdiction for a time (or even permanently) over certain kinds of cases. See Bickel, *The Least Dangerous Branch*, pp. 111–98; Bobbitt, *Constitutional Fate*, pp. 59–73.

39. Chambers v. Florida, 309 U.S. 227, 241 (1940).

40. Cf. Brest, "The Misconceived Quest for the Original Understanding," p. 234: "[I]f you consider the evolution of doctrines in just about any extensively-adjudicated area of constitutional law . . . explicit reliance on originalist sources has played a very small role compared to the elaboration of the Court's own precedents. It is rather like having a remote ancestor who came over on the Mayflower."

41. Cardozo, *The Paradoxes of Legal Science*, p. 30.

42. Holmes, "The Path of the Law," in *The Mind and Faith of Justice Holmes*, p. 83.

43. Cardozo, *The Nature of the Judicial Process*, p. 34.

44. Dworkin, *Law's Empire*, p. 95.

45. Farber, "Legal Pragmatism," p. 1332.

46. Cardozo, *The Paradoxes of Legal Science*, p. 59.

47. Ibid., p. 67.

48. Brennan, "The Constitution of the United States," p. 434.

49. Cardozo, *The Growth of the Law*, p. 95.

50. See, e.g., Clark v. Jeter, 486 U.S. 456, 461 (1988) (intermediate judicial scrutiny under the Equal Protection Clause requires that a challenged state action be substantially related to an important government objection); Boos v. Barry, 485 U.S. 312, 321 (1988) (content-based restrictions on political speech in a public forum are permissible only if they serve a compelling state interest and are narrowly tailored to achieve that end); Hobbie v. Unemployment Appeals Commission, 480 U.S. 136, 141 (1987) (state actions substantially burdening free exercise of religion are permissible only if they serve a compelling state interest by means narrowly tailored to that end); but see Employment Division v. Smith, 110 S. Ct. 1595, 1601 (1990) (religion-based exemptions to otherwise valid secular laws are not required except when petitioner's free-exercise claim also implicates other constitutional protections).

51. See Barnes v. Glen Theatre, Inc., 111 S. Ct. 2456, 2463–68 (1991) (Scalia, J., concurring).

52. See, e.g., United States v. O'Brien, 391 U.S. 367, 377 (1968). See, generally, Tribe, *American Constitutional Law*, pp. 977–1010.

53. See Wilson v. Seiter, 111 S. Ct. 2321, 2324 (1991); Whiteley v. Albers, 475 U.S. 312, 319 (1986); Rhodes v. Chapman, 452 U.S. 337, 347 (1981).

54. Palko v. Connecticut, 302 U.S. 319, 325–26 (1937); see also Bowers v. Hardwick, 478 U.S. 186, 191 (1986).

55. Snyder v. Massachusetts, 291 U.S. 97, 107 (1934). See also Moore v. East Cleveland, 431 U.S. 494, 503 (1977); and Michael H. v. Gerald D., 109 S. Ct. 2333, 2341 (1989) (plurality opinion).

56. I borrow this useful term from Joel Feinberg, *Harm to Others* (New York: Oxford University Press, 1984), p. 18.

57. Cf. Kaufman, "Judges or Scholars," p. 184.

58. See John Rawls, "The Idea of an Overlapping Consensus," *Oxford Journal of Legal Studies* 7 (1987), pp. 1–25.

59. Melvin A. Eisenberg, *The Nature of the Common Law* (Cambridge, Mass.: Harvard University Press, 1988), p. 16.

60. See ibid.

61. Ibid., p. 10.

62. Ibid.

63. Joseph Raz, "Legal Principles and the Limits of Law," *Yale Law Journal* 81 (1972), p. 849.

64. See p. 41.

65. Ely, *Democracy and Distrust*, p. 69 (emphasis added).

66. See, e.g., Thompson v. Oklahoma, 487 U.S. 815 (1988) (holding that states may not execute a person who was fifteen years old or younger at the time of his or her offense under current capital punishment statutes); Duncan v. Louisiana, 391 U.S. 145 (1968) (incorporating Sixth Amendment guarantee of a jury trial in criminal cases).

67. Cardozo, *The Paradoxes of Legal Science,* p. 124.

68. Cardozo, *The Nature of the Judicial Process,* p. 92.

69. Bickel, *The Least Dangerous Branch*, p. 26. See, e.g., Korematsu v. United States, 323 U.S. 214 (1943) (upholding internment of Japanese Americans at the beginning of World War II); Pierce v. Society of Sisters, 268 U.S. 510 (1925) (striking down a state law, enacted during a period of anti-Catholic feeling, that required all children who had not completed the eighth grade to attend public schools).

70. Cardozo, *The Paradoxes of Legal Science*, pp. 50–51.

71. Ibid., p. 50. Cf. ibid., p. 37 ("The law will . . . follow, or strive to follow, the principle and practice of men and women whom the social mind would rank as intelligent and virtuous").

72. Dworkin, *Taking Rights Seriously,* p. 254.

73. See Rawls, *A Theory of Justice,* pp. 48–51. Rawls discusses the method of reflective equilibrium as a means by which individuals may harmonize and systematize their personal moral beliefs. However, the method can equally well be used with shared moral judgments and principles. See Eisenberg, *The Nature of the Common Law,* p. 18.

74. For fuller explications of the method of reflective equilibrium, see Norman Daniels, "Wide Reflective Equilibrium and Theory Acceptance in Ethics," *Journal of Philosophy* 76 (1979), pp. 256–82; Robert Justin Lipkin, "Beyond Skepticism, Foundationalism, and the 'New Fuzziness': The Role of Wide Reflective Equilibrium in Legal Theory," *Cornell Law Review* 75 (1990), pp. 860–67. For discussions of how coherence methodologies such as Rawls's are consistent with a commitment to moral realism, see Perry, "The Legitimacy of Particular Conceptions of Constitutional Interpretation," p. 702, n. 93; Moore, "Moral Realism," pp. 1106–16.

75. See Dworkin, *Taking Rights Seriously*, p. 255.

76. 487 U.S. 815 (1988).

77. As we shall see, however, Justice Scalia does argue that the facial meaning of the amendment lends some support to his conclusion.

78. See *Thompson,* 487 U.S. at 832.

79. Ibid., p. 864.

80. See Scalia, "Originalism: The Lesser Evil," pp. 849–65.

81. See *Thompson*, 487 U.S. at 865.

82. See, e.g., Solem v. Helm, 463 U.S. 277, 285–86 (1983); Ford v. Wainwright, 477 U.S. 399, 405 (1986); Penry v. Lynaugh, 109 S. Ct. 2934, 2959 (1989).

83. See, e.g., Trop v. Dulles, 356 U.S. 86, 101 (1958); Estelle v. Gamble, 429 U.S. 97, 102 (1976); Stanford v. Kentucky, 109 S. Ct. 2969, 2974 (1989).

84. Gregg v. Georgia, 428 U.S. 153, 173 (1976) (opinion of Stewart, Powell, and Stevens, JJ.). See also Coker v. Georgia, 433 U.S. 458, 492 (1977); Enmund v. Florida, 458 U.S. 482, 498 (1982).

85. Gregg v. Georgia, 428 U.S. 153, 173 (1976) (opinion of Stewart, Powell, and Stevens, JJ.). See also Enmund v. Florida, 458 U.S. 482, 498 (1982).

86. Godfrey v. Georgia, 446 U.S. 420, 427 (1980) (plurality opinion). See also Caldwell v. Mississippi, 472 U.S. 320, 343 (1985).

87. *Thompson,* 487 U.S. at 815–38.

88. See ibid., pp. 848–55.

89. See ibid., pp. 858–59. In cases like *Thompson* in which there is no majority opinion, "the holding of the Court may be viewed as that position taken by those members who concurred in the judgment on the narrowest ground." Gregg v. Georgia, 428 U.S. 153, 169n. 15 (1976). Thus, what the Court officially held in *Thompson* is what Justice O'Connor held: that a person fifteen or younger at the time of his or her offense may not be executed under a death penalty statute that specifies no minimum age below which it ceases to apply.

90. See *Thompson,* 487 U.S. at 859–78. Cf. Harmelin v. Michigan 111 S. Ct. 2680, 2684–2701 (1991) (opinion of Scalia, J., and Rehnquist, C.J.) (arguing, largely on historical grounds, that the Eighth Amendment does not prohibit disproportionately severe punishments).

91. *Thompson,* 487 U.S. at 873.

92. Stanford v. Kentucky, 109 S. Ct. 2969, 2979 (1989).

93. See. e.g., Maynard v. Craig, 110 S. Ct. 3157, 3171–76 (1990) (Scalia, J., dissenting); K Mart Corp. v. Cartier, Inc., 108 S. Ct. 1811, 1831–34 (1988) (Scalia, J., concurring in part and dissenting in part). See, generally, William N. Eskridge, Jr., "The New Textualism," *UCLA Law Review* 37 (1990), pp. 621–91.

94. For a fuller discussion of textualism, see pp. 26–28.

95. See. e.g., United States v. American Trucking Association, 310 U.S. 534, 545 (1940) (rejecting the "Plain Meaning Rule," according to which courts were permitted to consult extratextual evidence of legislative intent only in cases in which the meaning of the text at issue was not "plain"). Cf. Thornburgh v. American College of Obstetricians and Gynecologists, 476 U.S. 747, 789 (1986)

(White, J., dissenting) ("As its prior cases clearly show, . . . this Court does not subscribe to the simplistic view that constitutional interpretation can possibly be limited to the 'plain meaning' of the Constitution's text").

96. See, generally, Levy, *Original Intent and the Framers' Constitution,* pp. 336–38.

97. Significantly, Scalia takes the word "unusual" in the phrase "cruel and unusual punishments" to mean "theoretically imposable in few if any jurisdictions," not "seldomly if ever imposed on eligible offenders." Capital punishment for juveniles is unusual in the second sense but not in the first. See Victor L. Streib, *Death Penalty for Juveniles* (Bloomington: Indiana University Press, 1987), pp. 24–30. As a matter of ordinary usage, Scalia's reading is possible but surely less intuitive than the alternative sense.

98. Stanford v. Kentucky, 109 S. Ct. 2969, 2980 (1989) (opinion of Scalia, J.). (In *Stanford,* the Court ruled, by a 5–4 majority, that the execution of persons who committed capital crimes at sixteen or seventeen years of age does not constitute cruel and unusual punishment. Justice O'Connor, in this instance, voted with the majority, as did Justice Kennedy.)

99. *Stanford*, 109 S. Ct. at 2986–87 (Brennan, J., dissenting).

100. West Virginia Board of Education v. Barnette, 313 U.S. 624, 638 (1943), quoted in *Stanford,* 109 S. Ct. at 2987 (Brennan, J., dissenting).

101. West Virginia Board of Education v. Barnette, 313 U.S. 624, 639 (1943).

102. See Ben M. Crouch and James W. Marquart, *An Appeal to Justice: Litigated Reform of Texas Prisons* (Austin: University of Texas Press, 1989), pp. 4–6.

103. 378 U.S. 546 (1964).

104. See, generally, Larry W. Yackle, *Reform and Regret: The Story of Federal Judicial Involvement in the Alabama Prison System* (New York: Oxford University Press, 1989); Crouch and Marquart, *An Appeal to Justice;* John J. DiIulio, ed., *Courts, Corrections, and the Constitution: The Impact of Judicial Intervention on Prisons and Jails* (New York: Oxford University Press, 1990).

105. See "Drug Cases Clog the Courts," *American Bar Association Journal* 76 (1990), p. 34.

106. See Crouch and Marquart, *An Appeal to Justice,* p. 1.

107. In a recent case, Justice Scalia acknowledges that the Eighth Amendment prohibits the deliberate, "wanton" mistreatment of prisoners. See Wilson v. Seiter, 111 S. Ct. 2321, 2326 (1991). He fails to explain, however, how this is consistent with his rejection of part (3) of the traditional Eighth Amendment analysis. Most recent prisoners' rights adjudication is explicitly premised on part (3) principles. See Gregory Bassham, "Rethinking the Emerging Jurisprudence of Juvenile Death," *Notre Dame Journal of Law, Ethics, and Public Policy* 4 (1990), p. 488 n. 130 (citing cases).

108. *Stanford,* 109 S. Ct. at 2980.

109. Ibid., p. 2970.

110. See Crouch and Marquart, *An Appeal to Justice*, p. 4; Yackle, *Reform and Regret,* pp. 108–67.

111. Coker v. Georgia, 433 U.S. 587, 592 (1977); *Stanford,* 109 S. Ct. at 2975.

112. See, e.g., Rhodes v. Chapman, 452 U.S. 337, 346 (1981); Solem v. Helm, 463 U.S. 277, 290–92 (1983); McCleskey v. Kemp, 481 U.S. 279, 300 (1987).

113. See *Thompson,* 487 U.S. at 832.

114. See Streib, *Death Penalty for Juveniles,* pp. 168–69.

115. See *Thompson,* 487 U.S. at 826.

116. See ibid., pp. 826–27.

117. See ibid., p. 829.

118. See ibid., pp. 865–68.

119. Ibid., pp. 871–72.

120. See ibid., p. 829.

121. See ibid., p. 833.

122. See, e.g., Webster v. Reproductive Health Services, 109 S. Ct. 3040, 3061 (1989) (O'Connor, J., concurring in part) (endorsing the traditional principle that the Court should not formulate a rule of law broader than the precise facts to which it is applied).

123. See *Thompson,* 487 U.S. at 857–58.

124. See, generally, Dworkin, *Law's Empire*, pp. 313–54; Ely, *Democracy and Distrust*, pp. 63–69; Mark Tushnet, "A Note on the Revival of Textualism in Constitutional Theory," *Southern California Law Review* 58 (1985), pp. 683–700; Eskridge, "Dynamic Statutory Interpretation," pp. 1498–1511.

125. See, generally, Furman v. Georgia, 408 U.S. 238, 342–45 (1972) (Marshall, J., concurring). Cf. Williams v. New York, 337 U.S. 241, 248 (1949) ("Retribution is no longer the dominant objective of the criminal law"); Morissette v. United States, 342 U.S. 246, 251 (1952) (speaking approvingly of the "tardy and unfinished substitution of deterrence and reformation in place of retribution and vengeance as the motivation for public prosecution").

126. See, generally, *Furman*, 408 U.S. at 345–54 (Marshall, J., concurring); ibid., p. 302 (Brennan, J., concurring); ibid., p. 312 (White, J., concurring).

127. See *Furman,* 408 U.S. at 391–96 (Burger, C.J., dissenting).

128. For recent defenses of retributivist theories of punishment, see p. 204, n. 96. For an influential but much-controverted defense of the deterrent efficacy of capital punishment, see Issac Ehrlich, "The Deterrent Effect of Capital Punishment: A Question of Life and Death," *American Economic Review* 65 (1975), pp. 397–417.

129. See, generally, cases cited in Bassham, "Rethinking the Emerging Jurisprudence of Juvenile Death," p. 488, n. 130.

130. See *Thompson,* 487 U.S. at 837–38.

131. Victor L. Streib, "Imposing the Death Penalty on Children," in K. Haas and J. Inciardi, eds., *Challenging Capital Punishment: Legal and Social Science Approaches* (Newbury Park, Calif.: Sage Publications, 1988), p. 251.

132. See *Thompson*, 487 U.S. at 832.

133. See ibid.

134. See ibid., pp. 832–33.

135. Ibid., p. 833, n. 39.

136. 481 U.S. 279 (1987).

137. Ibid., p. 308.

138. Ibid., pp. 322–24.

139. Gregg v. Georgia, 428 U.S. 153, 189 (1976) (opinion of Stewart, Stevens, and Powell, JJ).

140. See, e.g., Godfrey v. Georgia, 446 U.S. 420, 427 (1980) (plurality opinion); and California v. Brown, 479 U.S. 538, 541 (1987).

141. See, e.g., Coker v. Georgia, 433 U.S. 584, 598 (1977); Solem v. Helm, 463 U.S. 277, 292 (1983).

142. These organizations include, among others, the American Bar Association, the American Law Institute, the National Council of Juvenile and Family Court Judges, and the National Council on Crime and Delinquency. See *Stanford,* 109 S. Ct. at 2985 (Brennan, J., dissenting).

143. Ibid.

144. Ibid.

145. Eddings v. Oklahoma, 455 U.S. 104, 116 (1982).

146. See *Thompson,* 487 U.S. at 823–24.

147. Ibid., p. 824.

148. Franklin Zimring, *Twentieth Century Fund Task Force on Sentencing Policy Toward Young Offenders: Confronting Youth Crime* (1978), p. 7, quoted in *Stanford,* 109 S. Ct. at 2989 (Brennan, J., dissenting).

149. Ibid.

150. See *Eddings,* 455 U.S. at 104, 115 (1982).

151. Miller, "Adolescent Suicide: Etiology and Treatment," *Adolescent Psychiatry* 9 (1981), p. 329, quoted in *Stanford,* 109 S. Ct. at 2989 (Brennan, J., dissenting).

152. See, generally, Lawrence Kohlberg, *Essays on Moral Development,* 2 vols. (New York: Harper & Row, 1981–1984).

153. *Stanford*, 109 S. Ct. at 2990 (Brennan, J., dissenting).

154. See Lewis, et al., "Neuropsychiatric, Psychoeducational, and Family Characteristics of 14 Juveniles Condemned to Death in the United States," *American Journal of Psychiatry* 145 (1988), p. 584, quoted in *Stanford,* 109 S. Ct. at 2989 (Brennan, J., dissenting).

155. *Thompson,* 487 U.S. at 853 (O'Connor, J., concurring in the judgment) (emphasis added).

156. See Mullaney v. Wilbur, 425 U.S. 684 (1975).

157. See *In re* Winship, 397 U.S. 358 (1970).

158. See Duncan v. Louisiana, 391 U.S. 145 (1968).

159. See Gideon v. Wainwright, 372 U.S. 335 (1963).

160. See, e.g., Sheppard v. Maxwell, 384 U.S. 333 (1966); Tumey v. Ohio, 273 U.S. 510 (1927); Moore v. Dempsey, 261 U.S. 86 (1923).

161. *In re* Winship, 397 U.S. 358, 364 (1970).

162. Mill v. Maryland, 486 U.S. 367, 383–84 (1988).

163. See, generally, Kaufman, "Judges or Scholars," p. 184 (noting that "[n]ever in the history of constitutional scholarship in this country have the views from academia, almost all of them, been so different from the practice of judges").

Selected Bibliography

Allen, C. K. *Law in the Making*, 6th ed. Oxford: Clarendon Press, 1958.

Amar, Akhil Reed. "Philadelphia Revisited: Amending the Constitution Outside Article V." *University of Chicago Law Review* 55 (1988): 1043–1104.

Anderson, William. "The Intention of the Framers: A Note on Constitutional Interpretation." *American Political Science Review* 49 (1955): 340–52.

Antieau, Chester J. *Constitutional Construction.* New York: Oceana, 1982.

———. "Constitutional Construction: A Guide to the Principles and Their Application." *Notre Dame Lawyer* 51 (1976): 358–95.

———. *The Original Understanding of the Fourteenth Amendment.* Tucson, Ariz.: Mid-America Press, 1982.

Bach, Kent. *Thought and Reference.* Oxford: Clarendon Press, 1987.

Bacon, Matthew. *A New Abridgment of the Law*, 7th ed. 8 vols. London: Strahan, 1832.

Barber, Sotirios A. *On What the Constitution Means.* Baltimore: Johns Hopkins University Press, 1984.

Beard, Charles. *An Economic Interpretation of the Constitution of the United States.* New York: Free Press, 1965.

Berger, Raoul. *Death Penalties: The Supreme Court's Obstacle Course.*

Cambridge, Mass.: Harvard University Press, 1982.

———. *Government by Judiciary: The Transformation of the Fourteenth Amendment.* Cambridge, Mass.: Harvard University Press,1977.

———. "New Theories of 'Interpretation': The Activist Flight from the Constitution." *Ohio State Law Journal* 47 (1986): 1–45.

———. "'Original Intention' in Historical Perspective." *George Washington Law Review* 54 (1986): 101–42.

Bickel, Alexander M. *The Least Dangerous Branch: The Supreme Court at the Bar of Politics*, 2d ed. New Haven, Conn.: Yale University Press, 1986.

———. "The Original Understanding and the Segregation Decision." *Harvard Law Review* 69 (1955): 1–43.

Black, Henry Campbell. *Handbook on the Construction and Interpretation of the Laws,* 2d ed. St. Paul, Minn.: West, 1911.

Bobbitt, Philip. *Constitutional Fate.* New York: Oxford University Press, 1982.

Bork, Robert. "Neutral Principles and Some First Amendment Problems." *Indiana Law Journal* 47 (1971): 1–35.

———. *The Tempting of America: The Political Seduction of the Law.* New York: Free Press, 1990.

Brennan, William J. "The Constitution of the United States: Contemporary Ratification." *South Texas Law Review* 27 (1986): 433–45.

Brest, Paul. "The Misconceived Quest for the Original Understanding." *Boston University Law Review* 60 (1980): 204–38.

Brink, David O. "Legal Theory, Legal Interpretation, and Judicial Review." *Philosophy and Public Affairs* 17 (1988): 105–48.

Cardozo, Benjamin. *The Nature of the Judicial Process.* New Haven, Conn.: Yale University Press, 1921.

Chemerinsky, Erwin. *Interpreting the Constitution.* New York: Praeger, 1987.

Choper, Jesse H. *Judicial Review and the National Political Process: A Functional Reconsideration of the Role of the Supreme Court.* Chicago: University of Chicago Press, 1980.

Clinton, Robert A. "Original Understanding, Legal Realism, and the

Interpretation of 'This Constitution.'" *Iowa Law Review* 72 (1987): 1177–1280.

Cooley, Thomas M. *A Treatise on the Constitutional Limitations Which Rest Upon the Legislative Power of the States of the American Union*, 5th ed. Boston: Little, Brown, 1883.

Cord, Robert. *Separation of Church and State: Historical Fact and Current Fiction.* New York: Lambeth Press, 1982.

Cross, Rupert. *Statutory Interpretation.* London: Butterworths, 1976.

Crosskey, William W. *Politics and the Constitution in the History of the United States.* 2 vols. Chicago: University of Chicago Press, 1953.

Curry, Thomas J. *The First Freedoms: Church and State in America to the Passage of the First Amendment.* New York: Oxford University Press, 1986.

Curtis, Michael Kent. *No State Shall Abridge: The Fourteenth Amendment and the Bill of Rights.* Durham, N. C.: Duke University Press, 1986.

Devitt, Michael, and Kim Sterelny. *Language and Reality: An Introduction to the Philosophy of Language.* Cambridge, Mass.: MIT Press, 1987.

Dickerson, Reed. *The Interpretation and Application of Statutes.* Boston: Little, Brown, 1985.

Dworkin, Ronald. "The Bork Nomination." *New York Review of Books* (August 13, 1987): 3–10.

———. *Law's Empire.* Cambridge, Mass.: Harvard University Press, 1986.

———. *A Matter of Principle.* Cambridge, Mass.: Harvard University Press, 1985.

———. *Taking Rights Seriously.* Cambridge, Mass.: Harvard University Press, 1977.

Easterbrook, Frank. "Ways of Criticizing the Court." *Harvard Law Review* 95 (1982): 802–32.

———. "Statutes' Domains." *University of Chicago Law Review* 50 (1983): 533–52.

Ely, John Hart. *Democracy and Distrust: A Theory of Judicial Review.* Cambridge, Mass.: Harvard University Press, 1980.

Epstein, Richard A. *Takings: Private Property and the Power of Eminent Domain.* Cambridge, Mass.: Harvard University Press, 1985.

Eskridge, William N. "Dynamic Statutory Interpretation." *University of Pennsylvania Law Review* 135 (1987): 1479–1555.

———. and Philip P. Frickey. "Statutory Interpretation as Practical Reason." *Stanford Law Review* 42 (1990): 321–84.

Fairman, Charles. "Does the Fourteenth Amendment Incorporate the Bill of Rights? The Original Understanding." *Stanford Law Review* 2 (1949): 5–139.

Fallon, Richard H. "A Constructivist Coherence Theory of Constitutional Interpretation." *Harvard Law Review* 100 (1987): 1189–1286.

Farber, Daniel. "The Originalism Debate: A Guide to the Perplexed." *Ohio State Law Journal* 49 (1989): 1085–1100.

———. and Philip P. Frickey. "Legislative Intent and Public Choice." *Virginia Law Review* 74 (1988): 423–69.

The Federalist Papers. Edited by Jacob E. Cooke. Middletown, Conn.: Wesleyan University Press, 1961.

Grannuci, Anthony. "'Nor Cruel and Unusual Punishments Inflicted': The Original Meaning." *California Law Review* 57 (1969): 839–65.

Gray, John Chipman. *The Nature and Sources of Law,* 2d ed. New York: Macmillan, 1924.

Grey, Thomas C. "Do We Have an Unwritten Constitution?" *Stanford Law Review* 27 (1975): 703–18.

Hand, Learned. *The Bill of Rights.* New York: Atheneum, 1972.

Hart, H. L. A. *The Concept of Law.* Oxford: Clarendon Press, 1961.

Holmes, Oliver Wendell Jr. *Collected Legal Papers.* New York: Harcourt, Brace, 1920.

Kay, Richard S. "Adherence to the Original Intentions in Constitutional Adjudication: Three Objections and Responses." *Northwestern University Law Review* 82 (1988): 226–92.

Kelly, Alfred H. "Clio and the Court: An Illicit Love Affair." In *1965*

Supreme Court Review. Edited by Philip B. Kurland. Chicago: University of Chicago Press, 1965.

Kripke, Saul. *Naming and Necessity*. Cambridge, Mass.: Harvard University Press, 1970.

Kurland, Philip B. and Ralph Lerner, eds. *The Founders' Constitution*. 5 vols. Chicago: University of Chicago Press, 1987.

Land, Stephen K. *From Signs to Propositions: The Concept of Form in Eighteenth-Century Semantic Theory*. London: Longmans, 1974.

Laycock, Douglas. "Text, Intent, and the Religion Clauses." *Notre Dame Journal of Law, Ethics, and Public Policy* 4 (1990): 683–97.

Levy, Leonard W. *Original Intent and the Framers' Constitution*. New York: Macmillan, 1988.

———. *Emergence of a Free Press*. New York: Oxford University Press, 1985.

———. *The Establishment Clause: Religion and the First Amendment*. New York: Macmillan, 1985.

Lieber, Francis. *Legal and Political Hermeneutics*. Boston: Little, Brown, 1839.

Locke, John. *An Essay Concerning Human Understanding*. Edited by Peter N. Nidditch. Oxford: Clarendon Press, 1975.

Lyons, David. "Constitutional Interpretation and Original Meaning." *Social Philosophy and Policy* 4 (1986): 76–101.

MacCallum, Gerald. "Legislative Intent." *Yale Law Journal* 75 (1966): 754–87.

Macedo, Steven. *The New Right v. the Constitution*. Washington D.C.: Cato Institute, 1987.

Malbin, Michael J. *Religion and Politics: The Intentions of the Authors of the First Amendment*. Washington D.C.: American Enterprise Institute for Public Policy Research, 1978.

Maltz, Earl. "Some New Thoughts on an Old Problem: The Role of the Intent of the Framers in Constitutional Theory." *Boston University Law Review* 63 (1983): 811–36.

———. "The Failure of Attacks on Originalism."*Constitutional Commentary* 4 (1987): 43–56.

———. "Foreword: The Appeal of Originalism." *1987 Utah Law Review* (1987): 773–805.

Martin, Robert M. *The Meaning of Language*. Cambridge, Mass.: MIT Press, 1987.

Meese, Edwin. "Toward a Jurisprudence of Original Intent." *Benchmark* 2 (1986): 1–10.

Miller, Charles. *The Supreme Court and the Uses of History*. Cambridge, Mass.: Harvard University Press, 1969.

Monaghan, Henry P. "Our Perfect Constitution." *New York University Law Review* 56 (1981): 353–96.

———. "Stare Decisis and Constitutional Adjudication." *Columbia University Law Review* 88 (1988): 723–73.

Moore, Michael S. "The Semantics of Judging." *Southern California Law Review* 54 (1981): 151–294.

———. A Natural Law Theory of Interpretation." *Southern California Law Review* 58 (1985): 277–398.

Munzer, Stephen. "Realistic Limits on Realist Interpretation." *Southern California Law Review* 58 (1985): 459–75.

Munzer, Stephen and James Nickel. "Does the Constitution Mean What It Always Meant?" *Columbia University Law Review* 77 (1977): 62–77.

Murphy, Paul L. "Time to Reclaim: The Current Challenge of American Constitutional History." *American Historical Review* 69 (1963): 64–79.

Original Meaning Jurisprudence: A Sourcebook. Washington, D.C.: Justice Department Office of Legal Policy, 1987.

Perry, Michael. *The Constitution, the Courts, and Human Rights: An Inquiry into the Legitimacy of Constitutional Policymaking by the Judiciary*. New Haven, Conn.: Yale University Press, 1982.

———. "The Authority of Text, Tradition, and Reason: A Theory of Constitutional 'Interpretation.'" *Southern California Law Review* 58 (1985): 551–602.

———. *Morality, Politics, and Law: A Bicentennial Essay*. New York: Oxford University Press, 1988.

———. "The Legitimacy of Particular Conceptions of Constitutional Interpretation." *Virginia Law Review* 77 (1991): 669–719.

Powell, H. Jefferson. "The Original Understanding of Original Intent." *Harvard Law Review* 98 (1985): 885–948.

Putnam, Hilary. *Philosophical Papers.* 3 vols. Cambridge: Cambridge University Press, 1975.

Radin, Max. "Statutory Interpretation." *Harvard Law Review* 43 (1930): 863–85.

Rehnquist, William H. "The Notion of a Living Constitution." *Texas Law Review* 54 (1976): 693–706.

Riley, Laurence J. *The History, Nature, and Use of Epikeia in Moral Theology.* Washington D.C.: Catholic University Press of America, 1948.

Rostow, Eugene. *The Sovereign Prerogative: The Supreme Court and the Quest for Law.* New Haven, Conn.: Yale University Press, 1962.

Salmon, Nathan. *Reference and Essence.* Princeton, N.J.: Princeton University Press, 1981.

Sandalow, Terrance. "Constitutional Interpretation." *Michigan Law Review* 79 (1981): 133–72.

Scalia, Antonin. "Originalism: The Lesser Evil." *University of Cincinnati Law Review* 57 (1989): 849–65.

Sedgwick, Theodore. *A Treatise on the Rules Which Govern the Interpretation and Construction of Statutory and Constitutional Law*, 2d ed. New York: Baker, Voorhis, 1874.

Seigan, Bernard. *The Supreme Court's Constitution: An Enquiry into Judicial Review and its Impact on Society.* New Brunswick, N.J.: Transaction Books, 1987.

———. *Economic Liberties and the Constitution.* Chicago: University of Chicago Press, 1980.

Simon, Larry G. "The Authority of the Framers of the Constitution: Can Originalist Interpretation Be Justified?" *California Law Review* 73 (1985): 1482–1539.

Story, Joseph. *Commentaries on the Constitution of the United States*, 3d ed. 2 vols. Boston: Little, Brown, 1858.

ten Broeck, Jacobus. "Admissibility and Use by the United States Supreme Court of Extrinsic Aids in Constitutional Construction." *California Law Review* 26 (1938): 287–308, 437–54, 664–81; and 27 (1939): 157–81, 399–421.

Thayer, James B. "The Origins and Scope of the American Doctrine of Constitutional Law." *Harvard Law Review* 7 (1893): 129–52.

Tribe, Laurence. *American Constitutional Law*, 2d ed. Mineola, N.Y.: Foundation Press, 1988.

Tushnet, Mark. *Red, White, and Blue: A Critical Analysis of Constitutional Law.* Cambridge, Mass.: Harvard University Press, 1988.

———. "The U.S. Constitution and the Intent of the Framers." *Buffalo Law Review* 36 (1987): 217–26.

Wofford, John G. "The Blinding Light: The Uses of History in Constitutional Interpretation." *University of Chicago Law Review* 31 (1964): 502–33.

Wolfe, Christopher. *The Rise of Modern Judicial Review: From Constitutional Interpretation to Judge-Made Law.* New York: Basic Books, 1986.

Index

About the Author

Gregory Bassham is assistant professor of philosophy at King's College in Pennsylvania. He has his Ph.D. in philosophy from the University of Notre Dame. His publications include articles in constitutional theory, philosophy of law, and causation theory.